CW00384025

THE ROYAL
AUXILIARY
AIR FORCE

THE ROYAL AUXILIARY AIR FORCE

COMMEMORATING 100 YEARS OF SERVICE

DR LOUISE WILKINSON AND
SQUADRON LEADER TONY FREEMAN (RTD)

AIR WORLD

AIR WORLD

THE ROYAL AUXILIARY AIR FORCE
Commemorating 100 Years of Service

First published in Great Britain in 2023 by
Air World
An imprint of
Pen & Sword Books Ltd
Yorkshire – Philadelphia

ISBN 978 1 39906 218 3

Typeset by SJmagic DESIGN SERVICES, India.
Printed and bound in the UK by CPI Group (UK) Ltd.

Pen & Sword Books Limited incorporates the imprints of Atlas, Archaeology,
Aviation, Discovery, Family History, Fiction, History, Maritime, Military, Military
Classics, Politics, Select, Transport, True Crime, Air World, Frontline Publishing, Leo
Cooper, Remember When, Seaforth Publishing, The Praetorian Press, Wharncliffe
Local History, Wharncliffe Transport, Wharncliffe True Crime and White Owl.

For a complete list of Pen & Sword titles please contact

PEN & SWORD BOOKS LIMITED
George House, Units 12 & 13, Beevor Street, Off Pontefract Road,
Barnsley, South Yorkshire, S71 1HN, England
E-mail: enquiries@pen-and-sword.co.uk
Website: www.pen-and-sword.co.uk

or
PEN AND SWORD BOOKS
1950 Lawrence Rd, Havertown, PA 19083, USA
E-mail: uspen-and-sword@casematepublishers.com
Website: www.penandswordbooks.com

High Flight

Oh, I have slipped the surly bonds of earth
And danced the skies on laughter-silvered wings;
Sunward I've climbed and joined the sun-split mirth
Of sun-split clouds – and done a hundred things
You have not dreamed of; wheeled and soared and swung
High in the sun-lit silence. Hovering there
I've chased the shouting wind along, and flung
My eager craft through footless halls of air;
Up, up the long, delirious, burning blue
I've topped the windswept heights with easy grace,
Where never lark or even eagle flew;
And while, with silent lifting mind I've trod
The high un-trespassed sanctity of space,
Put out my hand and touched the face of God.

John Gillespie Magee

In memory of Queen Elizabeth II Air Commodore-in-Chief Royal Auxiliary Air Force 1953-2022

This book is dedicated to all those who have served in the Auxiliary Air Force and its successor, the Royal Auxiliary Air Force, from 1924 to the present day, remembering especially all those who have given their lives in the cause of freedom. *Per Ardua.*

For Pam, Lyndsey and Kerrianne, Che and Lenna, and my beautiful Great Niece Robyn. Thank you all for the love that you bring to my life. I love you all beyond measure.
Louise

Contents

Acronyms

Air Member for Personnel Development — AMP
Air Observation Post — AOP
Air Transport Auxiliary — ATA
Aircraftsman Second Class — AC2
Auxiliary Air Force — AAF
Auxiliary Territorial Service — ATS
Commanding Officer — CO
Distinguished Flying Cross — DFC
Distinguished Flying Medal — DFM
Elementary and Reserve Flying Training School — ERFTS
Maritime Headquarters Units — MHU
Navy Army Air Force Institute — NAAFI
Non-Commissioned Officer — NCO
North Atlantic Treaty Organization — NATO
Operational Record Book — ORB
Royal Aero Club — RAeC
Royal Air Force — RAF
Royal Auxiliary Air Force — RAuxAF
Royal Flying Corps — RFC
Special Reserve — SR
Territorial Army — TA
Territorial Force Association — TFA
The National Archives — TNA
University Air Squadron — UAS
Women's Auxiliary Air Force — WAAF
Women's Royal Air Force — WRAF

Introduction

'To be a member of an AAF squadron was to belong to a jealously guarded elite, access to which was barred by social and financial hurdles which were impassable for many who might have wished to fly with them.'[1]

This book has been published to commemorate the 100th Anniversary of the formation of the Royal Auxiliary Air Force (RAuxAF) on 24 October 1924 and to record and celebrate its many achievements for posterity during the past century. For many historians and local enthusiasts, discussions about the Auxiliary Air Force represent preconceived ideas about a 'gentleman's flying club' composed of rich young men from socially high-ranking families who used the AAF in the period between 1930 and 1957 as an extension of their social lives whilst still fulfilling their patriotic role to the country. My recent book, *The Territorial Air Force. The RAF's Voluntary Squadrons 1926-1957,* documents in great detail who the men of the Auxiliary Air Force were, their social backgrounds, education and employment. For this book, the focus has moved away from this perspective to focus on the different roles of the personnel, squadrons, and units of the Auxiliary Air Force.

There have been many books about the Auxiliary, subsequently Royal, Auxiliary Air Force, predominantly about the auxiliary flying squadrons which have been described as the 'Flagship' of the Force. Moreover, such books as the excellent *Twenty-One Squadrons* by Leslie Hunt and the many other individual squadron histories, such as *The Flying Sword (601 Squadron)* and so on, deal with the auxiliary flying squadrons only. Moreover, most of the aircrew that took part in those squadrons were not members of the AAF, they came from all the other portals of entry into the RAF, the RAFVR, and overseas etc. For example, of the 3,038 pilots who flew in the Battle of Britain, just 178 were auxiliary officers, although just fourteen of the sixty fighter squadrons that took part were AAF.

Who knew that of the 100 Balloon Squadrons that defended the UK during the Battle of Britain in 1940 and beyond, half of them were formed and manned by the Auxiliary Air Force (AAF) before the war?

After the Great War in 1918 the size of Britain's armed forces was drastically reduced as the nation returned its ex-servicemen and women to civilian life. In times of national emergency, nations can implement conscription and mobilize its reserves, for very few, and usually totalitarian, states can afford large standing armies in peacetime. After the First World War, the size of the new Royal Air Force was reduced so dramatically that the only way a sufficient number of squadrons could be mustered to make an independent air force viable and affordable was that the retention of a single air service was to include a number of part-time reservist squadrons to 'make up' the required numbers and to placate The Treasury. The Navy and the Army remained unconvinced. This resulted in the formation of twenty squadrons of the AAF by the outbreak of war in 1939. In fact, the number of squadrons in Fighter Command available to defend the United Kingdom in 1939 was just thirty squadrons and that included fourteen squadrons of the AAF.

After the Second World War, the AAF was disbanded, as was the Women's Auxiliary Air Force, (WAAF) many of whom had served as radar operators and plotters, (some of whom re-enlisted in the Fighter Control Units from 1947), as it has been recorded that 'their natural temperament gave them a clear advantage over men in those trades.' Demobilization was rapid and by 1949, the number of women still serving was small. However, in the latter part of that decade the Korean War broke out, the Berlin Airlift took place, and the Soviet Union exploded its first nuclear bomb. This heralded the beginning of what was to become known as the Cold War.

The advent of the Cold War highlighted the parlous state of the UK air defences. What became known as 'The Dowding System' that had served the nation so well during the war was run down and radar and other systems became obsolete and no match for the task of intercepting high flying and nuclear-armed Soviet bombers. Something had to be done so a major construction and re-equipment programme codenamed ROTOR was put in place to modernize and improve the UK Air Defence System. But there were two major problems, the first being that it would not be completed before 1957 when a new search radar became operational and just as importantly, the RAF did not have the personnel to man it – remember, most of the plotters and operators had been de-mobbed at the end of the war when the WAAF was also disbanded. The ROTOR plan was eventually to solve that problem by establishing thirty Royal Auxiliary Air Force (RAuxAF)

Fighter Control and Radar Reporting Units which served from 1947 until 1961. It is a matter of public record that, during the early and uncertain days of the Cold War, the Air Defence of the UK would have been largely in the hands of the auxiliaries, many of whom had re-enlisted in their old trades.

The WAAF, despite its name, was never originally legally part of the AAF/ RAuxAF. When the Air Companies of the Auxiliary Territorial Service (ATS) came under Air Ministry Control in 1938, they became 'affiliated' with AAF squadrons for administrative purposes when they were issued with RAF uniforms with the auxiliary 'A' on the shoulder under the eagle badge. Moreover, they were given a Service Number in the 800000 series which was allocated to the AAF. However, they were not considered members of the Armed Forces of the Crown until 1941 and were 'enrolled' and not enlisted, so they could leave if they wanted to, and some did! The WAAFs who worked as plotters and radar operators in Fighter Command during the Battle of France and Britain in 1940 were volunteers who were not part of the Armed Forces of the Crown until 1941. During the Battle, three of them were awarded the Military Medal for gallantry. It is a moot point whether female plotters who provided information to fighter controllers who were thus enabled to direct fighters to destroy the enemy, should have not been members of the Armed Forces of the Crown at that time. It has been possible to identify those early members of the WAAF who gave their lives in the cause of freedom by their service number, so due recognition of their patriotism and sacrifice has been included in the RAuxAF Roll of Honour in the RAF Church, St Clement Danes.

The AAF was disbanded at the end of the war in 1945, but by the end of that year, it had been proposed to re-form the original flying squadrons to bring the order of battle once more up to the strength of the pre-war RAF, plus five Army Co-operation Squadrons, jointly manned by the RAuxAF and the TA. In 1947, the force was honoured to receive the prefix 'Royal'. Under the ROTOR programme, twenty RAuxAF Regiment Squadrons were also proposed to operate anti-aircraft guns, but in the event, only twelve were formed. By 1957, it had become apparent that it was no longer possible to train auxiliary aircrew, as the fat provided by ex-wartime aircrew was running out and the modern swept-wing fighters were proving too sophisticated to operate. By March 1957, the auxiliary flying squadrons were disbanded. At the same time, the ROTOR Plan to modernize the air defences was completed and as the original Dowding Plan had proved to be extremely manpower-intensive, it was replaced by technology, so the Fighter Control and Radar Reporting units of the RAuxAF were also disbanded, as were the Regiment AA Squadrons. By 1961, the RAuxAF had virtually ceased to exist.

However, whilst these disbandments were taking place, three Maritime Headquarters Units of the RAuxAF (MHU) were being formed, along with a Maritime Support Unit in Ulster (since disbanded). These Units were to cement the continuity of service of 100 years that will be commemorated and celebrated in 2024. Unfortunately, until 1979, these few units meant that the RAuxAF was virtually in the wilderness and remained largely unknown to a generation of RAF personnel and the general public. It was to be nearly twenty years before the expansion of a resurgent RAuxAF really began.

In July 1979 it had been decided to form, on a trial basis, three RAuxAF Regiment Field Squadrons followed by a further three by 1982/3. Following lessons learned from the recent Falklands Conflict, a Movements Squadron was also formed in 1982, followed by an Aeromedical Evacuation Squadron the following year. Both were to be mobilized for the First Gulf War in 1991, more about which is covered elsewhere. In addition, four Airfield Defence Flights were formed at key locations in the UK which have since been disbanded.

In 1997, at a ceremony at the RAF College Cranwell, the four remaining war appointable flights of the RAF Volunteer Reserve were amalgamated with the RAuxAF but retained the letters 'VR' in their new squadron titles. Following an earlier decision, it had been decided to number new multi-role squadrons with former RAuxAF flying squadron numberplates as it was envisaged that auxiliary squadrons would never again fly their own aircraft. Single role squadrons such as movements and medical evacuation were to be found in the 4000 series and Regiment field squadrons in the 2000 series. As an aside, the Fighter Control Units (FCUs) in their day were numbered in the 3000 series. Between 1999 and 2017, a further fourteen squadrons were formed or re-formed, most of them with former flying squadron numberplates. There are currently thirty-two RAuxAF Squadrons and units still serving, including a RAuxAF band. Those squadrons that were allocated former flying squadron number plates have, or are due to have, a Squadron Standard, had its illustrious ancestor been awarded one, and the regulation regarding a 25-year qualifying period is met.

In 2004, a National Memorial to the RAuxAF was dedicated and the National Roll of Honour to those who gave their lives in the cause of freedom was dedicated and laid in the RAF Church, St Clement Danes, London, in October 2012, and is reproduced in this book. Full details of all current and past AAF and RAuxAF squadrons and units are also to be found within the pages of this book, or by accessing the Royal Auxiliary Air Force Foundation site (rauxaf.net) or the RAuxAF Wikipedia site (rauxaf.org) as well as the RAF web site.

Chapter 1

The Origins of the Auxiliary Air Force

In 1909, Louis Bleriot became the first man to fly across the English Channel, leaving Calais and arriving in Dover, twenty-one miles. This flight had major implications for the defence of Great Britain because, as an island, Britain always had a large navy and a land army to protect it from attack. Bleriot's flight meant that this island status could now be challenged. At the end of 1911 the Prime Minister, Asquith, appointed a Sub-Committee of Imperial Defence, chaired by Lord Haldane, whose role it was to decide what measures would be needed to ensure that Britain developed an 'an efficient aerial service.'[2] The sub-committee's membership included proponents of an aviation corps, Colonel David Henderson and Captain Frederick H. Sykes, men with army careers and backgrounds, who could both fly.[3] The sub-committee recommended an aeronautical service comprising the Royal Flying Corps (RFC), with a Naval wing and a Central Flying School. The RFC was constituted by Royal Warrant on 13 April 1912 and was controlled by the Army Council and commanded by Captain Sykes.[4] Given the Admiralty's resistance to inter-service links, the Royal Flying Corps was forced to cede the Naval wing, which was renamed the Royal Naval Air Service on 1 July 1914.[5]

Those who wished to join the Royal Flying Corps had first to qualify for the Royal Aero Club (RAeC) Pilot Certificate by taking a civilian flying course at their own expense. The Royal Aero Club had been created in 1901 and was itself very influential in the growth of aviation in Britain. It was responsible for the training of most military pilots up to 1915 when military schools took over the job. The club controlled all private and sporting flying

---

2 Sir Maurice Dean, *The Royal Air Force and Two World Wars,* (London, 1979) p 7.

3 Michael Armitage, *The Royal Air Force – An Illustrated History,* (London, 1993) p 37.

4 Stephen E Koss, *Lord Haldane: Scapegoat for Liberalism*, (USA, 1969) p 103.

5 Chaz Bowyer, *History of the* RAF, (London, 1977) p 21.

in the United Kingdom and regulated flying records and competitions. By the end of the First World War, more than 6,300 military pilots had taken the RAeC Aviators Certificates, and a new Light Aeroplane Club scheme was formed ensuring that between 1925 and 1939 about sixty Flying Clubs were started, training over 5,000 pilots, supporting the aircraft industry and providing a nucleus of RAF and AAF pilots for the Second World War.

The First World War allowed for the expansion of the RFC and highlighted the crucial role that aircraft could play in future conflicts. As the war progressed, the British Government entered into discussions to decide the future of aviation within the military and in June 1917, a Cabinet Committee was formed, chaired by General Jan Christiaan Smuts, Minister of Defence of South Africa and a member of the War Cabinet. As he was not British, he was detached from the inter-service rivalry that existed between the Army and the Royal Navy and also in many ways, from the influence of Government. The first report of the committee recommended that a single command be established for all fighter aircraft, anti-aircraft and search batteries and all observation posts. The second report was even more far reaching, arguing for the creation of a separate Air Ministry, since Smuts believed that aerial operations would in fact supersede the operations of the navy and army given their potential to devastate enemy territory, centres of industry and cities. [6] Parliament passed The Air Force (Constitution) Act on 20 November 1917. The RNAS and the RFC were merged on 01 April 1918 and on that day, a new third service, the Royal Air Force, was created. By the end of the war, the RAF possessed more than twenty-two thousand aircraft making it the world's largest air force. [7]

The war had heralded much loss of life, but enormous advances in both aeroplane and engine design and performance had taken place. Throughout the 1920s there was also a feeling of both relief and euphoria at the end of hostilities which, despite the austerity of the time, meant that those who could afford it were determined to enjoy themselves, a time that gave rise to the term 'the roaring twenties.'

In November 1919, Winston Churchill was appointed to the post of Secretary of State for War and Air and Hugh Trenchard accepted the post of Chief of the Air Staff and produced a White Paper called 'An Outline of the Scheme for the Permanent Organization of the Royal Air Force'

---

6 Jan Christian Smuts, *J C Smuts*, (London, 1952) p 107.
7 John D.R. Rawlings, *The History of the Royal Air Force*, (Feltham, 1984) p 52.

in December 1919. Trenchard wanted to create an air force reserve that would be raised on a territorial basis, and which would allow for the skills and expertise that had been developed within the RFC to be preserved, thus allowing for future expansion when the political climate was more propitious. In July 1920, a confidential document originating from the Air Ministry, entitled 'Territorial Air Force' (TAF), proposed a scheme in which a new organization would be created.

The TAF would take over the responsibility for the aerial defence of the United Kingdom; furthermore, should a war begin, the TAF would be able to reinforce the RAF. [8] Trenchard saw the TAF as an alternative to increased military spending on the RAF, which would enable him to gain support for his air reserves, without challenging the Government's position on disarmament and reduction of military spending.[9]

Churchill stated that the beginning of a very small TAF, made up of six squadrons, would commence in 1920. This started during a period of economic depression which resulted in increased taxation and a massive increase in unemployment. Public expenditure was blamed for this, and Sir Edward Geddes was appointed to prepare a report on National Expenditure. The final report put forward a round of public service cuts in several areas including the Army, Navy, education, and public health.

So, as the reserve squadrons began to be talked about, the concerns of many were raised regarding whether proficiency in the air could be achieved when the reserve personnel were working on a part-time basis. During 1923, discussions continued resulting in the decision to form two different categories of reserves. The Auxiliary Air Force and the Special Reserve. The two kinds of reserves would be in competition with each other to see which was the most popular. Key differences between the two were that the SR squadrons were to be commanded by a regular officer, there would be a Headquarters (HQ) and one flight of regulars plus one or two SR flights. The squadrons were sited near engineering centres and there was a limited attendance for the SR for service familiarisation and discipline. Officers and men would be recruited directly by the units, those who became officers would learn to fly in the unit, whereas the men had to be skilled tradesmen prior to volunteering and remained within their trade throughout their service. The squadrons were numbered in the 500 series.

---

8 National Archives, Air 2/273.

9 Andrew Boyle, *Trenchard,* (London, 1962) p 203.

The AAF on the other hand enlisted all their personnel through a local County Association. Officers had to be licensed pilots, the airmen were also recruited differently, they did not need to be skilled tradesmen because they were taught their trades in their squadrons. The organization consisted of three flights of AAF personnel with a small HQ staff of regulars. Squadrons were located close to centres of population with frequent attendance at a town HQ and local airfield plus annual camp. Auxiliary squadrons were also established for medical officers and chaplains. These squadrons were numbered in the 600 series.

In 1924 the Auxiliary Air Force and Air Forces Reserve Act was passed allowing for six auxiliary squadrons and seven Special Reserve squadrons. It was thought that the auxiliary squadrons would appeal to officers and airmen who wanted to serve together within individual localities, whereas the SR squadrons would appeal to men who wanted more of a connection with the regular air force.

In June 1925, Air Ministry Pamphlet No. 2 entitled 'Notes for the information of candidates for commissions in the General Duties Branch for service in Special Reserve Squadrons' stated:

> Special Reserve Squadrons will be raised and maintained in certain localities as part of the air defence of Great Britain. In peacetime each of these squadrons will be located at an aerodrome in the vicinity of the town from which the Special Reserve personnel of the squadron are recruited. Each squadron is associated for purposes of Home Defence with a regular air force aerodrome which will form its war station and to which it will proceed when called out to take its place in the air defences of the country, they will be keeping themselves efficient by attendance at the aerodrome and compliance otherwise with the conditions of their service. These conditions are made as elastic as possible to minimise interference with the civil life of officers and airmen.[10]

These conditions of service were different from those of the AAF. Selection of officers to new AAF squadrons was left to the Commanding Officer of

---

10 Leslie Hunt, *Twenty-One Squadrons. The History of the Royal Auxiliary Air Force 1925-1957,* (London, 1972), p10.

each squadron who 'will nominate to the Air Ministry gentlemen to fill the remaining vacancies on the establishment of his unit'.[11]

In an era when flying was a growing sport and air displays a popular form of entertainment, the reserve units had little difficulty in attracting recruits. Many squadrons ran an active social programme, and some took on the characteristics of a club. Publicity surrounding aviation was very exciting with the exploits of Charles Lindbergh, Amy Johnson and Amelia Earhart appearing regularly in the newspapers and magazines. Civil air travel blossomed, the creation of new and more expansive routes across the world, a string of airports, embracing the opening of Croydon Airport, the founding of Imperial Airways and the establishment of a chain of refuelling stops across the Pacific Ocean, pioneered by Pan American with their huge Clipper Flying Boats. It comes as no surprise that the Auxiliary Air Force captured the public imagination, particularly after the first flight over Mount Everest was completed in April 1933 by Sir Douglas Douglas-Hamilton and David Fowler McIntyre, both of 602 (City of Glasgow) Squadron. Enormous crowds attended the annual Empire Air Days at Hendon which featured AAF squadrons in their brightly coloured biplanes in immaculate formation.

The AAF soon acquired a somewhat flamboyant image, indeed, Goering, head of the German Luftwaffe referred to 'long haired weekenders' and, because it had its own culture it soon was able to ingratiate its squadrons with the local county associations and communities, holding open days for the public and hosting local dignitaries and business. Squadron badges reflected this county or city affiliation and the squadrons soon belonged to their individual local communities. This was an important factor in attracting recruits which led to the transfer of the Special Reserve Squadrons to the AAF in 1936.

From 1926 onwards, the RAF Establishment Committee began to discuss the merger of the SR squadrons into the AAF. The evidence seemed to suggest that the auxiliaries were proving to be a much more attractive proposition. Recruiting for the AAF units was easier as there were fewer restraints. The AAF units were more economical as there were fewer regular personnel and also the morale was higher because there was a stronger sense

---

11 TNA, AIR2/696, Re-organisation of Special Reserve Squadrons as Auxiliary Air Force Squadrons, 'Notes regarding the formation of Special Reserve and Auxiliary Air Force squadrons, Necessity for two separate organisations, 6 September 1931.'

of belonging to the local area. In 1933, it was pointed out that there was no doubt that in 'general *espirit de corps* and efficiency in doing the duties assigned to them, the auxiliary squadrons are far superior. I find that in past discussions of the subject, it has been generally agreed that it would be advantageous to do away with the distinctive features of the SR squadrons in favour of the AAF. Furthermore, a decision to convert SR squadrons into AAF squadrons would be a timely recognition of the progress of the AAF and one which full advantage could be taken in the Estimates Speech.'[12]

It was also mentioned that 'speaking very broadly the SR squadrons have been more difficult to recruit and somewhat less successful in the result than the AAF squadrons, more especially as regards airmen. This may arise from the fact that the latter have the civic, and tradition, of a county association behind them, an advantage which the SR squadrons do not enjoy.'[13] Other reasons given were that officers were not taught to fly in the AAF units whilst some SR officers are already pilots on joining. Skilled tradesmen did not desire to work in their spare time at their own trades. They joined the SR units to learn to do something different. The sub-committee claimed that these reasons coupled with the great success in efficiency achieved by AAF squadrons suggested that all units ought to be on AAF lines.[14]

The arguments put forward, in favour of the merger were that there would be a greater economy of personnel. There would also be a greater ease in recruiting men, because choice would be limited to one rather than two organizations. This would mean that those who wanted to become members of the RAF volunteers would know exactly what they were volunteering for and what was required of them, rather than having to look at two different sets of rules, regulations and opportunities. Another reason given for the merger was the possibility of higher professional standards because recruiting procedures would be strictly adhered to due to the lack of choice available. Also, there was the idea that the unit belonged to the volunteers and there was likely to be a greater *espirit de corps* if the men were largely reserves as opposed to being largely regulars with a small number of volunteers. Another idea put forward was that an AAF unit which was fostered by the town or country would have much more local

---

12 TNA, AIR2/696, Re-organisation of Special Reserve Squadrons as Auxiliary Air Force Squadrons, 'Notes regarding the formation of Special Reserve and Auxiliary Air Force squadrons, Air Council, The future of the Special Reserve Squadrons,' 5 April 1935.

13 Ibid.

14 Tom Moulson, *The Flying Sword, the Story of 601 Squadron,* (London, 1964), P93.

influence and atmosphere than a regular squadron because the men would all have dual roles in both the local community and as part of the squadron as a whole. Finally, there was at the time more interest in the AAF than in the SR squadrons. After much discussion and debate, the SR squadrons were merged into the AAF squadrons in 1936.

The members of the AAF always appeared to be very pleased with themselves. There was a great deal of elitism due to education in prestigious public schools and universities, their employment as financiers and bankers and owners of family businesses. The elite sports that they took part in such as riding and yachting and rowing. They believed themselves to be gentleman amateurs, with the notion that they could do in their spare time what other regulars had to devote all their energies too.

This gave rise to a feeling of effortless superiority. It might be thought that 'the auxiliaries were the snobbish preserve of the rich.' There is an element of truth in this but the social strictures of the 1920s and 30s, once the decision was made that all auxiliary pilots should either hold a pilot's licence or be able to afford one, the die was cast as only those wealthy enough would be selected. The culture of the auxiliaries was a direct result of the recruiting and selection policy at the time that restricted entry to those who were rich enough to fly.

The appointment of Adolf Hitler to the post of Chancellor in Germany in January 1933 prompted a realisation that a new threat to national security was emerging. Viscount Swinton, Secretary of State for Air, was given the challenge in 1935 of expanding the Royal Air Force. He has been described as 'the architect of the renaissance of the Royal Air Force and the most emphatic (Cabinet) exponent of effective rearmament.'[15] Subsequently, as the need to recruit more reserve pilots increased, it became clear that since the Auxiliary Air Force was something of a *corps d'elite* and was composed of formed units, it was an unsuitable organization to handle the vast number of reserve pilots who had to be recruited and trained. The idea of a Volunteer Reserve was developed in 1936. Its purpose was to fill the gaps between the entry requirements of the Auxiliary Air Force and the regular RAF, 'the intention was to convey a clear message that whilst there was an educational hurdle to be surmounted there were to be no social barriers for reservists to cross.'[16]

---

15 J.A. Cross, *Lord Swinton*, (Oxford, 1982) p 144.
16 Tony Mansell, *The Royal Air Force Volunteer Reserve 1936-1939* in *RAF Reserve and Auxiliary Forces*, (Oxford, 2003) p 30.

Thus, the RAFVR would have a wider appeal to potential pilot recruits and would ensure that background and status did not become an obstacle for enlistment, as perceived to be the case in the AAF. The decision to create the RAFVR was significant since:

> In January 1938 the AAF was running at only fifty-one per cent of its peacetime establishment of pilots and following a committee of enquiry chaired by Under Secretary of State Harold Balfour, it was forced to begin – in the face of opposition from amongst its squadrons – to train some of its own non-commissioned ground and aircrew members as pilots to compensate for the shortfall of its officer numbers. Even so, it entered the war still seriously below its established strength.[17]

By 1937 the recruitment of officers for the AAF was satisfactory on some squadrons, but the overall recruiting was never up to requirements. No squadron was fully up to strength in all ranks. AAF squadrons were regarded as part of the first line defence and the recruiting position was such as to cause serious concern in 1937. Pay and allowances were insufficient to cover out-of-pocket expenses. The annual cost of belonging to an AAF squadron was between £30 and £50 for an officer and £20 for an airman. These expenses were due, in the main, to the large number of attendances the AAF personnel were required to make and the distance they had to travel without adequate financial compensation. Thus, financial considerations were the main reason for low AAF recruiting, and for attracting potential new recruits to the newly formed RAFVR, for which more generous terms had been authorised. Other factors in addition to finance influenced the rate of AAF recruiting. These included the demands on the spare time demanded of personnel in carrying out the training expected of them, the shortage of aircraft for training purposes which restricted the recruitment of pilots to full establishment, insufficient publicity as compared to other branches of non-regular service and the expense of meeting the extra premium required by insurance companies to cover flying risks.

In an attempt to stimulate AAF recruiting and to remove the growing sense of injustice experienced by many officers and airmen of the AAF, a

---

17 Ibid, p 32.

committee was set up, under the chairmanship of the Under Secretary of State for Air in January 1938 to examine the recruitment, training and terms and conditions for the Auxiliary Air Force.

At that time, the AAF consisted of eleven Bomber, five Fighter and three Army Co-operation squadrons, a total of nineteen. The total personnel strength of the Bomber and Fighter squadrons was 237 officer pilots, 49 other officers and 1,985 airmen. These figures represent only fifty-one per cent of the peacetime establishment of officers and seventy-seven per cent of that for airmen. In view of the role in which the squadrons would be expected to play in the event of war, it was a most unsatisfactory position.

The committee issued its report in April 1938 and its recommendations led to great improvements in the terms and conditions of the AAF which was reorganised on a more realistic basis. The committee recommended that the emoluments of officers and airmen should be increased; that the aircraft for the AAF squadrons under the approved expansion scheme should be supplied up to establishment with the least possible delay; that there should be additional publicity and that a reasonable level of assistance from public funding should be provided towards the expense of private insurance towards accident or death undertaken by individuals accepting flying duties in the non-regular forces. In addition, all those members of the AAF who were provisionally accepted for commissioning for pilot duties, subject to them being able to produce evidence of qualifying for a pilot's licence, were now able to claim up to £117 reimbursement towards the cost of taking private flying lessons to enable them to join the AAF. Needless to say, if they failed to qualify, no such claim was possible.[18]

The committee recommended that personnel establishments, which then included trained personnel as well as those under training, on the basis that squadrons were both operational and training units and were thus higher than war establishments should be related to the number that would be required to enable the squadron to function in war.

The committee considered the current policy whereby pilot duties in auxiliary squadrons were carried out solely by commissioned officers. The AAF differed in that respect from the RAF, where airmen pilots occupied a definitive place in the establishment of all squadrons, except Army Co-operation squadrons. The committee recommended that airmen pilots should be introduced into AAF squadrons. This change was strenuously

---

18 A.M. Pamphlet No 1 dated January 1938.

9

opposed by many AAF squadrons, but reluctantly accepted. Airmen pilots were to be drawn both from airmen already serving in the AAF squadrons and from volunteers entering the AAF specifically for pilot duties. In the event, just nineteen AAF SNCO pilots were to take part in the Battle of Britain.

In the light of the recently approved organization which involved the grouping of all AAF squadrons with the appropriate regular formations and the consequent disappearance of the distinctive Auxiliary Group, the committee considered an appointment within the Air Ministry of an officer of senior rank for the purpose of effecting liaison in Auxiliary Air Force matters. As a result of their consequent recommendations, an AAF officer was appointed Director of the Auxiliary Air Force in the autumn of 1938.[19] He was responsible to the Air Council for liaison between the Air Ministry, Groups, Commands, AAF squadrons and TAVRA, but he was given no executive powers.

It can, therefore, be seen that, by the end of the decade, the AAF had been formed and expanded, and regulated to the point that it was made more ready to meet the challenges of the war to come. During the 1920s and 1930s, the AAF had spawned a (not entirely undeserved) reputation for being socially exclusive, mainly from its recruiting and selection policy which was predicated on those from the wealthy and titled echelons of society.

Sir Thomas Inskip, Minister for the Co-ordination of Defence, carried out a review of defence expenditure and his report was submitted to the Cabinet on 15 December 1937. His review, entitled 'Interim Report on Defence Expenditure' marked the start of a fundamental change in British preparations for any future war in the air. He argued that the role of the RAF should not be to deliver an early knockout blow to the Germans but instead to prevent them from knocking out the British.[20] This was a complete reversal of priorities. The emphasis had moved from long-range bomber production to that of fighter plane production. As a consequence of German rearmament, the Spanish Civil War, and the Munich crisis of 1938, the RAF began an expansion programme which resulted in a further eight AAF squadrons being formed.

---

19 A.M. File 699153/37
20 Barry D. Powers, *Strategy without Slide Rule. British Air Strategy 1914-1939*, (London, 1976) p 243.

In 1937, priority was given to bomber production, then a year later fewer bombers and more fighters. After the Munich crisis, by late 1938, the emphasis was on creating modern fighter aircraft. At the start of 1939, RAF strength stood at 135 squadrons, and in addition to this, the Auxiliary Air Force comprised nineteen squadrons.[21] In August 1939 members of the AAF and RAFVR were embodied into the RAF. There were twenty Auxiliary Air Force squadrons at the outbreak of war, fourteen squadrons who were fighter units, four squadrons who operated under the control of Coastal Command and two squadrons whose duties were army co-operation. Shores notes:

'At this stage, as the AAF was being mobilised, all units were undoubtedly at their most "pure" as "auxiliary" squadrons. Certainly, their ground crew personnel were essentially those who had faithfully served their chosen units throughout much of the 1930s and who were all enlisted under provisions which allowed the AAF personnel to refuse a posting to any other unit.'[22]

The other reserve organization was of course the Royal Air Force Volunteer Reserve (RAFVR), and it is appropriate at this point to appraise its formation and present a brief illustration of its purpose and principals. The RAFVR was formed in 1936 and was the brainchild of two men, Arthur Tedder who was an air commodore in the Air Member for Personnel's Department, and W.E. Scott, an Assistant Secretary in S7 which was part of the Air Ministry Secretariat serving AMP. I am grateful to Dr Tony Mansell of Kings College London for his permission to quote from his paper, presented to the Royal Air Force Historical Society and published in their Journal No. 11 in 1993. His paper was titled 'Professionals, Amateurs and Private Armies.'[23] W.E. Scott wrote a memo in February 1936 which contained the blueprint for the new reserve. His paper made it clear that a mass direct entry reserve would have to be created which would appeal to popular sentiment at the time. What was that sentiment?

---

21 John, D.R. Rawlings, *The History of the Royal Air Force,* (Feltham, 1984) p 87.
22 Christopher Shores, The Auxiliary Air Force in WWII, in *Royal Air Force Reserve and Auxiliary Forces,* (Oxford, 2003) p 40.
23 *Professional, Amateurs and Private Armies,* Mansell published by the RAF Historical Society Journal No 11, 1993.

In 1933, the journalist, novelist and playwright, J.B. Priestly, although not a sociologist or historian, set off on a tour around England looking at things and talking to people. These activities call for very accurate observation and interpretation of affairs. In 1934, just about the time when the RAF was beginning its expansion, he published his findings in a book called *English Journey*. There are three Englands, he wrote:

> The first is that of the history books, with its castles, cathedrals and great estates, the sort of things that the tourist comes to see. It has long since ceased to earn its living of course. The second England is that of the Industrial Revolution, mainly located in the north-east and the north-west. That was already beginning to show the signs of decay that we now see in such places. The Third England is the England of the cinema, the dance hall, greyhound racing and the wireless; of motor cars and filling stations; of Woolworths and the department store, of factories that didn't look like factories and factory girls that looked like actresses. An essentially democratic England this, where what you could actually do was beginning to matter more than who you were or liked to believe you were.

The young people in this Third England, Priestley claimed, did not content themselves with playing chorus in an opera where the leading roles had been taken by their social superiors. Their heroes and heroines were meritocrats, sportsmen and sports women, film stars and the likes of Amy Johnson or Malcolm Campbell. It was for this third England that this new reserve was designed.

The proposal called for a direct entry reserve on what were described as democratic principles. By the 1930s there were strong feelings in the country against any pre-determined social hierarchy, caste, or old school tie distribution of commissions; all men should enter at the same level – that of airmen pilot. Commissioning might take place later, or even at entry in a minority of cases, but always according to proven aptitude. This question of social or democratic hierarchy commissioning was really a matter of choosing between public schoolboys who might be lost by democratic entry and secondary schoolboys who might be lost by special hierarchy commissions. The secondary schoolboys won the day, but Etonians were to be found in the Volunteer Reserve![24] In fact, Dr Louise Wilkinson's research shows us that larger numbers of men who joined the RAFVR came from better backgrounds than those who joined the AAF.

Another popular mood at the time was anti-militarism, so the sporting and recreational aspects of flying were to be emphasised in recruiting. Every attempt was made by bringing the reserve to the men by making access to it in geographic terms. Flying at weekends or on summer evenings was to be supplemented by ground training at conveniently located town centres providing good social facilities and helping to build up *esprit de corps*. Tedder saw that the organization must be quite different from that of the AAF, although the new reserve would also consist of weekend fliers. The AAF was bound up with the Territorial Associations and they, like their country gentlemen members, were in Tedder's view, moribund.

The new reserve was a brilliant concept, the product of forward-thinking minds. What should it be called? Citizen's Air Force was one proposal considered by the Air Ministry, because flying training was carried out by civilian flying clubs, but the one chosen was, of course, the Royal Air Force Volunteer Reserve. Through this portal was to pass the overwhelming majority of those who fought and died in the ensuing war, but it is important to remember that all those who enlisted or were commissioned, except for overseas personnel, after the outbreak of war were in the RAFVR. However, research into all those RAFVR members who served in AAF squadrons up to and including the Battle of Britain in 1940 shows that most were pre-war weekend fliers.

Finally, the RAFVR differed from the AAF in one other aspect. The AAF was formed into squadrons, whereas the RAFVR was not, as it was originally created to form a pool of reservist pilots, which, on completion of flying training, would be posted and sent to fill vacancies on any RAF squadron, in any role. The airmen of the AAF, on the other hand, who enlisted before April 1939, could not be posted away from their parent squadron without their consent, due to their terms and conditions of service, which in many cases did not end until their current engagement which expired as late as 1943. Thereafter, they were either transferred to the RAFVR or discharged from the Service.

All members of the RAFVR were required to wear the insignia 'VR' on their uniforms until 1943 when the regulation was withdrawn as it was

---

24 Dr Louise Wilkinson, *The Territorial Air Force*, (Barnsley, 2020)

thought to be divisive. For the record, the trained strength of the RAFVR on the outbreak of war in September 1939 was 6,646 pilots, 1,623 had been trained as observers and 1,948 as wireless operators/air gunners.[25]

The twenty squadrons of the Auxiliary Air Force at the start of the Second World War

600 (City of London) Squadron, formed on 15 October 1925 at Northolt, before moving to Hendon in 1926; it was affiliated to the City of London Territorial Association, and most of its members worked in the City at Lloyds, the Stock Exchange, or in other financial firms and legal institutions.

'The Millionaires Mob', otherwise known as 601 (County of London) Squadron, born in White's Club, St James', W1, the idea of Lord Edward Grosvenor who very much wanted to create a civilian air force. It was formed on 14 October 1925, and based at Northolt, before moving to Hendon.

602 (City of Glasgow) Squadron, formed on 15 September 1925 at Renfrew, with Captain J.D. Latta as Commanding Officer.

603 (City of Edinburgh) Squadron, formed on 14 October 1925 at RAF Turnhouse as a day bomber squadron with an establishment of twenty-three officers and 158 airmen. The first Commanding Officer was Squadron Leader J. McKelvie.

604 (County of Middlesex) Squadron, formed on 17 March 1930 at Hendon. Its CO was Lieutenant Colonel A.S.W. Dore, DSO, TD, a former soldier in the Worcester Regiment who had transferred to the Royal Flying Corps in 1917.

605 (County of Warwick) Squadron, formed on 5 October 1926 at Castle Bromwich, Birmingham. For some reason the number 606 was never allocated or used by any other air force formation until 1996.

607 (County of Durham) Squadron, formed at Usworth on 17 March 1930.

608 (North Riding) Squadron, formed on 17 March 1930. It was assigned to No. 6 Auxiliary Group as a bomber squadron and located at Thornaby.

609 (West Riding) Squadron, formed on 10 February 1936 at Yeadon near Leeds. Its CO was Squadron Leader Harald Peake. He was a retired officer of the Yorkshire Dragoons Yeomanry.

---

25 Patrick Bishop, *Air Force Blue*, (London, 2017)

610 (County of Chester) Squadron formed in 1936 at Hooton Park.

611 (West Lancashire) Squadron, formed in name only on 10 February 1936 at RAF Hendon, London, five days after the Liverpool City Council had granted a tenancy to the Air Ministry of five acres of land to the east of the Chapel House Farm Speke.

612 (County of Aberdeen) Squadron, formed on 1 June 1937 at Dyce Aerodrome as an army co-operation unit.

613 (City of Manchester) Squadron, formed at Ringway on 1 March 1939, the last of the original AAF squadrons to be formed before the start of the Second World War.

614 (County of Glamorgan) Squadron, formed on 1 June 1937 at Llandow in Wales.

615 (County of Surrey) Squadron, formed on 1 June 1937 at RAF Kenley.

616 (South Yorkshire) Squadron, formed on 1 November 1938 at Doncaster. Squadron Leader the Earl of Lincoln was posted in from 609 Squadron to command the unit.

500 (County of Kent) Squadron, formed at RAF Manston on 15 March 1931 as a Special Reserve Squadron.

501 (County of Gloucester) Squadron, formed at Filton on 14 June 1929 as a Special Reserve Squadron.

502 (Ulster) Squadron, formed on 1 May 1925, as the only Irish Special Reserve Squadron, commanded by Squadron Leader R.D. Oxland.

503 (County of Lincoln) Squadron, formed at Waddington on 5 October 1926 however, recruiting and retention problems led to the disbandment of this squadron in 1938, with a nucleus of personnel transferring to the newly formed 616 (South Yorkshire) Squadron at Doncaster that same year.

Finally, 504 (County of Nottingham) Squadron, formed at Hucknall on 26 March 1928.

A major change in recruitment took place in 1939 when a committee under the chairmanship of Sir James Barnes, Under Secretary of State for Air, recommended increases in pay and allowances for the AAF and required them to accept airmen pilots, first by training some of their own ground crew and then by taking in direct-entry men. Many AAF squadrons reacted violently to this order but were forced to comply and this resulted in a handful of AAF sergeant pilots in British AAF squadrons. On enlistment, recruits for other ranks were guaranteed that they would never be called upon to serve further than five miles from their home airfield.

Initially the majority of squadrons were formed in the light bomber role, being equipped with the DH9, the Westland Wapiti, Hawker Hind, Hart and Demon and other similar types. However, by the outbreak of war, all the auxiliary squadrons which had hitherto been part of No. 6 (Auxiliary Group) had been re-roled, fourteen of them as fighter squadrons, coming under the appropriate regular RAF formation (Fighter Command).

The following table shows the Auxiliary Air Force Order of Battle at the outbreak of the Second World War. They were or were in the process of equipping with the aircraft types shown.

Fighter Command

Unit	Aircraft
501 Squadron	Hurricane
504 Squadron	Hurricane
601 Squadron	Hurricane
605 Squadron	Hurricane
607 Squadron	Gladiator
615 Squadron	Gladiator
600 Squadron	Blenheim 1f
604 Squadron	Blenheim 1f
602 Squadron	Spitfire
603 Squadron	Spitfire
609 Squadron	Spitfire
610 Squadron	Spitfire
611 Squadron	Spitfire
616 Squadron	Spitfire

Coastal Command

Unit	Aircraft
500 Squadron	Avro Anson
502 Squadron	Avro Anson
608 Squadron	Avro Anson
612 Squadron	Avro Anson

Army Cooperation

Unit	Aircraft
613 Squadron	Lysander
614 Squadron	Lysander

Whilst most of the accolades go to the auxiliary fighter squadrons for their contribution to the Battle of Britain, a glance at these tables will show the other varied roles that the Auxiliary Air Force undertook both during the Battle of Britain and thereafter, in support of the Royal Air Force in its many and varied wartime operations.

The history of the Auxiliary's formation and the overview of the defence policies of the 1920s and '30s helps to underpin the thinking behind building up a trained reserve of pilots and air crew from 1924. It is also clear that a great deal is known about the men who became pilots prior to the Second World War. Indeed, much has been written about their social backgrounds and their antics primarily during the period 1924-1939. What is also apparent is that these men were excellent, efficient, and daring in fulfilling their duties. Details about these officers can be found in Dr Wilkinson's book, *The Territorial Air Force. The RAF's Voluntary Squadrons 1926-1957,* published by Pen and Sword in September 2020. On the other hand, the Auxiliary Air Force did not just contain pilots and aircrew. This book is about all the men and women who served within the Auxiliary Air Force, the ground crew, the radar and wireless operators, the women in the fighter control and radar reporting units, and in the women's auxiliary air force. They all gave up their time to volunteer for the AAF. They all did different jobs within the AAF, and all had a vital role to play from 1924 to 2024.

It has been said that the AAF was a 'gentlemen's flying club' A recent book by Dr Louise Wilkinson certainly paints that picture.[26] It would be easy to cite the fact that AAF pilots had to hold a pilot's licence in order to be commissioned as AAF pilots but there is more to it than that. To begin with, the sobriquet 'Gentlemen's Flying Club' with its overtones of elitism can hardly be laid solely at the door of the AAF. When Dr Wilkinson undertook research for her excellent book, she started by tracking down the history of every aircrew member of the AAF. She then trawled through electronic records from the *Times* newspaper and other sources to identify those members who had

---

26 Dr Louise Wilkinson, *The Territorial Air Force*, (Barnsley, 2020)

submitted birth, deaths, and marriage announcements in those publications, on the not unreasonable assumption that only the well-heeled or socially conscious would do that kind of thing, so that she could statistically analyse the social and economic background of as many former AAF members as possible, in order to arrive at her conclusions. In fairness, this was an innovative approach and with the passage of time, with so many former AAF personnel since deceased, it would have been impossible to do otherwise.

The AAF was formed as a separate Air Force when creating national air forces was in vogue amongst nations which could afford it and which wanted a seat at the international aviation table. It should also come as no surprise that the AAF soon aquired a somewhat flamboyant image (Goering, head of the Luftwaffe, referred to 'long-haired weekenders') and, because it had its own culture it soon was able to ingratiate its squadrons with the local county associations and communities, holding open days for the public and hosting local dignitaries and businesses. Squadron badges reflected this county or city affiliation, and the squadrons became 'their' adopted squadron. This was an important factor in attracting recruits which led to the transfer of the Special Reserve Squadrons to the AAF in 1936.

Recruiting and Retention

From the start all applicants for a commission had to be in possession of a civil pilot's licence. This inevitably meant that applicants (or the Bank of Mum and Dad) had to be in a position of some wealth. Moreover, as caring (and wealthy) parents, there was a natural tendency to give their offspring the best possible education, which usually meant paying for education at public or private schools. In most cases this led to university qualification and the award of degrees which, in turn, led to employment in the Civil Service, government or senior appointments in finance, commerce and industry etc, and such appointments usually resulted in those applicants themselves becoming successful and wealthy, passing on the same benefit to their children, thereby perpetuating the same cycle of privilege.

This was the culture and society that prevailed (and still does exist to some extent) at the time. However, this was not unique to the recruiting and selection of candidates for the AAF. In his light-hearted account of flying between the wars, Wing Commander S.J. Carr recounts an interview he attended at Adastral House in London in February 1929.[27] In addition to some general knowledge questions, he was asked if he played rugby and if so, what position, cricket and if not, why not, could he ride a horse, sail a boat, drive a car or shoot, to which, apart from not playing cricket, which raised a few eyebrows, he affirmed. Now, in the light of all the foregoing, the reader might be forgiven for thinking that the said candidate was applying for a commission in the AAF. Not so. He was applying for a Permanent Commission at the Royal Air Force College at Cranwell which was 'soaked in the public-school ethos' and which cost £100 a term plus another £100 for uniform and books and which had, amongst its excellent sporting facilities, two packs of foxhounds![28]

During 1936, the AAF was asked if it would be able to help with the training of pilots for the newly formed RAF Volunteer Reserve and to agree to the formation of a Branch of Accountants, both of which were so strenuously opposed that the ideas were hastily dropped. In his paper 'Professionals, Amateurs and Private Armies', Dr Tony Mansell argues that 'the AAF was not prepared to sacrifice its exclusive character to serve wider interests.'[29] A more pragmatic view might suggest that the AAF was formed to be part of the Front Line and was organised as such, and simply not structured or established otherwise. Final judgement should be withheld until we come to look at the evidence.

Personalities

The exclusive nature of recruiting into the Auxiliary Air Force before the war meant that it was inevitable that the Force would attract people with a privileged background, or many with wealth and influence. That said, the AAF had, amongst its members, personnel of great courage and fame, as well as fortune. One of the earliest celebrities was Squadron Leader The Marquess of Douglas and Clydesdale, OC 602 (City of Glasgow) Squadron who, in 1933, became the first to fly over Mount Everest, (a private venture sponsored by Lady Houston), awarded the Air Force Cross for his achievement, along with Flight Lieutenant McIntyre, the pilot of the second machine.

---

27 S.J. Carr *You Are Not Sparrows,* (London, 1975)

28 Patrick Bishop, *Air Force Blue*, (London, 2017)

29 Dr Tony Mansell, 'Professional Amateurs and Private Armies', in the proceedings of the RAF Historical Society No 11 1993.

Probably the bravest, if somewhat unknown officer was Squadron Leader Roger Bushell, a pre-war barrister from South Africa, so successful in defending wayward RAF miscreants that it was eventually deemed a conflict of interest. This officer was commissioned with 601 Squadron (The Millionaires) and posted to command 92 Squadron RAF in 1940, probably the first auxiliary to command a regular squadron. He was shot down over Dunkirk and ended up incarcerated in Stalag Luft III. He became the legendary 'Big X' of the 'Great Escape', portrayed by Richard Attenborough in the film of the same name. Bushell was recaptured and executed by the Gestapo. In the film, Attenborough is shown wearing the ribbon of the Distinguished Flying Cross, although Bushell was never decorated, other than a belated Mentioned in Despatches.

Other auxiliary luminaries include Group Captain John 'Cats Eyes' Cunningham, the celebrated night fighter pilot, who earned his nickname not because he consumed a regular diet of carrots to improve his night vision (a story put out by the press), but because of the need to protect the security surrounding the development of Airborne Interception Radar (AI). After the war Cunningham went on to become Chief Test Pilot for De Havilland. A dozen of the survivors of the Battle of Britain days later achieved group captain rank, including Group Captain Max Aitken, son of Lord Beaverbrook.

Born on 15 February 1910, Max Aitken was the son of Max Aitken Senior, who later became better known as the press baron Lord Beaverbrook and later the Minister of Aircraft Production under Winston Churchill. Treading the traditional education path through Westminster and Pembroke College, Cambridge, the young playboy then entered civil aviation before returning to England to join his father's newspaper empire. Aitken joined No. 601 (County of London) Squadron AAF in 1935, known variously as 'The Millionaires' being almost entirely populated by other wealthy young men, or 'The Legion' because of the colourful composition of its members. Aitken was a nationally recognised figure, and the press soon dubbed the AAF 'Max Aitken's Air Force' (doubtless due to his press connections.) He habitually disdained RAF Dress Codes and was rarely seen without a silk cravat or scarf around his neck and his top button undone. In truth, these were habits from the First World War when pilots wore silk scarves to counter the soreness caused by the stiff collars they wore, when rapidly turning the head from side to side. Members of 601 Squadron lined their uniforms with red silk and wore red socks. It is claimed that Aitken also lined his battledress jacket with the same silk material, and some AAF squadrons followed suit and do so still. He ended the war in command of the Banff Strike Wing with fifteen credited victories, although none of them during the Battle of Britain. This lengthy discourse about just one pilot has been chosen to illustrate the flamboyant reputation of the AAF.[30].

Four auxiliaries ended up as wing leaders, including Hugh 'Cocky' Dundas, in command of fighter wings and another three as wing commanders. Many others became station commanders or were involved in training at this rank. Squadron Leader Andy McDowell was in command of 616 Squadron in 1944 when it became the first squadron to be equipped with the Meteor jet fighter, and the first to destroy an enemy V1 Flying Bomb by tipping it over with his wing tip; he was subsequently reprimanded for damage to that wing tip. He was followed the same afternoon by a fellow squadron colleague who used more conventional means. Incidentally, two AAF squadrons were chosen to introduce new aircraft into the RAF: 601 Squadron with the unpopular Bell Aircobra in 1941 and 616 Squadron with the Meteor in 1944. These are not large numbers compared to the other successful pilots of the regular squadrons, but it must be remembered that only 100 or so auxiliary pilots survived the Battle of Britain and many of them went on to provide notable leaders for the later years of the war, and the AAF continued to exert a notable influence on the later conduct of hostilities.

Finally, amongst the highest scoring pilots in the Battle of Britain were Squadron Leader Archie McKellar (605 Squadron), a pre-war auxiliary officer and Sergeant 'Ginger' Lacey, an RAFVR man, serving with 501 Squadron. Wing Commander James Bazin who, as an auxiliary fighter pilot, scored ten victories in 1940 and went on to command 9 Squadron, RAF, flying twenty-five sorties on Lancaster bombers. Given that, numerically, members of the AAF were far fewer than their counterparts, they showed that they were capable of comparison with the best.

Personal Stories

Geoffrey Shaw 608 (North Riding) Squadron

Geoffrey originated from Nunthorpe, Teesside and his family owned W.G. Shaw Engineering Co in North Ormesby. His father W.G Shaw

---

30 Les Taylor, *Banff Strike Wing at War: A Unique Photographic History 1939–45*, (Wellington, 2010)

was the President of the Middlesbrough branch of the Institute of British Foundrymen. Geoffrey was educated in Scotland but then attended Cambridge University where he learned to fly as part of the University Air Squadron. He also owned his own aeroplane that he used for long business trips. On 28 September 1930 he was commissioned as a pilot officer in the Auxiliary Air Force. He took part in the MacRobertson Air Race from England to Australia in October 1934.[31] There was a £10,000 prize for the pilot or pilots who came first in the race. The race was organised by the Royal Aero Club in London, and it started at RAF Mildenhall in East Anglia and finished at the Flemington Racecourse in Melbourne. The total distance was 11,300 miles. On the route there were five compulsory stops at Baghdad, Allahabad, Singapore, Darwin, and Charleville, but the individual pilots could choose any route that they liked. Furthermore, along the route there were a further twenty-two airfields which were provided with supplies of fuel and oil by Shell and Stanavo. Also, three days rations for each person on the aircraft, floats, smoke signals and well-maintained instruments. Geoffrey's aeroplane was a B A Eagle, which was a light three-seat aircraft manufactured in the United Kingdom by the British Klemm Aeroplane Company. His plane was named 'The Spirit of WM Shaw and Co Ltd' and was numbered G – ACVU.

Geoffrey did not complete the race, landing at Busherh in Western Iraq, when his landing gear collapsed. In terms of his time with 608 Squadron, he was awarded the Distinguished Flying Cross, as a Wing Commander on 21 February 1941.[32]

Willard Whitney Straight 601 (County of London) Squadron

Whitney was born in New York on 6 November 1912 and the family moved to England in 1925. His father died at the end of the First World War and his mother eventually married Leonard Elmhurst. They then set up a progressive school at their home, Dartington Hall, near Totnes. Whitney attended this school before going to Cambridge University. He was fascinated with aeroplanes and by the age of sixteen he had logged 60 hours of solo flying even though he was not old enough to get a pilot's licence.

---

31 The *Times*, Monday, 24 December 1934, p8
32 https://www.thegazette.co.uk/London/issue/35083/data.pdf page 1077.

Whilst at university he began racing cars, and he used to cycle to the aerodrome where he could then fly to any race meetings. His first continental race was the Swedish Winter Grand Prix held at Lake Ramen. In 1934 he set up his own Grand Prix team racing Maseratis which were painted white and blue, the colours of the United States. He finished seventh in the Monaco Grand Prix and then went on to achieve wins in the Donnington Park Trophy, the Brooklands Mountain Race and the inaugural South African Grand Prix in East London. Due to his success, he was invited to join the best German Auto Union team in 1935, but he turned down the offer primarily because he was anti-fascist and the German team was funded by Hitler's Nazi Government, also, he had promised his fiancé that he would stop racing. He was the head of the Straight Corporation Ltd and he joined the Auxiliary Air Force on 18 July 1938.

Chapter 2

To Dunkirk and the Battle of Britain

At the outbreak of war in September 1939, the AAF had stopped recruiting and was 'embodied' with the RAF. The word 'embodied' means 'included with' so, contrary to popular belief, the AAF was not officially part of the RAF and continued to enjoy its own identity and ethos to a certain extent, whilst being on Active Service along with everybody else. The officers could be posted away from their parent squadrons, but the other ranks could not, without their consent, until their current four-year period of engagement expired when they were given the option to discharge or transfer to the RAFVR. This resulted in manning difficulties for the RAF as the war progressed.[33] By September 1939, there were just thirty squadrons in total available for the air defence of the United Kingdom, including the fourteen newly transferred squadrons of the AAF.

On 16 October 1939, both 602 (City of Glasgow) and 603 (City of Edinburgh) Squadrons destroyed the first enemy aircraft in combat over the British Isles, followed on 28 October by both squadrons bringing down the first enemy aircraft to be shot down over British soil during the war. The newspapers trumpeted *'FIRST BLOOD TO THE AUXILIARIES'* and telegrams of congratulation were sent from the Chief of the Air Staff, AOC-in-C Fighter Command and the AOC 13 Group flew up in person to add his congratulations along with the Honorary Air Commander (HAC) of 602 Squadron and the AOC-in-C Coastal Command.[34] This was a welcome piece of news at the start of a war that harbingered uncertain times to come. A more considered view of these achievements would acknowledge that both squadrons had been left up north to defend that

---

33 RAF Manning Plans and Policy AHB.
34 Leslie Hunt, *Twenty-One Squadrons, The History of the RAuxAF*, (London 1972).

part of the UK and the German bombers were unescorted due to the long range from their bases in Norway which was too far for the single engine Me 109 escort fighter to fly. A question of being in the right place at the right time may be more apt.

On 10 May 1940, the Germans invaded France and the Low Countries. Four AAF squadrons formed part of the Allied Expeditionary Force (AEF) and were despatched to bases in France where they fought with great distinction. However, by 26 May the AEF had been forced back to Dunkirk. Earlier, on 23 May, No. 92 Squadron which had been formed from a nucleus of 601 Squadron AAF on 10 October 1939 under Squadron Leader Roger Bushell, was in action over Calais when he was shot down and taken prisoner. An inveterate escaper, he managed to escape captivity twice before finally being incarcerated in Stalag Luft III where he organised the Great Escape of 1944 when he was finally recaptured and shot by the Gestapo.

The evacuation from Dunkirk took place from 25 May to 2 June 1940. During this time, when over 300,000 troops were rescued from the beaches, some twenty-one squadrons of the RAF and AAF were in action, including nine squadrons of the latter. Indeed, during the whole Battle of France in May 1940, the RAF lost some 900 aircraft to all causes, 250 by 15 May alone, and destroyed some 1,400 of the Luftwaffe. In fact, over Dunkirk, the nine AAF squadrons that were in action included some from bases in the South of England. The RAF suffered sixty-three pilots killed and an additional 108 were shot down and survived during this period, whereas the Luftwaffe, during the Dunkirk fighting, lost 202 aircraft destroyed.[35] Much has been said about the absence of the RAF over Dunkirk but many of the air combats either took place inland, over the sea, or at such a high altitude that only the contrails were visible from the ground.

During the Battle of Britain, of fifteen top scoring squadrons credited with over fifty victories, eight were AAF Squadrons These squadrons came under 11 Group which saw the brunt of the fighting in the south-east of England. These figures are derived from a contemporary record kept by HQ 11 Group at RAF Uxbridge at the end of the Battle.

---

35 Norman Franks, *Air Battle Dunkirk*, (London, 2000).

Squadron Kills

Squadron Number	Number of kills
303 (Polish) Sqn RAF	120
501 (County of Gloucester) Sqn AAF	100
609 (West Riding) Sqn AAF	84
607 (County of Durham) Sqn AAF	84
41 Sqn RAF	82
603 (City of Edinburgh) Sqn AAF	71
72 Sqn RAF	71
602 (City of Glasgow) Sqn AAF	65
43 Sqn RAF	65
213 Sqn RAF	65
249 Sqn RAF	64
601 (County of London) Sqn AAF	57
32 Sqn RAF	56
605 (County of Warwick) Sqn AAF	53
610 (County of Chester) Sqn AAF	51

Battle of Britain 10 July to 31 October 1940

Squadron Commanders[36]

Squadron Number	Commanding Officer (All holding the rank of Squadron Leader)	Branch
501 Squadron	H.A.V. Hogan	RAF College Cranwell
504 Squadron	J.C. Sample DFC	AAF
600 Squadron	D. DeB Clarke	AAF
601 Squadron	M. Aitken DFC	AAF

---

36 RAF Uxbridge 11 Group Contemporary Record 1946. Kenneth G Wynn, *Men of the Battle of Britain*, (Croydon, 1999).

26

Squadron Number	Commanding Officer (All holding the rank of Squadron Leader)	Branch
	W.F.C. Hobson	RAF College Cranwell
	A.P. Hope	AAF
602 Squadron	A.V.R Johnstone DFC	AAF
603 Squadron	G.L. Denholm DFC	AAF
604 Squadron	M.F. Anderson	AAF
605 Squadron	W. Churchill DSO DFC	AAF
	A.A. McKellar DSO	AAF
607 Squadron	J.A. Vick	AAF
609 Squadron	M. Lister-Robinson	RAF/SSC
610 Squadron	J. Ellis DFC	RAF
611 Squadron	M. McCombe	AAF
615 Squadron	J.R. Kayall DSO DFC	AAF
616 Squadron	M. Robinson	AAF
	H.F. Burton	RAF College Cranwell

AAF Squadrons in the Battle of Britain 10 July to 31 October 1940

Service Background	Number
Auxiliary Air Force (AAF)	159
AAF Sergeants	29
Royal Air Force Volunteer Reserve (RAFVR)	286
Short Service Commission	110
Royal Air Force	15
Direct Entry Airman Pilots (DEAC/P)	7
Royal Air Force of Oman (RAFO)	3
Fleet Air Arm	1
Royal Navy (RN)	1
Military Aid Programme	3
University Air Squadrons (UAS)	31
Halton	20
Polish	30

Service Background	Number
Cranwell	9
Canada	2
Free French	4
Belgium	1
New Zealand	5
Czech	2
AC1/AC2 (AAF)	2
Total	**719**[37]

The above table shows the service background of all the personnel who flew with Auxiliary Air Force Squadrons, including multi-crew personnel such as air gunners as well as pilots.

Who Were The Few?

Entry Method Regulars	Number
Cranwell	88
Direct Entry Permanent Commission	18
Short Service Commission	665
Aircraft Apprentices	116
Aircraftmen	48
Direct Entry Airmen Pilots	30
Total	**965**

Entry Method Reserves	Number
Auxiliary Air Force	159
University Air Squadron	99
Auxiliary Air Force Ground & Aircrew	29
Royal Air Force Volunteer Reserve	797
Total all Reserves	**1084**

---

37 Kenneth G. Wynn, *Men of the Battle of Britain*, (Croydon, 1999).

Other Categories	Number
European Air Force pilots	271
Dominion Air Force pilots	66
Fleet Air Arm pilots	59
Total	**396**

Aircraft Crew	Number
Air Gunner	295
Wireless Operator/Air Gunner	96
Radar Operator	101
Observer	102
Total	**595**

Total pilots 2445 [38]

All AAF Aircrew in the Battle of Britain Who Flew from 10 July to 31 October 1940

KIA - Killed in Action   KSB – Killed since Battle

Rank	Name	Squadron	Role	Confirmed	Remarks
PO	Adams D.A.	611	Pilot	1	Also served with 41 Squadron
Flt Lt	Aitken J.W.M.	601	Pilot		OC 601 Squadron
Sgt	Albertini A.V.	600	Pilot		
PO	Aldridge K.R.	501	Pilot	1	Also served 32 Sqn
Sqn Ldr	Anderson M.F.	604	Pilot		OC 604 Sqn
PO	Appleby M.J.	609	Pilot	3	
Sgt	Baker A.C.	610	Pilot	2	
Sgt	Bamberger C.S.	610	Pilot	1	Also served with 41 Sqn

---

38 Mansell The Battle of Britain Memorial Trust 70th Anniversary Publication

Rank	Name	Squadron	Role	Confirmed	Remarks
Fg Off	Barnes J.G.C.	600	Pilot		Wg Cdr 1946
PO	Barnes W.	504	Pilot		
Flt Lt	Barran P.H.	609	Pilot		**KIA 11/07/1940**
Flt Lt	Bazley S.H.	266	Pilot		KIA 02/03/1941
Flt Lt	Bazin J.M.	607	Pilot		
Flt Lt	Beaumont S.G.	609	Pilot		
Fg Off	Bell J.S.	616	Pilot		**KIA 30/08/1940**
Flt Lt	Blackadder W.F.	607	Pilot	1 + 1 shared	
PO	Bland J.W.	501/601	Pilot	1 + 1 shared	**KIA 18/08/1940**
Fg Off	Blayney A.J.	609	Pilot		
Sgt	Booth J.J.	603/213	Radar Op		
Fg Off	Bowring B.H.	600	Pilot	3	Also served with 111 Sqn
Flt Lt	Boyd R.F.	602	Pilot	11 + 1 shared	
Fg Off	Branch G.R.	145	Pilot	2	**KIA 11/08/**1940
Fg Off	Brewster J.	615/616	Pilot		KIA 06/04/1941
Flt Lt	Budd G.O.	604	Pilot		
PO	Carnaby W.F.	264/85	Pilot		KIA 05/02/1943
PO	Casson L.H.	616	Pilot	1	
Sgt	Chandler H.H.	610	Pilot	4	
Fg Off	Chisholm R.A.	604	Pilot		Air Cdr 1946
Sqn Ldr	Churchill W.M.	605/71	Pilot		OC 605 Sqn KIA 26/08/1942
Flt Lt	Clackson D.L.	600	Pilot		Wg Cdr 1946
Sqn Ldr	Clark D. De B.	600	Pilot		OC 600 Sqn
Fg Off	Cleaver G.N.S.	601	Pilot		
Flt Lt	Clyde W.P.	601	Pilot	5 + 1 shared	
Fg Off	Collard P.	615	Pilot	1 +1 shared	
Sgt	Corfe D.F.	610	Pilot	1	Also with 73 and 66 Sqn KIA 25/04/1942

Rank	Name	Squadron	Role	Confirmed	Remarks
Flt Lt	Craig G.D.	607	Pilot		
PO	Crook D.M.	609	Pilot	3 + 2 shared	KIA 18/12/1944
Flt Lt	Cunningham J.	604	Pilot		Post war test pilot with DH
Flt Lt	Cunningham J.L.G.	603	Pilot	1 shared	**KIA 28/08/1940**
PO	Davies A.E.	610	Pilot		KIA 30/10/1940
Sqn Ldr	Davies J.A.	604	Pilot		Killed in accident 16/10/1940
Sgt	Davies L.	151	Pilot		
Fg Off	Davis C.R.	601	Pilot	10 + 1 shared	KIA 06/09/1940
Fg Off	Deanesley E.C.	152	Pilot		
Fg Off	Demetriadi R.S.	601	Pilot		**KIA 11/08/1940**
Sqn Ldr	Denholm G.I.	603	Pilot	2 + 1 shared	OC 603 Sqn Gp Capt 1947
Sqn Ldr	Devitt P.K.	152	Pilot		OC 152 Sqn
PO	Douglas W.A.	610	Pilot		
Fg Off	Doulton M.D.	601	Pilot	2 + 2 shared	**KIA 31/08/1940**
Fg Off	Dundas H.S.L.	616	Pilot	1 + 1 shared	
Fg Off	Dundas J.C.	609	Pilot	11 + 2 shared	KIA 27/11/1940
Fg Off	Dunning-White P.W.	29/145	Pilot	3 + 2 shared	
Flt Lt	Edge A.R.	607	Pilot		
Flt Lt	Edge G.R.	605	Pilot	1	Also served with 253 Sqn
Fg Off	Eyre A.	615	Pilot	4 + 2 shared	
Wg Cdr	Farquhar A.D.	257	Pilot		
PO	Fenwick S.D.	601	Pilot		.

Rank	Name	Squadron	Role	Confirmed	Remarks
Flt Lt	Ferguson P.J.	602	Pilot	1	
Sgt	Fletcher J.J.	604	Air Gunner		**KIA 28/08/1940**
Fg Off	Forster A.D.	607	Pilot		Also with 151 Sqn
Fg Off	Frisby E.M.	504	Pilot		KIA 05/12/1941
Sgt	Gadd J.E.	611	Pilot		
PO	Gaunt G.N.	609	Pilot		**KIA 15/09/1940**
Fl Lt	Gaynor J.R.H.	615	Pilot	1 shared	
Fg Off	Gilroy G.K.	603	Pilot	3 + 1 shared	Gp Capt RAuxAF
Sgt	Goodman M.V.	604	Air Gunner		
Fg Off	Goodwin H.McD.	609	Pilot	3	**KIA 13/08/1940**
Flt Lt	Gore W.E.	607	Pilot		Also with 54 Squadron KIA 25/10/1940
Flt Lt	Gray A.P.	615	Pilot	1	
Flt Lt	Green C.P.	421	Pilot		Gp Capt 1947
Sgt	Green W.J.	501	Pilot		
Flt Lt	Haig J.G.E.	603	Pilot	1	
PO	Hamilton C.E.	234	Pilot		KIA 15/05/1941
Sgt	Hardwick W.R.H	600	Wop. AG		
Sgt	Hawke S.N.	604	Air Gunner		(KSB) Killed 29/05/1941
Flt Lt	Hayes T.N.	600	Pilot		OC 600 Sqn Post war
Flt Lt	Heal P.W.D.	604	Pilot		Gp Capt 1962
Flt Lt	Heath B.	611	Pilot		
Flt Lt	Hellver R.O.	616	Pilot		
Flt Lt	Hillcoat H.B.L.	1	Pilot	1 + 1 shared	MIA 08/01/1943
Fg Off	Holden K.	616	Pilot	1 + 1 shared	Wg Cdr 1965

Rank	Name	Squadron	Role	Confirmed	Remarks
Flt Lt	Hope Sir A.P.	601	Pilot	1 + 1 shared	OC 601 Sqn
Fg Off	Hope R.	605	Pilot		**KIA 14/10/1940**
Flt Lt	Hubbard T.E.	601	Pilot	2 shared	
Flt Lt	Hunter A.S.	601	Pilot		Killed in accident 23/10/1940
Fg Off	Irving M.M.	607	Pilot	1 shared	**KIA 29/09/1940**
Flt Lt	Jack D. McF.	602	Pilot	2	
PO	Johnson S.F.F.	600	Pilot		KIA 28/02/1941
Sqn Ldr	Johnstone A.V.R.	602	Pilot	6 + 2 shared	AVM 1968
PO	Joll I.K.S.	604	Pilot		
Sqn Ldr	Kayll J.R.	615	Pilot	3 + 1 shared	OC 615 Sqn
Fg Off	Keighley G.	610	Pilot		
Sqn Ldr	Kellett R.G.	249/303	Pilot	4	OC 03 Sqn
Sgt	Keast F.J.	600	Air Gunner		**KIA 08/08/1940**
PO	Kershaw A.	1	Pilot		KIA 01/01/1941
Sgt	Kirk T.B.	74	Pilot		Died 22/07/1941
Flt Lt	Lamb P.G.	610	Pilot	4	
Flt Lt	Lawton P.C.F.	604	Pilot		
Flt Lt	Leather W.J.	611	Pilot	3 shared	
Sgt	Lipscombe A.J.	600	Wop/ AG		(KSB) Killed 20/09/1941
Flt Lt	Little B.W.	609	Pilot		
Flt Lt	Little J.H.	219	Pilot		KIA 12/06/1943
Fg Off	Lofts K.T.	615	Pilot	4 + 1 shared	Also with 249 Sqn
Fg Off	Looker D.J.	615	Pilot		
Fl Lt	Macdonald H.K.	603	Pilot	3	**KIA 28/09/1940**
Sgt	McDougall C.W.	111	Pilot		KIA 05/03/1941

Rank	Name	Squadron	Role	Confirmed	Remarks
PO	Macfie C.H.	611/616	Pilot		Sqn Ldr 1963
PO	Mackay R.	234	Pilot		
Sqn Ldr	Maclachlan A.M.	92	Pilot		OC 92 Sqn
PO	Maclaren A.C.	604	Pilot		
Flt Lt	Maclean C.H.	602	Pilot		
Sgt	Manton E.	610	Pilot		**KIA 29/08/1940**
PO	McClintock J.A.P.	615	Pilot	1 shared	KIA 25/11/1940
Sqn Ldr	McCombe J.E.	611	Pilot	2 + 1 shared	OC 611 Sqn
PO	McGrath J.K.U.B.	601	Pilot		
Flt Lt	McKellar A.A.	605	Pilot	19 + 1 shared	KIA 01/11/1940
Sgt	Metcalf A.C.	604	Air Gunner		
Flt Lt	Miller A.G.	Fighter Interception Unit	Pilot		
PO	Mitchell G.T.M.	609	Pilot		**KIA 11/07/1940**
Sqn Ldr	Mitchell H.M.	25	Pilot		OC 25 Sqn
Fg Off	Moberley G.E.	616	Pilot		**KIA 26/08/1940**
Fg Off	Morton J.S.	603	Pilot	4 + 3 shared	
Flt Lt	Mount C.J.	602	Pilot	1	Air Cdre 1965
PO	Mudie M.R.	615	Pilot		**KIA 15/07/1940**
PO	Murray T.B.	616	Pilot	2	
PO	Niven H.G.	601/602	Pilot		
Sgt	Oldfield T.G.	64/92	Pilot		**KIA 27/09/1940**
Wg Cdr	Parker I.R.	611	Pilot		
PO	Parnall S.B.	607	Pilot		**KIA 09/09/1940**
PO	Parsons P.T.	504	Pilot	1 + 1 shared	KIA 02/10/1942

Rank	Name	Squadron	Role	Confirmed	Remarks
Sgt	Peacock W.A.	46/151	Pilot	1	**KIA 11/09/1940**
Fg Off	Peel C.D.	603	Pilot		**KIA 17/07/1940**
Sgt	Phillips R.F.P.	602	Pilot		
Flt Lt	Pritchard C.A.	600	Pilot		
Flt Lt	Rabone J.H.M.	604	Pilot		
Fg Off	Rawlence A.J.	600	Pilot		
Fg Off	Rhodes-Moorhouse W.	601	Pilot	5 + 1 shared	**KIA 06/09/1940**
Flt Lt	Riddle C.J.H.	601	Pilot	1 shared	
Fg Off	Riddle H.J.	601	Pilot	1 shared	
Flt Lt	Richie I.S.	603	Pilot	1 shared	
Fg Off	Roberts R.	615	Pilot	1	Also with 64 Sqn
Sqn Ldr	Robinson M.	616	Pilot		OC 616 and OC 602 post war
Fg Off	Robinson P.B.	601	Pilot	2	Sqn Ldr 1965
Flt Lt	Rook A.H.	504	Pilot	1	OC 504 Sqn post war
Fg Off	Rook M.	504	Pilot	1 + 1 shared	Killed in flying accident 13/03/1948
Fg Off	Rowley R.M.B.	145	Pilot		Died 1941
Fg Off	Royce M.E.A.	504	Pilot	1 shared	
Flt Lt	Royce W.B.	504	Pilot		
Flt Lt	Rushmer F.W.	603	Pilot	1 shared	**KIA 05/09/1940**
Flt Lt	St Aubin E.F.	616	Pilot		KIA 27/05/1941
Sqn Ldr	Sample J.	504	Pilot	1 + 1 shared	OC 504 Sqn KIA 28/10/1941
Sgt	Scott A.E.	73/442	Pilot		KIA 19/08/1942
Sqn Ldr	Scott D.R.	605	Pilot		KIA 08/11/1941
Flt Lt	Scott R.H.	604	Pilot		
Fg Off	Scrase G.E.T.	601	Pilot		KIA 28/09/1941
Fg Off	Selway J.B.	604	Pilot		
Sgt	Shepherd F.E.R.	611	Pilot		**KIA 11/09/1940**

Rank	Name	Squadron	Role	Confirmed	Remarks
Sgt	Shepherd J.B.	234	Pilot		(KSB) Killed in flying accident 22/01/1946
Sgt	Shirley S.H.	604	Air Gunner		(KSB) (KSB) Killed 27/07/1941
Flt Lt	Skinner C.B.E.	604	Pilot		
Flt Lt	Skinner S.H.	604	Pilot		KIA 19/08/1942
Flt Lt	Smith A.T.	610	Pilot		OC 610 Sqn **KIA 25/07/1940**
Flt Lt	Smith E.B.B.	610	Pilot	2	
Flt Lt	Smith E.S.	600	Pilot		
PO	Smithers J.L.	601	Pilot		**KIA 11/08/1940**
Flt Lt	Speke H.	604	Pilot		KIA 26/07/1941
Flt Lt	Stoddart K.M.	611	Pilot		
Fg Off	Straight W.W.	601	Pilot		
PO	Strickland C.D.	615	Pilot		KIA 27/10/1941
Sgt	Stewart C.N.D.	604	Air Gunner		(KSB) Killed 31/05/1942
PO	Sutton J.R.G.	611	Pilot	2 shared	KIA 27/03/1941
PO	Sutton N.	611	Pilot		*KIA 05/10/1940*
Sgt	Swanwick G.W.	54	Pilot		Wg Cdr 1965
PO	Sylvester E.J.H.	501	Pilot		**KIA 20/07/1940**
Sgt	Taylor R.H.	604	Air Gunner		(KSB) Killed 26/11/1940
Sgt	Townsend T.W.	600	Air Gunner		
PO	Turan A.J.J.	615	Pilot		KIA 25/11/1940
Sqn Ldr	Urie J.D.	602	Pilot		
Sqn Ldr	Vick J.A.	607	Pilot		OC 607 Sqn
Sgt	Walley P.K.	615	Pilot		**KIA 18/08/1940**
Fg Off	Warner W.H.C.	610	Pilot		**KIA 16/08/1940**
Fg Off	Waterson R. McG.	603	Pilot	1 + 1 shared	**KIA 31/08/1940**
Flt Lt	Watkins D.H.	611	Pilot	2	

Rank	Name	Squadron	Role	Confirmed	Remarks
Flt Lt	Webb P.C.	602	Pilot	6	Air Cdre 1973
PO	Welford G.H.E.	607	Pilot		
Flt Lt	Whitty W.H.R.	607	Pilot		
PO	Williams T.D.	611	Pilot	1 shared	
Flt Lt	Wilson D.S.	610	Pilot	2	

Summary:

188 Members of the AAF flew in the Battle of Britain from 10 July to 31 October 1940.

Of these, twenty-nine were sergeants as follows:

Pilots	17
Wop/AG	11
Radar Op	1

Fifty-nine AAF aircrew were Killed in Action, of whom thirty-five died during the Battle of Britain. (Shown in bold)

AAF pilots accounted for some 196 confirmed victories during the Battle of Britain. Those with five or more credited victories during the Battle can be classed as 'aces' although there are some who claimed victories both before and after, but none during the battle, for example Aitken (14).

Twenty-five AAF pilots flew with regular RAF squadrons only, whilst a further ten pilots flew with both their own AAF Squadron and with a regular squadron.[39]

Numbers of all the AAF aircrew that flew with auxiliary squadrons

501 (County of Gloucester)	4
504 (County of Nottingham)	8
600 (City of London)	14

---

39 Tony Freeman, Royal Auxiliary Air Force Foundation, 28 June 2020. Kenneth Wynn, *Men of the Battle of Britain,* (Croydon, 1999)

601 (County of London)	18
602 (City of Glasgow)	10
603 (City of Edinburgh)	10
604 (County of Middlesex)	21
605 (County of Warwick)	5
607 (County of Durham)	11
609 (West Riding)	10
610 (County of Chester)	13
611 (West Lancashire)	13
615 (County of Surrey)	14
616 (South Yorkshire)	11
Total	**162**

Total aircrew is less than 188 because some twenty-five other AAF men flew with regular RAF squadrons only.

Balance Sheet

RAF Airmen Killed	537
Luftwaffe Airmen Killed	2662
BF109 and BF110 Airmen Killed	549
RAF Aircraft Lost	1017
Luftwaffe Aircraft Lost	1882
BF109 and BF110 Aircraft Lost	871[40]

AAF Fighter Squadrons in the Battle of Britain

No.	Aircraft	Sqn Code
501 (County of Gloucester)	Hurricane	SD
504 (County of Nottingham)	Hurricane	HX
600 (City of London)	Blenheim	ZO
601 (County of London)	Hurricane	UF

40 Source *The Battle of Britain – Then and Now*, Battle of Britain Printers Ltd London 1980

No.	Aircraft	Sqn Code
602 (City of Glasgow)	Spitfire	LO
603 (City of Edinburgh)	Spitfire	XT
604 (County of Middlesex)	Blenheim	NG
605 (County of Warwick)	Hurricane	UP
607 (County of Durham)	Hurricane	HF
609 (West Riding)	Spitfire	PR
610 (County of Chester	Spitfire	DW
611 (West Lancashire)	Spitfire	FY
615 (County of Surrey)	Hurricane	KW
616 (South Yorkshire)	Spitfire	YQ

Airfields used by AAF Fighter Squadrons during the Battle of Britain

Squadron Number	Airfield	Date
501 (County of Gloucester)	Middle Wallop	4 July 1940
	Gravesend	25 July 1940
	Kenley	10 September 1940
504 (County of Nottingham)	Catterick	2 September 1940
	Hendon	6 September 1940
	Filton	26 September 1940
600 (City of London)	Manston	20 June 1940
	Hornchurch	24 August 1940
	Redhill	12 September 1940
	Catterick with detachments to Drem, Acklington and Prestwick	12 October 1940
601 (County of London)	Tangmere	17 June 1940
	Debden	19 August 1940
	Tangmere	2 September 1940
	Exeter	7 September 1940
602 (City of Glasgow)	Drem	22 May 1940
	Westhampnett	13 August 1940

Squadron Number	Airfield	Date
603 (City of Edinburgh)	Turnhouse with detachments to Montrose and Dyce	5 May 1940
	Hornchurch	28 August 1940
604 (County of Middlesex)	Gravesend	3 July 1940
	Middle Wallop	27 July 1940
605 (County of Warwick)	Drem	28 May 1940
	Croydon	7 September 1940
607 (County of Durham)	Usworth	4 June 1940
	Tangmere	1 September 1940
	Turnhouse	10 October 1940
609 (West Riding)	Middle Wallop	6 July 1940
	Warmwell	2 October 1940
610 (County of Chester	Biggin Hill	6 July 1940
	Acklington	31 August 1940
611 (West Lancashire)	Digby	10 October 1939
615 (County of Surrey)	Kenley, with detachment to Manston	22 May 1940
	Prestwick	29 August 1940
	Northolt	19 October 1940
616(South Yorkshire)	Leconfield	6 June 1940
	Kenley	19 August 1940
	Cotishall	3 September 1940[41]

---

41 Wing Commander C.G. Jefford, *RAF Squadrons*. (Shrewsbury, 1988)

Chapter 3

The Second World War

The 1920s and the early part of the 1930s were characterised by the development of the bomber, at the expense of fighter production, to the extent that, when Fighter Command was formed in 1936, under the command of Air Chief Marshal Sir Hugh Dowding, as part of his plan to improve the fighter defences of the United Kingdom, eight AAF squadrons were transferred to Fighter Command, followed by four newly formed units, and one day and one night-fighter squadron. September 1939 saw the invasion of Poland by Germany and Britain responding with a declaration of war. All the Auxiliary Air Force squadrons, along with the Royal Air Force Volunteer Reserve, were embodied with the Royal Air Force in August 1939. The Auxiliary Air Force played a key role within all the squadrons of the Royal Air Force throughout the duration of the Second World War. However, throughout the period 1939-1945, the AAF ceased recruiting, as all its personnel had been embodied with the full-time Royal Air Force. Many of the pre-war auxiliaries chose to wear their 'A' s on their uniforms to show their pride in their pre-war auxiliary squadrons.

After the Battle of Britain was over, the twenty squadrons of the AAF continued to serve in a variety of roles until the end of the war. Amongst the day fighter units 501, 504, 601, 602, 603, 609, 611 and 616 Squadrons soon all equipped with the Spitfire, continued to be based in the United Kingdom during 1942, taking part in the continued defence of the country and in the costly sweeps and bomber escort duties over occupied Europe.

Charles Arthur Pritchard from New South Wales in Australia joined 600 (City of London) Squadron in 1936 and was called in for full time service on 24 October 1939. On the night of 15/16 September 1940 he destroyed a Ju 88, that he saw in his spotlights and shot down. The aircraft crashed into the sea near Bexhill. The squadron was involved in the defence of the United Kingdom, and as part of Fighter Command, they were active in the Battle of Britain, by which time they had converted from the Beaufighter to the Hurricane.

601 (County of London) Squadron, the fabled 'Millionaires, or 'The Legion', spent the first part of 1940 helping with the Evacuation of Dunkirk and then defending their country during the Battle of Britain. Squadron members who were active during the Battle of Britain included John William Maxwell Aitken who joined the AAF in 1935 and was, along with the rest of 601 Squadron, embodied with the RAF on 26 August 1939. In November 1939 he joined five other Blenheims from the squadron to meet up with 25 Squadron for the purpose of attacking the German seaplane base in Borkum. Then in May 1940 he flew with A Flight of 601 Squadron to reinforce 3 Squadron in Merville in France. He was successful there, shooting down an He 11 871 over Brussels on 18 May. The following day he shot down another He111 and a Junkers 87. He was promoted and took over command of 601 Squadron in June of 1940. On 26 June he destroyed another He 111 and was awarded the Distinguished Flying Cross (DFC). On 20 July 1940 he was posted away from 601 Squadron. Another 601 Squadron pilot was Gordon Neil Spencer Cleaver who joined the squadron in 1937. He also went to Merville in France as part of A Flight. Whilst there he destroyed a Bf 109 on 26 May and claimed two other victories before his flight left. On 11 July 1940 he claimed a Ju 87 and an He 111 and then on 26 July he claimed a further two Bf 110s. He was shot down over Winchester, with his eyes full of splinters from a cannon shell which landed on his hood. He was awarded the DFC in September of that same year.

William Pancoast Clyde joined 601 Squadron in 1935. Whilst a member of A Flight in France, he destroyed a Bf 110 on 27 May. He was awarded the DFC at the end of May. On 6 June he destroyed a Do 17, and he shared a Ju 88 with Max Aitken on 7 July. He also claimed two Bf 110s on 13 August, a Ju 87 on 16 August, a Do 17 on 31 August and a Bf 110 on 7 October 1940, Another 601 man was Thomas Edward Hubbard, who joined the squadron in 1937. He flew one of the six Blenheims that attacked the seaplane base at Borkum. He claimed a Bf 110 over Dunkirk on 27 May 1940 and then an He 59 on 20 July 1940. John Keswick Ulick Blake McGrath joined 601 Squadron in early 1939 and was called to full time service on 25 August of that year. On 22 May he destroyed a Bf 109 over Arras and then on 26 May he destroyed a Bf 110 over Dunkirk. On 11 July he claimed an He 111, on 8 August two Bf 109s, on 11 August two Bf 110s and on 13 August a Ju 88 and a Bf 109. He was awarded the DFC on 27 August 1940.

William Henry Rhodes-Moorhouse, the son of a First World War Victoria Cross holder, joined 601 Squadron in 1937, after being educated at Eton and gaining his pilot's licence at the age of seventeen. He was one of the six pilots flying Blenheims who attacked the German seaplane base in November 1939. He also was a member of A Flight who flew to Merville in May 1940. He shot down an He 111 just east of Brussels on 18 May and a Bf 109 on 22 May 1940. He destroyed a Ju 88 on 16 July and two Bf 109s on 31 July and on 4 September he claimed a Do 17. He was awarded the DFC on 30 July 1940. He was shot down and killed in combat over Tunbridge Wells on 6 September 1940.

Squadron Leader Roger Bushell, an auxiliary officer with 601 Squadron and a barrister in his civilian life, masterminded and led the Great Escape on 24 March 1944. He was caught and, along with forty-nine other prisoners, was murdered on or around 29 March 1944, on the direct orders of Hitler. Hugh Joseph Riddle also joined 601 Squadron in 1937 and was called up to full time service on 25 August 1939. He shared in the destruction of a Bf 110 on 11 July 1940. Finally, Julian Langley Smithers joined 601 Squadron in 1938. On 11 August 1940 he was shot down and killed in Hurricane P 3885 during combat over Portland.

601 Squadron was re-equipped with the unsuccessful America Bell AiraCobra in August 1941, the only squadron to do so. This unique aircraft had the engine *behind the pilot,* with the long crankshaft passing between his legs to the propeller in front. His fate, in the event of a crash landing, without the protection of the engine in front, can only be imagined. The aircraft also had two cab-like side doors, hinged at the front which made bailing out in the slip stream in the conventional way (although there was an escape hatch in the roof of the cockpit) a bit of a challenge, if not impossible, (indeed, its successor, the King Cobra even had two extra winding door handles with which to lower sliding windows up and down!) and to cap it all, the fighter had a tricycle undercarriage! Technical problems abounded and the aircraft was soon withdrawn from service and sold to the Russians who successfully used it in the ground attack role.

If that were not enough, the squadron was posted in 1942 to RAF Acaster Mabis, an airfield just south of York and situated within a curve of the River Ouse which was beset by damp and foggy conditions, leading to many accidents. In fact, 601 Squadron was the *only* squadron during the entire war ever to operate from Acaster Mabis – for just 3 months, from January to March 1942 which, together with being issued with such a radical and unsuccessful aircraft makes one wonder what the hapless squadron had done to deserve it all! They remained in the United Kingdom, re-equipped with the Spitfire, and were involved in home defence until April 1942 when they relocated to Malta and then on to Egypt and Libya during that year.

February 1943 saw them move to Tunisia and then back to Malta, Sicily and then to Italy in October 1943, where they remained until the end of the war.

602 (City of Glasgow) Squadron remained in the United Kingdom throughout the early years of the war, concentrating on the defence of the country. The top-scoring Auxiliary 'Ace' in the Battle of Britain was Squadron Leader Archie McKellar DSO DFC*, OC 605 (County of Warwick) Squadron, who was killed on the morning of 1 November, hours after the Battle of Britain had officially ended. McKellar, a plasterer in civilian life, served initially on 602 Squadron and was credited with twenty-one confirmed victories and three probables. He was also Mentioned in Dispatches (MiD) following his death. Robert Findley Boyd joined 602 Squadron in 1935 before being called up for full time service in September 1939. On 7 July 1940 he shared in the destruction of a Ju 88. On 15 August he claimed a Do 215, a Ju 87 and an He 111, followed by a Ju 87 and a Bf 109 on 18 July 1940. He then shot down two Bf 109s. In September he claimed a Do 17 and a Bf 109 on the 4th and then a Bf 109 on the 11th and a Bf 109 on the 26th. After a shared kill on 2 October his final victory in 1940 was a shared Ju 88 on 13 November. He was awarded the DFC on 29 September 1940 and in December 1940 he was given command of 54 Squadron.

Another 602 pilot was Peter John Ferguson who joined the squadron in 1936 and was taken into full time service on 24 August 1939. He claimed a Ju 87 on 18 August and was then attacked by a Bf 109 which hit the port wing of the aircraft and the fuel tank. Ferguson was wounded but managed to land at Norway Farm after breaking through power lines. He was no longer able to fly following this incident.

Donald MacFarlane Jack joined 602 Squadron in 1936. He damaged a Ju 88 on 9 July 1940 followed by a Bf 110 which was destroyed on 25 August and a Bf 109 on 26 August 1940. He was then posted to the Air Staff at HQ13 Group on 27 December 1940. Another member of 602 Squadron was Alexander Vallance Riddell Johnstone. He joined the squadron in 1934 and took command of the squadron on 12 July 1940. On 13 August 602 Squadron went south to RAF Westhampnett, and here he shared in destroying a Ju 88 on 19 August and a Bf 110 and a Bf 109 on the 25th, followed by a Ju 88, a Bf 109 and an He 111 on 7 September. He shared a Do 17 on 9 September and destroyed a Ju 88 on 30 September. He was awarded the DFC on 1 October 1940.

Charles Hector Maclean joined 602 Squadron in 1936 and was called up for full time service on 24 August 1939. On 7 July 1940 he shared a Ju 88 before being shot down on 26 August 1940, crash landing at Tangmere he was sent to hospital where his right leg was amputated. John Dunlop Urie joined 602 Squadron in June 1935. In April 1940 he was appointed as a Flight Commander, and he damaged a Ju 88 on 9 July. On 1 August he tore a wing of Spitfire P 9461 managing to land at RAF Drem. On 18 August he landed at RAF Westhampnett minus flaps and with one burst tyre after his Spitfire X 4110 was severely damaged in combat. He was wounded in both legs. Finally, Paul Clifford Webb had joined 602 Squadron in late 1937. On 1 July 1940 he attacked and damaged a Ju 88 which jettisoned its bombs in the sea close to Dunbar. On 16 August he claimed a Bf 110 destroyed, two more on the 25th and on the 26th, an He 59. In September he destroyed an He 59 on the 7th and on the 9th an unidentified enemy aircraft. His Spitfire K 9910 was damaged in combat with Bf 109s, and he had to crash-land in Boxgrove, breaking his wrist in the process. In June 1944, 602 Squadron moved to France, and then Belgium in September of the same year. They then returned to England until the war ended in 1945.

603 (City of Edinburgh) Squadron concentrated on the defence of Great Britain between September 1939 and March 1941, being actively involved in the Battle of Britain. George Lovell Denholm joined 603 Squadron in 1933. On 3 July 1940 he shared in the destruction of a Ju 88, on 28 August he claimed a Bf 109 and he was shot down himself on 30 August over Deal. He managed to bale out and his Spitfire L 1067 crash-landed. On 15 September he claimed a Bf 109 and on same day he was hit by return fire from a Do 17. Again, he baled out and whilst his Spitfire R 7019 crash-landed, he again was unhurt. Finally, he shared a Bf 109 on 27 September before being awarded the DFC on 22 October 1940.

George Kemp Gilroy, a sheep farmer before the war, joined 603 Squadron in 1938. On 3 July 1940 he claimed a share in the destruction of a Ju 88 and a share in the destruction of a Do 25 on 6 July and then a share of an He 111 on 12 July. On 27 August the squadron were sent to RAF Hornchurch, and here he claimed the destruction of a Bf 109 on both 28 and 31 August. He was shot down over London on 31 August and baled out wounded. He was awarded the DFC on 13 September 1940. He then claimed a Bf 109 on 28 October and shared an He 111 on 21 November. On 17 December 1940 he was badly hurt in an accident.

Harold Kennedy MacDonald joined 603 Squadron in 1935, after being called up to full time service, he destroyed Bf 109s on 31 August, 18 September, and 27 September. On 28 September he was attacked by a group of Bf 109s and eventually shot down. He was killed at the age of twenty-eight. Another 603 Squadron pilot was James Storrs Morton who joined the squadron in 1939. On 15 and 16 July he claimed a share in the destruction of two He 111s, on 28 August he destroyed a Bf 109 and on the thirty-first a Do 17. On 1 September he destroyed a Bf 109 and was awarded the DFC. Charles David Peel also joined 603 Squadron in early 1938. Sadly, on 17 July he was reported missing after failing to return from an operational sortie.

Ian Small Ritchie joined 603 Squadron in early 1938. On 3 July he claimed a share in the destruction of a Ju 88 and he also shared an He 111 on 16 July. He was wounded in combat with Bf 109s on 28 August 1940. Another 603 Squadron pilot was Frederick William Rushmer who had joined the squadron in 1934. He was the leader of Red Section and on 30 July he claimed a share in an He 111. On 29 August he had to make a forced landing after combat over Deal. He failed to return from combat with Do 17s on 5 September 1940. Finally, Robin McGregor Waterston joined 603 Squadron in 1937. On 20 July 1940 he shared a Do 17 and a Bf 109 on 30 August. He was killed in action over London aged twenty-three. After the Battle of Britain 603 Squadron remained in England until April 1942 when they moved to Malta before moving to Egypt until December 1944. Then they finished the war back in England.

604 (County of Middlesex) Squadron concentrated on the defence of the United Kingdom between September 1939 and July 1944, playing a part in the Battle of Britain. John Cunningham, together with his navigator, Sergeant C.F. Rawnsley, became the best night-fighting partnership of the war. Michael Frederick Anderson joined the squadron in October 1930 and after several courses, he took command of the squadron in March 1940, leading them throughout the Battle of Britain.

605 (County of Warwick) Squadron were involved in the Evacuation of Dunkirk and the Battle of Britain. Gerald Richmond Edge joined the squadron in 1936. He claimed a share in the destruction of a Do 17 on 9 May 1940 and he destroyed a Ju 87 on the 25th and shared another Do 17 the next day. He was promoted to squadron leader and posted to command 253 Squadron on 5 September. Ralph Hope joined the squadron in 1938. He was shot down on 28 September by Bf 109s and baled out unhurt. On 14 October he flew into the Inner Artillery Zone during a patrol, and he crashed and was killed by either anti-aircraft fire or by hitting a balloon cable. The squadron remained in England until November 1941 before being sent to Malta and then moving on to Batavia, Java and Netherlands East Indies.

607 (County of Durham) Squadron were part of the British Expeditionary Force and played an important role during the Battle of Britain. James Michael Bazin joined the squadron in May 1935. He claimed a Do 215 on 15 September and a Ju 88 on 30 September. He transferred to Bomber Command in 1944 and completed a full tour of twenty-five operations flying Lancaster's. George Dudley Craig joined 607 Squadron in May 1937 and flew with them throughout the Battle of Britain. Maurice Milne Irving joined the squadron in 1934, he claimed a share in the destruction of a Ju 88 on 14 September 1940 and was then shot down in combat with Bf 109s. On 28 September he was reported missing at the age of twenty-nine. Another pilot to be killed during the Battle of Britain was Stuart Boyd Parnell who had joined 607 before the war. On 9 September 1940 he was shot down and killed whilst in combat with Do 17s and Bf 109s aged thirty. Finally, William Hubert Rigby Whitty joined the squadron in 1938 and flew with them throughout the Battle of Britain. In May 1942 607 Squadron were sent to India and served in Bengal before moving to Burma in 1945.

609 (West Riding) Squadron spent the war years within the United Kingdom apart from helping with the evacuation of Dunkirk and the Battle of Britain in 1940. One of the squadron pilots who had joined in early 1937 was Philip Henry Barran. He became one of the first casualties of the Battle of Britain when on 11 July 1940 his Spitfire I 1069 was severely damaged in morning combat with Bf 109s. He tried to reach the coast at Portland but bailed out and was picked up wounded and badly burned. He sadly died before reaching land. John Charles Dundas joined the squadron in 1938. He destroyed several German aircraft in the skies above Dunkirk, and then on 13 July he claimed a Bf 109 and then another one on 19 July. He then shot down two Bf 110s on 11 and 12 August, a Ju 87 on 13 August a Do 17 destroyed and a share of a Ju 88 on 15 September. Continuing in September 1940 he claimed a shared Do 17 on the 15th, a Bf 110 on the 24th, a Do 17 and a Bf 110 on the 25th, a Bf 110 on the 27th, a Bf 110 on 7 October and finally a Bf 109 on 15 October. He was awarded a DFC on 22 October 1940 and then was lost at sea on 27 November 1940. having been chased out to sea and then shot down. He received a Bar to the DFC on 7 January 1941, aged twenty-four. In 1942, 609 Squadron converted to the more powerful Hawker Typhoon, ultimately being incorporated in the 2nd Tactical Air Force (TAF) during the campaigns in Normandy in 1944 and into Holland and Germany. 602 Squadron was also part of 2nd TAF before returning to the UK for air defence duties in June 1944, and with the appearance of the

V1 flying bomb in 1944, 601 Squadron took part in many interceptions of these missiles, joined by 616 Squadron, the first to be equipped with the new jet fighters to see action, the Gloster Meteor.

610 (County of Chester) Squadron spent the war between United Kingdom bases. Peter Gilbert Lamb joined the squadron in early 1938. On 24 and 26 August he claimed a number of Bf 109s destroyed. On the 29th he claimed a Bf 110 and on the 30th an He 111, he was posted to another squadron on 28 October 1940. Another 610 pilot was Edward Manton, who had joined the squadron prior to the war. On 29 August 1940 he was shot down and killed over Mayfield at the age of twenty-five. Andrew Thomas Smith was also killed on 25 July 1940 when he stalled his Spitfire whilst attempting to land after combat with Bf 109s. Edward Brian Bretherton Smith joined 610 Squadron in 1936. He took part in the fighting over Dunkirk in May 1940 and then destroyed several Bf 109s on 24 and 25 July. The following day he was shot down in flames over New Romney and baled out and was rescued from the sea with burns. Finally, William Henry Cromwell Warner had joined 610 Squadron in 1937. He failed to return from conflict off Dungeness on 16 August 1940 aged twenty-one.

611 (West Lancashire) Squadron were involved in the Evacuation of Dunkirk and the Battle of Britain and remained in United Kingdom bases throughout the war. William Johnson Leather joined the squadron in May 1936. On 2 July 1940, he claimed a share of a Do 17 and on 15 September he claimed a Do 17 destroyed and another shared. On 11 October he shared in destroying two Do 17s. He was awarded the DFC on 8 October 1940. James Ellis McComb transferred into 611 Squadron from 600 Squadron on 25 September 1936. He took part in the battle over Dunkirk, and then in August 1940 he claimed a Do 17 destroyed and a share in the destruction of another one. On 15 September he also claimed another Do 17. He was awarded the DFC on 22 November 1940. Finally, Douglas Herbert Watkins joined the squadron in 1938. On 21 August 1940 he destroyed a Do 17. He claimed another on 11 October. He was awarded the DFC on 29 April 1941.

615 (County of Surrey) Squadron were part of the British Expeditionary Force in France and were then involved in the Battle of Britain. Peter Collard joined the squadron in late 1937 and he claimed a Ju 87 on 14 July 1940 and a share of an He 59 on 27 July. On 14 August 1940 he failed to return from combat off the coast of Dover aged twenty-four. He was awarded the DFC on 23 August 1940. Anthony Eyre joined 615 Squadron

in 1938. On 20 July 1940 he claimed a Bf 109 and on 14 August he destroyed a Ju 87 and shared another. The next day he shared a Bf 109 and, on the 20th, he destroyed a Do 17. On the 26th he claimed a Bf 109 and on 28th a Do 17. He was awarded the DFC on 30 August 1940. John Richard Hensman Gayner joined the squadron on 1 June 1937. On 14 July 1940 he shared the destruction of a Ju 87 before being posted away from the squadron. Joseph Robert Kayll joined 607 Squadron in 1934 and was posted to command 615 Squadron in March 1940. During the Battle of Britain, he claimed several aircraft destroyed: an He 59 on 27 July, an He 111 on 16 August, a Do 17 on the 20th and a Do 17 on the 28th. In December 1940 he was posted to HQ Fighter Command. Finally, Peter Kenneth Walley joined the squadron in March 1938. He shared the destruction of a Bf 109 on 16 August 1940 and then two days later he was shot down and killed by Bf 109s. He was twenty years old. In 1942 615 Squadron was sent to Bengal and then in June 1945 they went to Burma.

616 (South Yorkshire) Squadron took part in the Evacuation of Dunkirk and the Battle of Britain. The squadron took some pilots from the disbanded 503 (City of Lincoln) Squadron Special Reserve on 1 November 1938. John Swift Bell had joined 503 Squadron in 1935 and had moved to 616 Squadron. He had a number of kills over Dunkirk, but on 30 August 1940, he was shot down in his Spitfire X 4248 over West Malling in a head-on attack of Bf 109s. He was killed at the age of twenty-three. Richard Owen Hellyer was another pilot who had transferred from 503 Squadron, where he had been a founder member, to 616 Squadron. He was wounded when he was shot down over Dunkirk on 28 May 1940, landing on the beach. He continued to fly with the squadron until 1 October 1940, when he was posted to 56 OTU. George Edward Moberley joined 609 (West Riding) Squadron in 1938 but transferred to 616 Squadron when it began to be formed on 1 November 1938. He was in action over Dunkirk but was shot down and killed in combat off Dover on 26 August 1940. Finally, Thomas Burnley Murray claimed two Ju 88s on 15 August. After the Battle of Britain, the squadron stayed on bases in the United Kingdom before leaving for Belgium and Germany in 1945.

The final Auxiliary Air Force squadron that was active during the Battle of Britain was 504 (County of Nottingham) Squadron. Phillip Trevor Parsons joined the squadron in 1938. On 15 September 1940 he claimed a Do 17 destroyed and shared an He 111. He was later killed on 2 October 1942. Finally, Michael Rook joined 504 Squadron in 1938. On

15 September 1940 he shared in the destruction of a Do 17 and on the 27th he claimed a Bf 109.

501 Squadron moved to Holland in December 1944, joining 2nd TAF to intercept the V1, launched from bombers at night. 600 and 604 Squadrons continued as night fighter units through 1941 and 1942, the latter continuing as such for the rest of the war, whilst 600 Squadron took its Beaufighters to Algeria in 1943.

Towards the end of 1941, 605 Squadron was dispatched to the Middle East, the air element being flown from an aircraft carrier to Malta, although some of the pilots and ground crew who were travelling by sea were sent to the Far East, following the Japanese entry into the war. During the latter stages of the fighting in the Dutch East Indies, the surviving pilots were amalgamated with the remains of other units and formed a new 605 Squadron until they were captured by the Japanese in 1942. Meanwhile, the original members of the squadron on Malta were absorbed with other units until a completely new 605 Squadron was formed in the UK in June 1942 to undertake night intruder operations.

In April 1942, 601 and 603 squadrons were flown to Malta on the US aircraft carrier USS *Wasp*, with their ground elements sailing around the Cape of Good Hope to Egypt. In June, 601 left Malta for Egypt to be reunited with its ground party. Meanwhile, 603 Squadron stayed in Malta where it was merged with two other Spitfire squadrons, effectively ceasing to exist. However, its ground party had stuck together and, in 1943, it formed the nucleus of a new 603 Squadron which operated maritime Beaufighters over the Aegean until it was disbanded in December 1944, only to be re-formed again in the UK.

In March 1942, 607 and 615 Squadrons were sent to the Far East for the remainder of the war. Of the other non-fighter units, 500, 502, 608 and 612 Squadrons had continued to fly with Coastal Command, continuing their anti-submarine patrols for the rest of the war, 500 and 608 Squadrons being sent to North Africa in late 1942. Meanwhile, 613 and 614 Squadrons had seen little activity, other than training and exercising with the army. At the end of 1942, 614 Squadron was re-designated as a bomber squadron and, equipped with the Blenheim V, it was sent to North Africa. 613 Squadron was re-formed as an intruder unit, continuing in this role as part of 2nd TAF until the end of the war. Lack of activity in the Mediterranean theatre by late 1944 led to the disbandment of 600, 608 and 614 Squadrons, although the number plates were allocated to disbanded or new regular units. It may thus be seen that by the later months of the war, the AAF had virtually ceased to exist, many of the squadrons operating during that period bearing no relationship to the original units of 1939/40. The only thing that they had in common with the AAF units was that these new squadrons continued to carry the same squadron numbers within a vastly expanded air force.

Most AAF ground crew were on a four-year engagement, the length of their remaining entitlement to auxiliary terms of service being governed by the date on which their current engagements had commenced, which, because the AAF had ceased recruiting on the outbreak of war, could be no later than 1939. Under the original AAF terms of service, an airman could not be posted away from his parent unit without his consent, which, in most cases was local to his home. This restriction led to a pool of immobile airmen which caused manning difficulties within the RAF. Therefore, by 1942-43, it became possible to persuade most auxiliary airmen to agree to be posted to other units without their consent under the veiled threat of being discharged from the AAF and re-enlisted in the RAFVR. This meant that the AAF squadrons were to lose more of their auxiliary personnel as the war went on.

However, as in the Battle of Britain, the squadrons of the AAF continued to be involved in some of the most significant episodes of the air war. 608 (North Riding) Squadron were part of Coastal Command during the war and spent much of their time protecting shipping convoys around Scotland and the north-east coastline. They went to Blida in Algeria in October 1942, before moving to Tunisia, Sicily, and Italy in 1943. The number of operational sorties increased month by month so that by April 1940 the monthly total was 131. These consisted of convoy escorts, anti-submarine patrols, air-sea rescue missions and coastal patrols searching for sight of possible German invasion forces.

During 1941, the squadron was re-equipped with Hudson aeroplanes and their airborne radar. They carried out offensive missions off the Norwegian and Dutch coasts and dropped leaflets over Denmark, which urged the Danish people to continue their resistance to the Germans, and on 3 October the squadron bombed the enemy airfield at Aalborg.[42] In January 1942, 608 Squadron moved base from Thornaby to Wick in North Scotland. Their brief was to continue coastal reconnaissance and to hunt for German U-boats. They were involved in hitting a tanker, attacking

---

42 National Archives, 608 Squadron Operational Record Book, 1941.

U-boats and attacking the German cruiser, *Prince Eugen*.[43] On 5 August 1942, the squadron moved up to the Shetland Islands, to Sumburgh, with a brief to attack targets off the Norwegian coast and to help protect convoys moving to North Russia. In November 1942 the squadron provided anti-submarine cover for Allied shipping transporting the invasion force to North Africa. By February 1944, the squadron had again moved its main base to Montecorvino, with a detachment at Bo Rizzo. Volcanic activity in March 1944 caused 608's Hudsons to be grounded after they were covered in volcanic dust from Mount Vesuvius, however, they eventually resumed their convoy duties until 7 July 1944 when the squadron was withdrawn from active duty. They were disbanded at Montecorvino on 31 July 1944.

612 (County of Aberdeen) Squadron worked from bases in the United Kingdom throughout the war. 613 (City of Manchester) Squadron was involved in the Evacuation of Dunkirk in 1940 and remained at bases throughout the United Kingdom for the remainder of the war. 614 (County of Glamorgan) Squadron remained in bases within the United Kingdom until November 1942 when they went out to Blida in Algeria, and then in August 1943 they moved on to Sicily before spending the last year of the war in Italy.

500 (County of Kent) Squadron remained in the United Kingdom until November 1942 when they were sent to Algeria, followed by Corsica in 1943, Italy in 1944 and finally Kenya in 1945. 501 (County of Gloucester) Squadron also remained in bases throughout the United Kingdom for the rest of the war. 502 (Ulster) Squadron also served in bases across the United Kingdom during the war.

The squadrons fought with great distinction in almost every theatre of operations equipped with almost every type of aircraft in the RAF inventory. The first enemy aircraft shot down over UK soil in 1939 was by 603 Squadron, closely followed by another by 602 Squadron. 616 Squadron, commanded by an AAF officer destroyed the first V1 flying bomb by air in 1944 and another AAF squadron, No. 613, carried out the pinpoint attack on the Gestapo headquarters in The Hague. The first U-boat sunk with the use of the new Anti-Surface Vessel (ASV) radar was credited to 502 Squadron. It would be wrong to credit these actions and successes solely to members of the AAF. The squadrons had progressively been leavened by the input of aircrew from every portal of entry into the RAF, particularly the RAFVR as

---

43 National Archives, 608 Squadron Operational Record Book, 1941.

the war progressed. However, they do show that the AAF squadrons were in the centre of operations throughout the Second World War, making no less of a contribution to the air war than the regular squadrons.

Personal stories

Squadron Leader Archie McKellar 602 Squadron

Archibald Ashmore McKellar was born in Paisley in 1912. The family moved to Glasgow in 1915 and he was educated at Shawlands Academy. He learned to fly in secret as his father was opposed to the idea and he was invited to join 602 (City of Glasgow) Squadron Auxiliary Air Force in 1936. [44]

In October 1939 he shared in the destruction of a Heinkel bomber, the first enemy aircraft to be brought down over the soil of the United Kingdom. This incident led to a national newspaper proclaiming 'First Blood to the Auxiliaries!' In June 1940 the Scotsman was posted to 605 (County of Warwick) Squadron Auxiliary Air Force and was promoted to flight lieutenant as a flight commander.

In September 1940 the squadron was deployed to Croydon in South London and it was during this period that he achieved his greatest success, being credited with seventeen enemy aircraft destroyed and becoming the highest scoring auxiliary pilot in the Battle of Britain. In the period 7 to 29 October, he accounted for five Messerschmidt fighters, testimony to his skill as a pilot and a marksman because he was flying the Hurricane, which was normally allocated the task of going after the bombers. For this feat, he was awarded the Distinguished Flying Cross and promoted to the rank of acting squadron leader. He received a bar to his DFC in October. Sadly, he was killed on 1 November, one day after the official end of the Battle of Britain, as can be seen in 605 Squadron Operations Record Book. [45]

He is buried in New Eastwood Cemetery in Glasgow and a memorial placed at the site of his crash at Woodlands Manor, Addisham, Kent. There is also a wing at the Erskine Hospital in Glasgow dedicated to his name. He was posthumously awarded the Distinguished Service Order and a Mentioned in Despatches in November 1940.

---

44 http://www.bbm.org.uk/airmen/McKellar.htm
45 National Archives, AIR 27/2088, 1 November 1940

Auxiliary Territorial Service (ATS)

In April 1938, the War Office informed the Air Ministry of their proposal to form a Reserve of Women which they visualised as providing for the RAF as well as the Army. The Air Ministry, while supporting the scheme for a common service under War Office control, wanted the segregation in special companies of women enrolled for duty with the RAF. This was agreed and, when the ATS came into being in September 1938 it contained separate RAF Companies. Following the Munich Crisis of 1938, it became apparent that the RAF Companies of the ATS should be brought more closely under RAF control, and in December 1938, the Air Council decided to move them to localities where they could be affiliated to an AAF unit. Experience proved, however, that administrative and training requirements necessitated a separate Women's Service for the RAF and, on 28 June 1939, the WAAF was constituted by Royal Warrant. On transfer from the ATS to the WAAF, Service numbers were allocated in the series 880000 to 897999.

In 1934, discussions took place for the first time on introducing women into the armed services on a part-time basis. However, in 1936, the Imperial Defence Committee concluded that the formation of a reserve of women in peace was neither desirable nor necessary. This view changed in 1938 with the very real threat of imminent war. In May of that year, following a change in Cabinet policy, it was decided to set up a part-time Auxiliary (Women's) Territorial Service under Army control. The Air Ministry supported a proposal that women enrolled in the service for duty with the Royal Air Force should be segregated into forty-eight separate companies and, whilst wearing khaki, should have a distinctive badge to show their light-blue affiliation. By the end of 1938, it had become evident that closer links were required between the forty-eight companies and the Royal Air Force. Consequently, in January 1939 the Air Council assumed responsibility for the companies which were then affiliated to the Auxiliary Air Force.

Six months later, all forty-eight of these companies became the nucleus of an entirely separate service known as the Women's Auxiliary Air Force. Despite the inclusion of the word 'Auxiliary' in the title, this new force no longer had an association with the part-time reservist Auxiliary Air Force. Thus, before the war, part-time female reservists were connected to the AAF for a mere six months. During this time, the AAF recruited applicants, issued them with uniforms bearing the distinctive 'A', issuing them with pay and allowances and service numbers in the 800000 series which was reserved for AAF personnel. Furthermore, women were not considered as Armed Forces of the Crown until April 1941. This is a sobering thought when considering the role of the airwomen during the Battle of Britain in 1940.

The Balloon Squadrons

The Auxiliary Air Force was also in control of a number of the anti-aircraft balloon defences of the United Kingdom. In 1939, as war was declared, there were around forty-two squadrons operating barrage balloons. All balloon squadrons which fell between numbers 900 and 947 were formed within the Auxiliary Air Force, higher numbers were subsequently formed within the RAF, as the AAF ceased recruiting on the outbreak of war. RAF Balloon Command itself was formed on 1 November 1938 at Stanmore Park in Middlesex, when it subsumed the No. 30 (Balloon) Group which had been formed earlier in 1937 within Fighter Command and was then split up into four centres, all of whom were operated by the Auxiliary Air Force as follows:

No. 1 Balloon Centre Kidbrooke	No. 2 Balloon Centre Hook	No. 3 Balloon Centre Stanmore	No. 4 Balloon Centre Chigwell
No. 901 (County of London) Balloon Squadron	No. 904 (County of Surrey) Balloon Squadron	No. 906 (County of Middlesex) Balloon Squadron	No. 908 (County of Essex) Balloon Squadron
No. 902 (County of London) Balloon Squadron	No. 905 (County of Surrey) Balloon Squadron	No. 907 (County of Middlesex) Balloon Squadron	No. 909 (County of Essex) Balloon Squadron
No. 903 (County of London) Balloon Squadron			No. 910 (County of Essex) Balloon Squadron

When the Second World War began in September 1939, Balloon Command was reorganised into a dedicated Command Headquarters, which was still stationed at Stanmore in Middlesex. The Command now controlled five groups. Each group was responsible for a number of individual Balloon Centres. Each Balloon Centre consisted of Balloon Squadrons which were numbered between 900 and 994. So, No. 30 Barrage Balloon Group was run by the AAF and was responsible for No. 1, No. 2, No. 3, No. 4, and eventually No. 22, No. 23 and No. 24 Balloon Centres, and so on. Finally, each Balloon Centre was responsible for a number of Balloon Squadrons which are shown in the following table.

Barrage Balloon Squadron Number	Location
901 County of London Sqn	Woolwich
902 County of London Sqn	Kidbrooke, Brixton
903 County of London Sqn	Brixton
904 County of Surrey Sqn	Clapham
905 County of Surrey Sqn	Kensington
906 County of Middlesex Sqn	Hampstead
907 County of Middlesex Sqn	Harringay
908 County of Essex Sqn	Wanstead
909 County of Essex Sqn	West Ham
910 County of Essex Sqn	Dagenham
911 County of Warwick Sqn	West Bromwich
912 County of Warwick Sqn	Brockworth
913 County of Warwick Sqn	Erdington
914 County of Warwick Sqn	Wythall
915 County of Warwick Sqn	Bourneville
916 County of Warwick Sqn	Coventry
917 County of Warwick Sqn	Coventry
918 County of Derby Sqn	Derby
919 County of West Lancashire Sqn	Birkenhead
920 Sqn	Derry
921 West Lancashire Sqn	Liverpool
922 West Lancashire Sqn	Warrington
923 West Lancashire Sqn	Runcorn
924 Sqn	Southampton
925 East Lancashire Sqn	Manchester
926 East Lancashire Sqn	Bowlee
927 County of Gloucester Sqn	Bristol
928 Sqn	Felixstowe
929 Sqn	South Queensferry

Barrage Balloon Squadron Number	Location
930 Hampshire Sqn	Southampton
931 Hampshire Sqn	
932 Hampshire Sqn	Portsmouth
933 Hampshire Sqn	Portsmouth
934 County of Devon Sqn	Plymouth
935 County of Glamorgan Sqn	Plymouth
936 County of Northumberland Sqn	Newcastle upon Tyne
937 County of Northumberland Sqn	Newcastle upon Tyne
938 County of Northumberland Sqn	Stockton on Tees
939 West Riding Sqn	Sheffield
940 West Riding Sqn	Sheffield
941 West Riding Sqn	Sheffield
942 East Riding Sqn	RAF Sutton on Hull
943 East Riding Sqn	RAF Sutton on Hull
944 East Riding Sqn	RAF Sutton on Hull
945 City of Glasgow Sqn	Glasgow
946 City of Glasgow Sqn	Renfrew
947 City of Glasgow Sqn	Glasgow

Recruitment for the Balloon Squadrons started in 1939 with a call for volunteers who were aged between twenty-five and fifty. They trained on weeknights and weekends in the same way as the pilots, aircrew and ground staff of the Auxiliary Air Force. By 1940, the decision was taken to train members of the Women's Auxiliary Air Force to operate the balloons, thus releasing men for active service. Double the number of women were needed as the balloons were very heavy and difficult to manoeuvre.

The purpose of the barrage balloons was to help defend cities, ports and industrial areas. They played a significant role in Britain's anti-aircraft defences. Their job was to restrict the movement of German aircraft so that they were forced to change their routes, or to fly into the anti-aircraft gun areas. The presence of these balloons raised the morale of the civilian population as they were so big, 62 feet long, 3 feet high and 25 feet in diameter, and although they were floated at around 5,000 feet, they could be seen from the ground as an active defence against German aircraft. However, they could also be viewed in a negative sense, as they in fact highlighted the areas, such as industrial and ports, that they were there to defend. The balloons themselves were not the deterrent to aircraft, Luftwaffe or RAF, it was the cables that held them which caused chaos. Apart from this, wind was often the downfall of the barrage balloons. Strong wind could cause the balloon cables to break away from their mooring and then the cable itself would be dragged in whatever direction that the wind blew causing destruction in its wake. Similarly, thunder and lightning could also prove dangerous to them.

Operation Starfish

RAF barrage balloon personnel often shared in the civil defence role during and immediately after air raids. As the threat of invasion grew in 1940, several industrial cities and towns were divided up into various defensive sectors, and in some of these it was the balloon squadrons that took on command and control. Personnel were given regular weapons training and, together with the Home Guard, had specific responsibilities for defence in the face of enemy infiltrations on the ground. This meant close liaison not only with the garrisons, but also with commanders of the Home Guard, both field force and factory units.

Another role bestowed on the RAF balloon squadrons was that of organising and operating decoy fires. Carefully laid out trench systems containing petrol could be ignited to simulate a town ablaze when viewed from the air. These special fires were first tried in late 1940. Subsequently they were known by the codename 'Starfish'. In January 1941, all Starfish sites became the responsibility of RAF Balloon Command.

Therefore, whilst the Balloon Barrage might seem to be the least glamourous of all the organizations during the war in the air, Balloon Command made a more significant contribution than has been appreciated. Its very presence forced enemy bombers to fly higher when bombing, thus being less effective and it played a key role in ground defence as well as operating the Starfish decoy target system.[46] Finally, the Balloon Barrage was responsible for the destruction of some 200 V1 flying bombs during the summer of 1944.

RAF Balloon Command was disbanded in February 1945, so its hard-working personnel took no part in the victory parades of 1945. These pages pay due homage to those involved.

---

46 Extract taken from *The Luftwaffe over Brum*, by Steve Richards www.birminghamairraids. co.uk, and published by *Flypast* Magazine April 2022.

Chapter 4

The Women's Auxiliary Air Force
1939–1946

The foundations for the Women's Auxiliary Air Force (WAAF) were laid by the Women's Royal Air Force which was formed early in 1918 soon after the RAF had come into being on 1 April 1918. At that time some 10,000 women of the Women's Royal Naval Service, and the Queen Mary's Women's Auxiliary Army Corps were serving with the Royal Naval Air Service and the Royal Flying Corps and, of these, nearly all selected to transfer to the new Service. Although many had served in the domestic or clerical side and others were found working on acetylene welding and mending balloon silk, there were no proper training facilities available for the women, although some women worked applying strong lacquer to the fabric covering aircraft which helped to make them weatherproof. These women were called aircraft dopers. Women were also working on switchboards, and some were telegraphists. Others were trained as carpenters, electricians, painters, engine fitters, riggers and salvage workers. By 1919 there was a total of 24,659 members of the Women's Royal Air Force (WRAF). Plans were formulated in 1919 for the continued employment of women with the RAF in peacetime but were abandoned on account of the drastic post-war economy. By April 1920, the disbandment of the WRAF had been completed.

During the 1930s some women's organizations began to be formed. For example, the Women's Voluntary Service (WVS) was formed in 1938, members of which drove ambulances, helped and organised evacuation and even worked with the Air Raid Precautions (ARP) services to help in the event of a war. The Townswomen's Guild (TG) was formed in 1929, made up of local branches who work together throughout the UK. There is also the Women's Institute (WI) which prides itself on being independent from all other groups. It does not particularly want to support any activity which could be seen as war work and during the Second World War its contribution

59

was limited to looking after evacuees and running the Preservation Centres which were sponsored by the Government and there, volunteers made jam out of excess produce which was then sent to depots across the country to be added to the rations.

The Emergency Service began in October 1936, led by Dame Helen Gwynne-Vaughan, who had been commandant of the WRAF between 1918 and 1920. Those who wished to join had to commit to attending training sessions once a week, to take part in summer camps and were prepared to accept a fee of 10 shillings a year. Many people, including the government, looked down at the women involved, and the women had to put up with poor conditions as well. September 1938 saw the Munich Crisis, which brought forward the development of the Auxiliary Territorial Service to 27 September, the idea being that each county of Britain would raise several companies which were affiliated to the male territorial unit. Finally, on 28 June 1939, the Women's Auxiliary Air Force was born and the ATS separated from it and went its own way.

The WAAF in 1939 had around 1,734 members and was commanded by Katherine Trefusis-Forbes,[47] who had been a chief instructor in the Emergency Service. The WAAF members were spread across the country in forty-seven companies, with each company having sixty-seven women each, serving as cooks, clerks, mess orderlies, mechanical transport drivers and equipment assistants. Also, Balloon Centres were to have five more women whose job was to work as fabric assistants.

Initially, women who joined the WAAF were enrolled rather than enlisted, which meant that they were able to leave if they decided it was not for them. Moreover, the Air Ministry, who had taken the view that it needed no women, was suddenly panicked into appealing for telephonists, teleprinter operators, plotters and radar operators. From 25 August 1939 telegrams went out and mobilised all of the WAAF. Then, when war was declared, the Air Ministry immediately began recruiting for a further 10,000 women. By 1941, however, due to the secret nature of some of the work undertaken by the WAAF, the Defence (Women's Forces) Regulations were passed making members subject to RAF discipline and rules. Furthermore, in 1942, the National Service Act of 1941 began to call up girls who were born in 1920 and 1921. This act was not popular with women who had

---

47 *The WAAF,* Beryl E. Escott, Oxford, 2012, p5

volunteered early to join the WAAF, as by the end of 1942 over 33,932 women had been enlisted, some not particularly willingly.

Hundreds of women volunteered to join the WAAF, from all over the country as well as those from countries in the Empire. However, there were major issues with unfinished accommodation, inadequate or no training and lack of uniforms. Many WAAFs were billeted with local families close to the aerodrome while they waited for accommodation to be built or completed. Early into the recruitment process there were not enough uniform items so often new recruits wore a mixture of civilian clothes and whatever uniform they had. What made up for all the upheaval was the friendships that developed between the groups of women, many of which lasted a lifetime.

A Substitution Committee was set up in 1941 with the role of working out how many women it would take to replace a man in order for him to be released to fight. Its key role was to monitor substitution rates and to review them in the light of changing technology and socio-economic factors. It was not only a gender issue but took into account the hours that some trades were required to work, especially twelve-hour shifts in the darkness of winter. When women were offered the chance of manning the balloon barrage, the substitution rate was sixteen women to ten men, but this ratio changed over time with the introduction of new winches that were easier to operate, the ratio was reduced from sixteen to ten. This meant that the substitution rate lessened to an equal number of women and men. The Substitution Committee only met five times during the war, the final one being in 1945.

In 1943, recruiting was temporarily suspended with 182,000 WAAFs appointed.[48] Basic training took two to three weeks, the first day being spent collecting uniform and equipment and having a medical inspection. Following days were spent undertaking a variety of tests for various trades. The women moved around the camp in full uniform, marching everywhere to lectures, fire, first aid, canteen, hygiene and gas training. If they were lucky enough, they got to sleep in huts, which slept 12-23 per room, in iron beds with straw mattresses. There were separate courses for officers and senior non-commissioned officers. The women were paid two-thirds of the pay allocated to their male counterparts. The next training that the women undertook was trade training. The biggest branch of the WAAF was the Domestic Group which included cooks, bat women and orderlies.

---

48 *The WAAF,* Beryl E. Escott, Oxford, 2012, p7

By 1943 there were 23,034 members of the WAAF, and together they represented sixty-one per cent of the catering services. Their trade training was based on preparing food and taught how to choose and cut a piece of meat, how to manage large quantities of food, health and safety at work and cooking out in the field. The training was very intensive and took into account many different scenarios, such as cooking through the night, early morning and big quantities for the daytime. Other women decided to go into the technical trades such as transport mechanic, radar mechanic and flight mechanic. Others became dental technicians or nurses or medical orderlies. Finally, there were those who worked in communications and intelligence. In September 1944 there were nearly 32,000 WAAF serving in the signals branch, many of whom were radar plotters providing a vital role in the defence of Britain. Initially women were considered to be not strong enough to cope with the large barrage balloons and the long wires which were used to tether the balloons to the ground. However, in May 1941, 257 women were posted to some balloon squadrons and performed so well that by 1943 there were women manning over 1,029 balloon sites which amounted to forty-seven per cent of all of Balloon Command personnel. Those women were given extra rations and better accommodation on their site and each crew was made up of twelve airwomen and two NCOs. In late 1940, in order to release more men for flying duties an Air Ministry Committee agreed that 'no work should be done by a man if a woman could do it or be trained to do it.'[49]

Recruiting

On the outbreak of war, the AAF was embodied with the RAF as was the WAAF. However, whilst the AAF stopped recruiting and all new wartime entrants were to the RAFVR, the WAAF retained its identity simply because there was no other organization to harbour them and the acronym 'WAAF' has been an everyday term for female members of the RAF to this day. For the first eight months of the war, entry to the WAAF was through the forty-eight RAF companies of the ATS, each of which had an establishment of seventy personnel, rising to 206, and which had originally been affiliated to the AAF squadrons. From July 1940, Service numbers allocated to WAAF recruits were in the series 420000 to 495000. The recruiting procedure for women closely

---

49 *The WAAF*, Beryl E. Escott, Oxford, 2012, p12.

followed the arrangements for men. Women were not considered members of the Armed Forces of the Crown until April 1941. The strength of the WAAF at the outbreak of war was 234 officers and 1,500 other ranks, a total of 1,734, whereas by 1 July 1940 it was 687 officers and 11,170 other ranks, a total of 11,857. The strength of the WAAF reached its peak of 181,835 in April 1943.

Enrolment into the RAF Companies of the ATS had been affected through the AAF organization, with AAF squadrons initially being responsible for recruiting, and the issue of the AAF series of Service numbers in the 880000 series took place, but when the Air Ministry decided to form a separate women's service, recruiting was taken over by WAAF officers working directly under the Air Ministry. In April 1940, the Inspector of Recruiting assumed responsibility and, by the end of June, recruiting was being affected at eight Area Headquarters. It was at this time that Service numbers for WAAF in the 420000 series were introduced in July 1940. Applicants were registered and had a preliminary medical examination at an Area Depot and were then sent on to the Reception Depot at West Drayton for a final medical examination and enrolment. In 1941, Northern Ireland Area Headquarters and certain combined Recruiting Centres were brought in to assist, as were twenty sub-depots in towns which had no Combined Recruiting Centres.

Wartime Growth

On the outbreak of war, the Women's Auxiliary Air Force consisted of 234 officers and 1,500 airwomen, a total of 1,734. The establishment for a General Duties Company was increased to 206 other ranks and a Record Office Company was set up with an establishment of 159. Companies allocated to balloon units were allowed twenty fabric workers in lieu of twenty cooks. Immediate authority was given for recruitment up to 10,000 and a later provision of 20,000 was approved. The original peacetime companies were not disbanded until March 1940. Therefore, in the period from 1 September 1939 until 31 March 1940, the ATS Companies of the RAF continued to provide recruits to the burgeoning WAAF.

The mobilisation of the WAAF on 28 August 1939, after only, two months existence, and its rapid expansion to some 8,000 personnel during the first five weeks of war produced acute clothing, accommodation and kindred difficulties. No uniforms were at first available, and for many weeks, WAAF officers were reduced to searching London and provincial cities for essential garments which they ordered from wholesale and retail houses. The accommodation position was equally unsatisfactory. It had been agreed in July 1939 that tentage for 5,000 should be earmarked for the use of WAAF on the outbreak of war, but as war broke out in September, the tentage was of little value. Consequently, airwomen had to be housed in all types of quarters, many of which were quite unsatisfactory from the administrative, hygienic and disciplinary aspects. Other airwomen had to return home on pay and allowances until some form of housing was available. The position improved on 26 October when the WAAF Depot at West Drayton was opened. It then became possible to give nearly all recruits a fortnight's disciplinary course. Previously, a number of them had to be sent directly for duty at their war stations or for initial or specialised training.

General recruiting had to be suspended when the strength reached 8,000 on 6 October owing to inadequate accommodation. All companies then compiled waiting lists of candidates, and as accommodation and training facilities improved, recruiting was resumed for specialised trades. Despite various restrictions imposed by the Schedule of Reserved Occupations and other Ministry of Labour controls, numbers increased rapidly, and by the spring of 1941, applications were outstripping requirements in certain trades. In order not to lose suitable applicants who would be required as personnel targets rose, the Air Ministry (DGM) opened a WAAF Deferred List in May 1941. Accepted recruits were then only provisionally enrolled and sent home on the understanding that they would be recalled within three months. A number of recruits continued to be drafted for immediate service.

Wastage

During the period 3 September 1939 to 31 December 1940, the wastage rate for the WAAF was 3,636 against an intake of 14,672 (25 per cent), a figure no doubt influenced by the 'enrolled' rather than 'enlisted' status of the newly formed WAAF. (It is a moot point that a female radar operator who provides a fighter controller with information concerning the height, bearing and speed of an enemy target which results in that target's destruction is or is not party to that act.)[50]

From the table below there is a variety of jobs available to recruits of the WAAF. In all, eighty of them, whilst a range of twenty-four different jobs where available to female officers.

---

50 https://www.iwm.org.uk/collections/item/object/10226

WAAF Trades (1946)

Group 1	Group 2	Group 3	Group 4	Group 5	Group M
Draughtswoman (Cartographical)	Acetylene Welder	Cook	Administrative	Aircraft hand General Duties	Chiropodist
Electrician I	Aircraft Finisher	Fabric Worker Aero	Air Movements Assistant	Armament Assistant	Dental Clerk Orderly
Fitter II (Air frame)	Armourer (Guns)	Fabric Worker Balloon	Clerk Equipment Accounting	Balloon Parachute Hand	Dental Hygienist
Fitter II (Engine)	Balloon Operator	Hairdresser	Clerk General Duties	Bat woman	Dispenser
High Speed Telegraphist	Carpenter	Radio Assistant	Clerk General Duties (Cypher)	Bomb Plotter	Laboratory Assistant
Instrument Repairer I	Cook	Safety Equipment Assistant	Clerk (Movement Control)	Cine Projectionist	Masseuse
Model Maker	Electrician Grade II	Shoe Repairer	Clerk Pay Accounting	Drogue Packer and Repairer	Nursing Orderly
Radar Mechanic	Flight Mechanic (Air Frame)	Tailor	Clerk Personnel Section	MT Driver	Operating Room Assistant
Wireless Mechanic	Flight Mechanic (Engine)	Telephonist	Clerk (Provisioning)	Maintenance Assistant	Optician Orderly
Wireless Operator Mechanic	Interpreter (Technical)		Clerk (Signals)	Mess Steward	Radiographer
	Instrument Repairer, Grade II		Clerk (Special Duties)	Orderly	
	Meteorologist		Clerk Special Duties (Watchkeeper)	Physical Training Instructor	
	MT Mechanic		Equipment Assistant	Waitress	

Group 1	Group 2	Group 3	Group 4	Group 5	Group M
	Photographer		Interpreter	WAAF Police	
	Radar Operator		Radar Operator		
	Safety Equipment Worker		RT Operator		
	Wireless Operator		Teleprinter Operator		
	WT (Slip Reader Operator)[51]		Tracer		

WAAF Officer Branches[52]

Accountant
Administrative
Catering
Code and Cypher
Equipment
Fitter
Intelligence
Interception Controller
Medical and Psychological Assistant
Meteorological
Motor Transport
Movements Liaison
Operations 'B'
Operations 'C'
Orthoptist
Personnel Selection

---

51 Aircraft Women's trades, Air Ministry Pamphlet 103, eighth edition, 1946
52 WAAF Officer Branches 1946 (AP3234)

Photographic Interpretation
Provost
Signals 'G'
Signals, Special Radar
Signals, Supervisory Radar
WAAF G (WAAF Only)
Dentist (RAF Branch)
Doctor (RAF Branch)

It is clear though that WAAF personnel did not fly, although thirty volunteers were allowed to join the Air Transport Auxiliary, to work as pilots.

Daily life as a WAAF was generally busy with work shifts, monthly kit inspections, visits out of camp to places like the cinema or local dances and time spent in the Navy, Army and Air Force Institute (NAAFI). There was a great sense of camaraderie among the WAAF with plenty of support available to them should they need it.

Demobilisation

Discharges from the WAAF commenced on 18 June 1945, but as late as April 1948, some 7,000 personnel had still not been discharged, indeed some soldiered on until the end of the year when they transferred to the re-formed Women's Royal Air Force.

The Roll of Honour

The AAF/RAuxAF Roll of Honour commemorates all those members of the Force who were enlisted or commissioned in the AAF or RAuxAF and who gave their lives in the cause of freedom and who died as a result of accidents or enemy action or otherwise whilst in service and on duty. The Commonwealth War Graves Commission (CWGC) holds a database of all such AAF casualties that were allocated the Service Numbers 90000 for officers and 800000 for other ranks. For at least the first eight months of the war, recruits were provided by the forty-eight former RAF companies of the ATS and were allocated the block of Service numbers reserved for the WAAF. These women were affiliated to an AAF squadron. It was not until July 1940 that the allocation was changed to the 420000 series. All casualties after this date are remembered in the Royal Air Force Books of Remembrance lodged in the RAF Church, St Clement Danes in London. Moreover, the CWGC lists forty-nine airwomen with a Service number in the 880000s. At least 1,734 members of the WAAF were transferred from the ATS before the war, and thereafter up to the end of March 1940, this block of numbers was replaced in July 1940 by those in the 420000 series.

Service Numbers

In July 1940, Sylvia Drake-Brockman applied to join the WAAF at the RAF's recruiting headquarters at Kingsway in London. Two weeks later she attended the West Drayton reception centre where recruits were arriving at the rate of 100 a day. The following day, she was enrolled and given the Service number 896991.[53] Presumably, she inherited her Service number from an unused batch of the earlier allocation. However, she survived the war so is not included in the CWGC list of casualties or the AAF/RAuxAF Roll of Honour.

In a cemetery at Closeburn, just north of Dumfries in Scotland is a CWGC headstone which reads:

443863 LACW
Louise McKie Age 23
13. 9. 43.

Women's Auxiliary Air Force

For the sake of completeness, shown below are the complete allocations for WAAF personnel Service Numbers 1939 to 1945.

880000 to 897999	Mar 1939	Ex ATS/WAAF
420000 to 430000	Jul 1940	WAAF West Drayton, Harrogate, Bridgenorth
430001 to 440000	Mar 1941	WAAF West Drayton, Harrogate, Bridgenorth

---

53 Patrick Bishop *Air Force Blue,* p.102 William Collins London 2017.

440001 to 450000	Feb 1941	WAAF Gloucester
450001 to 460000	June 1941	WAAF Gloucester
460001 to 465000	Dec 1941	WAAF No. 1 and No. 2 Depot
465001 to 475000	Nov 1942	WAAF No. 2 Depot
475001 to 485000	Jan 1943	WAAF Gloucester
485001 to 495000	Apr 1943	WAAF Gloucester
499000 to 499999	Sep 1942	WAAF NSA for ROC Duties.

Moreover, if, as is likely, service numbers were not allocated sequentially and from a single source, but issued in blocks to the forty-eight different RAF companies of the ATS or the AAF Squadrons, then taking the known strength of the WAAF at 1 July 1940 and adding that figure to the first in the 800000 series is not valid because of wastage during the period and blocks of numbers being exhausted or unused within the recruiting process. All such unallocated Service numbers, after March 1940 would have either been withdrawn or sent to the WAAF Depot at West Drayton.

Timeline

April 1920	Disbandment of the original WRAF.
October 1924	Formation of the AAF.
December 1925	Allocation of 800000 series of numbers to the AAF.
September 1938	Formation of the ATS.
December 1938	RAF Companies of the ATS. Affiliated to AAF Squadrons.
28 August 1939	WAAF embodied with a strength of 1,734.
6 October 1939	WAAF strength increased to 8,000.
31 March 1940	RAF companies of ATS disbanded.
April 1940	RAF Inspector of Recruiting assumes responsibility for WAAF.
July 1940	Strength of WAAF increases to 11,857.
July 1940	WAAF Service Numbers changed to 420000.
December 1940	Wastage of WAAF to date reaches 3636 (25 per cent).
April 1941	WAAF finally becomes Armed Forces of the Crown.

When the Fighter Control and Radar Reporting Units were formed in 1947 and 1948, they included a number of former experienced WAAF plotters and operators who had served during the war and now re-joined as members of the newly formed WRAuxAF.

Personal stories

Muriel Gane Pushman

Born in 1921 at Warren Farm House, located just outside Guildford, she was just eighteen when war was declared. Dreaming about the opportunity of enlisting to help her country she decided upon the Women's Auxiliary Air Force, primarily because she didn't want to wear Khaki and she didn't like the black silk stockings worn by the Women's Royal Naval Service. So, 'as a blue-eyed blonde, I had always been besotted with blue. It was my colour and so my conscience, my ego, and I met in agreement and the WAAF was elected.'[54] Having been to London to attend the WAAF Recruiting Office, she received her acceptance letter on 31 December 1939, requesting her to attend Bush House, the Air Ministry headquarters in London at 12 noon on 6 January 1940. Once there she was taken with several other women from Kings Cross Station to Harrogate, where they were to be billeted at the Majestic Hotel for three weeks of basic training. The next day they were issued with all their kit and shown the standard of cleanliness that they were expected to maintain.

Following basic training, Muriel was assigned to Special Duties and took a train south to Leighton Buzzard in Bedfordshire. She had a two-mile march, ending with a march down a long drive to an old house. Once here they were told that they were going to be trained as plotters to work with Fighter Command at Bentley Priory in Middlesex. Eventually she was told that she had been accepted for the Officer Training Unit at Loughborough where she would be based for a month. Following her ninety-six per cent pass of the course she was posted to RAF Station Pucklechurch near Bristol. By 1943 she had been posted to Cardiff and worked in the old stable block close to Cardiff Castle in Balloon Command. Then, towards the end of 1943 she received a letter from the Air Ministry stating that she had been selected to attend a four-week senior WAAF Officers Course at Bowness, Lake Windermere. On completion of the course, and after two weeks leave, she was posted to RAF Flying Training Command Brize Norton in Oxfordshire. There her role was to support the girls who had been taken from Balloon Command to be re-trained due to a shortage of flight mechanics. She remained there until she married George Pushman and,

---

54 *We All Wore Blue*, Pushman, Muriel Gane, Stroud, 2006, page 18.

once pregnant, she found that the RAF did not cater for pregnant women and so she was discharged back into civilian life.

Jane Trefusis-Forbes

Born on 21 March 1899 in Taital, Chile. During 1936, Jane and two other women, Helen Gwynne-Vaughan and Kitty Trenchard, had together set up the Emergency Service whose role was to select women and organise them so that they were prepared in case a war happened. She had been the chief instructor at the Auxiliary Territorial Service School of Instruction in 1938. On 1 July 1939, she was appointed as Director of the WAAF. She was an experienced WAAF and worked in Canada in October 1943 to consider the effectiveness of the Women's Division of the Royal Canadian Air Force and then had travelled to India to determine whether it was possible to employ women in the South East Asia Command. She retired from the WAAF in August 1944. She died on 18 June 1971.

Joan Elizabeth Mortimer

Born in 1912 in London, she worked as a political organiser before joining the WAAF in April 1939. By October 1939 she had been promoted to sergeant and was awarded the Military Medal on 1 September 1940 along with two other WAAFs. On that day RAF Biggin Hill was attacked by the Luftwaffe. Sergeant Mortimer was a teleprinter operator and was in the armoury when the air raid sounded, though she was surrounded by several tons of high explosives she remained at her telephone switchboard relaying messages to the defence posts around the airfield. Even before the all clear had been sounded she picked up a bundle of red flags and went outside to mark the many unexploded bombs which lay around the area. Eventually she was invalided out of the WAAF and settled in Suffolk as a poultry farmer. She died in 1997.

Conclusion

A total of 217,249 women served in the WAAF during the war, 183,492 volunteers and 33,757 under the National Service Act from 1 April 1942.

In the first five weeks of the war, the strength of the WAAF was some 8,000, rising to 11,170 by July 1940, well within the block of 18,000 Service numbers allocated for that purpose.

Therefore, the wartime criteria for inclusion in the AAF/RAuxAF Roll of Honour can be based solely on evidence that the woman was a CWGC casualty and allocated a Service number in the 880000 series.[55] It is not possible to determine the details of those members of the WAAF who were enrolled after the disbandment of the RAF companies of the ATS in March 1940, but before the introduction of the 420000 allocation of Service numbers the following July, without access to individual Service records. The CWGC lists twenty-two such members of the WAAF whose Service numbers are in excess of the known strength of the WAAF at 1 July 1940, but this does not take into account the wastage figures for the period which were considerable, so the number of those twenty-two WAAF could be overstated. In any event, if Service numbers for the WAAF were allocated in blocks to the forty-eight RAF Companies of the ATS or direct to AAF squadrons then such a numerical algorithm is flawed. For those who died before or after the Second World War, contemporary squadron records or other official documents should suffice.

---

55 RAF Monograph Manning Plans and Policy Air Historical Branch (1) Air Ministry.

Chapter 5

Post War Flying Squadrons 1947–1957

By the end of the Second World War all of the auxiliary squadrons had been disbanded, so there was no real surprise when on 14 November 1945, William Wedgewood Benn (Lord Stansgate), Secretary of State for Air, made a statement in the House of Lords with a view to resurrecting the Auxiliary and Reserve Forces. Once the speech had been made, King George VI agreed to the plan and the first step was to re-establish the Reserve Command of the RAF, which had been abolished in 1940. It was noted that 'the appropriate joint Territorial Army and Air Force County Associations, with the approval of the Treasury, have been asked to undertake certain preliminary steps towards the re-formation of the AAF squadrons which formed part of our first line air defence in 1939, and have since served with distinction in all theatres of war.'[56]

Over time there would be twenty-one new auxiliary squadrons which would be recreated on their old territorial basis, and by November 1946, recruiting for these squadrons had begun, recruiting in the first instance released officers and men 'who have been trained in the Air Force during the war and who therefore will only require refresher training.'[57] In terms of the AAF, the view was that:

'We have the AAF as a means of augmenting economically the front-line strength of the regular RAF by making use of the voluntary services of young men willing to devote most of their spare time to the work. That a standard of efficiency as high as that to be found in regular squadrons can be attained

---

56 The National Archives (TNA), AIR20/932, Auxiliary Air Force Reconstitution, 'Auxiliary and Reserve Air Forces', Note from Secretary of State for Air, 14 April 1946.

57 TNA, AIR20/932, Auxiliary Air Force Reconstitution, 'Memo from W.G. Clements F8 12,' 12 September 1946.

73

by the AAF squadrons was amply demonstrated in the opening stages of the war and there is no reason to believe that this performance could not be repeated in the future, provided that the incentive is there.'[58]

After several months of discussion, it was decided that the role of the new AAF squadrons would not include long range fighter or coastal shipping strike, nor would they be included in light bomber squadrons. Finally, the equipment which was used by long range strategical bomber, transport and general reconnaissance squadrons was considered to be too complicated to be operated and maintained by Auxiliary personnel.[59]

The Air Ministry believed men who had been demobbed from the Royal Air Force would be only too happy to join the Auxiliary Air Force as they would be able to maintain their contact with servicemen who were their friends, but that 'once that stock had been depleted, it would have to start using inexperienced crews, who would fly relatively infrequently and therefore might not be able to cope with the increasingly complex technology of aircraft.'[60] Furthermore, Air Vice-Marshal Douglas Macfadyen supported this view by concluding that there would be a major gulf between a man who could fly a modern fighter and a skilled pilot who could operate it effectively.[61]

It is clear that the shortcomings of part-time pilots and aircrew were apparent as early as February 1946, whilst discussions were taking place to re-form the auxiliary squadrons. Furthermore, a memo from the Assistant Chief of Air Staff, dated 10 September 1945 noted that 'in terms of the proposal to reconstitute a number of AAF squadrons as Night Fighter squadrons, I am of the opinion that it is unacceptable because it is extremely doubtful whether they could be trained to the high standard of efficiency in this specialised role.'[62] However, the decision made by the Air Ministry was

---

58 TNA, AIR20/932, Auxiliary Air Force Reconstitution, 'Air Ministry Minute Sheet' Note from E.L. Colbeck-Welch, DDFT Ops, 3 May 1946.

59 TNA, AIR 20/932, Auxiliary Air Force Reconstitution, Auxiliary Air Force Post-War, D D Pol (G) 2, 2 October 1945.

60 Squadron Leader F.A. Freeman, 'The Post-War Royal Auxiliary Air Force,' *Royal Air Force Reserve and Auxiliary Forces*, (Oxford, 2003), p99.

61 Ibid, p100.

62 TNA, AIR20/932, Auxiliary Air Force Reconstitution, 'Reconstitution of the Auxiliary Air Force,' Memo from the Assistant Chief of Air Staff, 10 September 1945.

that the twenty auxiliary squadrons should comprise thirteen day fighter (interceptor) squadrons, to be equipped with the Supermarine Spitfire F21/22/24, three night fighter squadrons equipped with the de Havilland Mosquito NF 20 and three light bomber squadrons equipped with the de Havilland Mosquito B 25. These squadrons would be the responsibility of Reserve Command. They would ensure the raising and initial training of the reconstituted AAF squadrons which were to be named and located as follows:[63]

Reconstituted Auxiliary Air Force squadrons name, classification and location

Squadron Number	Squadron Name	Squadron Classification	Squadron Location
500	County of Kent	Night Fighter	West Malling
501	County of Gloucester	Day Fighter	Filton
502	County of Ulster	Light Bomber	Aldergrove
504	County of Notts	Light Bomber	Syerston
600	City of London	Day Interceptor	Biggin Hill
601	County of London	Day Fighter	Hendon and later North Weald
602	County of Glasgow	Day Fighter	Abbotsinch
603	County of Edinburgh	Day Fighter	Turnhouse
604	County of Middlesex	Day Interceptor	Hendon and later North Weald
605	County of Warwick	Night Fighter	Honiley
607	County of Durham	Day Fighter	Ouston
608	North Riding	Light Bomber	Thornaby
609	West Riding	Night Fighter	Church Fenton
610	County of Cheshire	Day Fighter	Hooton Park
611	West Lancashire	Day Fighter	Speke
612	City of Aberdeen	Day Fighter	Dyce

---

63 TNA, AIR 20/932, Auxiliary Air Force Reconstitution, Auxiliary Air Force Post-War, D D Pol (G) 2, 2 October 1945.

Squadron Number	Squadron Name	Squadron Classification	Squadron Location
613	City of Manchester	Day Fighter	Ringway
614	County of Glamorgan	Day Fighter	Llandow
615	County of Surrey	Day Fighter	Biggin Hill
616	South Yorkshire	Light Bomber	Finningley

In September 1946, the Defence Committee decided to allow an active air force reserve of 72,000. Of those, 12,000 would be members of the AAF.[64] Wing Commander Jefford, speaking to the Royal Air Force Historical Society noted that 'in the event of an emergency the auxiliary units would be embodied and take their places in the front line, as they had done during the Second World War.'[65]

Matters become rather more complicated when discussing the post-war auxiliaries as it was decided to include two other types of squadrons within the AAF – the Light Anti-Aircraft ground-based squadrons of the AAF Regiment and the Auxiliary Fighter Control Units. These units will be discussed fully in the following two chapters. These extra units meant that the original figure of 12,000 had to be revised. The figure was increased in 1946 to 26,400.[66]

The squadrons maintained much of their pre-war framework and organization and 'were established on a pre-war basis'.[67] Advertisements that appeared in the press emphasised the specific requirements and conditions of service to ensure that men who volunteered were highly motivated and understood the commitment that they were making. For example, the *Yorkshire Post* noted on 7 November 1946:

> Recruiting for the new Auxiliary Air Force of twenty flying squadrons opens tomorrow and will be carried out by the individual squadrons. At present, only officers and men who have served in the Air Force during the war are eligible to join. Vacancies exist for flying members, for personnel for ground trades…officers will be commissioned for five years and

---

64 Wing Commander Jeff Jefford, 'Post-War Reserves to 1960,' *Royal Air Force Reserve and Auxiliary Forces*, (Oxford, 2003) p79.

65 Ibid, p82.

66 TNA, AIR20/932, Auxiliary Air Force Reconstitution, 'Note by the Secretary of State for Air,' 12 October 1945.

67 Ibid.

airmen will be enlisted for four years. Members must carry out certain training each year, to be undertaken during evenings, at weekends, and at the annual camp, which lasts fifteen days.[68]

The article went on to specify the conditions of service for both officers and airmen. Thus, men who volunteered to join the AAF were supposed to be very aware of their obligations towards the organization and were fully cognisant of the nature and purpose of the establishment that they were volunteering to join.

The changing technical demands of both flying and crewing aircraft became even more apparent when jet-engine aircraft became available to AAF squadrons in the late 1940s; aircraft which required large crews became obsolete with single-seat fighters that needed high level technical skills and knowledge to operate becoming much more common. A direct consequence of these technical changes was the acceptance of men as pilots who were not officers.[69] Whilst the initial level of interest was overwhelming, the actual number of men who met the criteria for enlisting was disappointing and reflected the new recruitment restrictions placed on all squadrons. Selection of officers, NCOs and airmen became much more demanding with particular emphasis on previous experience and knowledge. By June 1947 it had become apparent that auxiliaries were finding it difficult in maintaining currency on multi-engine aircraft, indeed, it was also becoming difficult to constitute multi-engine crews, so by the end of 1948, all auxiliary squadrons had converted to single-engine day fighters, a decision reinforced by the fact that the squadrons were living off the fat of ex-wartime aircrew and that new pilots joining them were likely to find flying single-engine fighters easier to cope with, although even they were becoming more complex to operate.

In 1948 the regular establishment of an auxiliary squadron stood at three officers, five NCOs and thirty-three airmen, a total of forty-one, although HQ Reserve Command had recently submitted a bid for this to be increased to sixty-four.[70] These demands were relaxed in 1948 to allow any ex-servicemen to join the AAF in an effort to increase recruitment.[71] However, in many ways this action was too late to enable the AAF squadrons to benefit

---

68 *Yorkshire Post*, 7 November 1946.
69 *Flying Review*, 17 August 1948.
70 Freeman, *The Post-War Royal Auxiliary Air Force*, p100.
71 *North Eastern Daily Gazette, 15 March* 1948.

from the immediate post-war wave of enthusiasm which subsequently waned as men successfully re-entered civilian life.

Another significant factor in slowing down recruitment was the conditions of service, which required the attendance for twelve weekends and fifteen days at annual camp, as well as the completion of one hundred hours of non-continuous training. Many potential recruits could not meet this level of commitment. Volunteers had to be prepared to give up a significant amount of their free time in order to fulfil their obligations to the AAF.[72] For airmen, wartime aircrew categories and ground crew classifications were superseded by peacetime ones, sometimes requiring higher qualifications.[73] On 19 January 1948 a memo was sent to all AAF squadrons informing them that in recognition of their outstanding service in the Battle of Britain and in many of the other campaigns, King George VI had conferred upon the AAF, the pre-fix 'Royal'.[74] This title remained until all of the squadrons were disbanded in March 1957.

Recruiting by the end of March 1948 was at thirty-nine per cent of the establishment figures for the Royal Auxiliary Air Force (RAuxAF) across the country.[75] National attention turned to new conscripts who were being compelled by the National Service Act of 1948 to join HM Forces. Initially the time period of National Service was eighteen months, but this was extended to two years following the outbreak of the Korean War in 1950. An agreement was made that 300 National Service conscripts would be selected for flying training each year and these men would fulfil their subsequent reserve obligation by either becoming members of the Royal Air Force Volunteer Reserve (RAFVR) or of an auxiliary squadron. In this way it was hoped that the poor number of recruits for the RAuxAF squadrons could be boosted.[76]

Overall recruiting figures showed that there were significant numbers of pilots, around seventy-three per cent across England, who had served in the AAF during the 1930s and were eager to continue flying, and wanted the opportunity to fly. Many were officers who had attained high ranks or had been decorated for their skill and bravery; others were NCOs who had been

---

72 Jefford, 'Post-War Reserves to 1960, 'p89.

73 TNA, AIR20/932, Auxiliary Air Force Reconstitution, 'Minute Sheet – Reserve Air Forces,' D D B Ops, 23 January 1946.

74 TNA, AIR2/13172, 'Memo from Air Ministry,' 19 January 1948.

75 Freeman, *The Post-War Royal Auxiliary Air Force,* p98.

76 Ibid, p99.

able to fly and had enjoyed successful careers. Members from both groups were very willing to rejoin the RAuxAF as soon as it was reformed, but these men were in the minority compared to the larger number of ex RAF personnel.

During the mid to late 1940s and throughout the 1950s the auxiliary squadrons struggled to recruit sufficient numbers to maintain efficiency. Indeed, there had been concern about their efficiency since they had been reformed in 1946. By 1948, the Minister of Labour appealed to young men and women to join one of the auxiliary or reserve forces. He also asked employers to give their employees all possible facilities.[77] Lord Pakenham, Minister of Civil Aviation urged more volunteers to come forward, stating that the RAuxAF still needed some 25,000 volunteers. He noted that the country would remain in danger, along with the rest of Europe, until Western Europe was very much stronger both economically and militarily.[78] In early 1949, Arthur Henderson, Secretary of State for Air, noted that to fit the squadrons of the RAuxAF for their role as part of the first line of Britain's defence they were to be re-equipped with jet fighters. He hoped that as a result of special measures to be taken that year a steadily increasing number of auxiliary pilots would be able to gain jet flying experience.[79] The Auxiliary and Reserve Forces Bill was presented to the House of Commons on 23 May 1949. 'It is designed to extend the powers and duties of the territorial and auxiliary forces associations and to facilitate calling out reserve and auxiliary forces to meet either an actual or an apprehended attack upon the United Kingdom.'[80] At the end of October 1949 the twenty fighter squadrons of the RAuxAF were transferred to Fighter Command, which emphasized their place in the wartime front line defences of Great Britain. 'Since their reforming in 1946, the squadrons have been training and have now reached a sufficiently high standard to be transferred into the Command who would control them in a time of war.'[81]

During March 1950, a new Air Ministry Scheme which enabled the twenty squadrons of the RAuxAF to have combined training with the regular fighter squadrons every month, was unveiled. This scheme would enable the auxiliaries to get the most out of their weekend flying by operating under conditions similar to wartime. Each auxiliary unit was

---

77 *The Times*, 24 September 1948, p4.

78 *The Times*, 29 October 1948, p6.

79 *The Times*, 3 February 1949, p3.

80 *The Times*, 24 May 1949, p2.

81 *The Times*, 31 October 1949, p4.

affiliated to a regular squadron, and each auxiliary squadron would visit their regular station to help them gain a close understanding and develop a common operating system and technique. The pilots and ground crews would live on the RAF station during their training weekend. 'For the auxiliary pilots, the greatest benefit will be that they become accustomed to being directed from the ground, which they cannot do unless they are operating under a Fighter Command sector control.'[82] In 1949, approval was given to form five Air Observation Post Flying Squadrons (AOPF), equipped with Austers to support the Territorial Army. These squadrons were manned jointly by the Army and the Royal Air Force and were numbered:

661 AOP Squadron Royal Auxiliary Air Force
662 AOP Squadron Royal Auxiliary Air Force
663 AOP Squadron Royal Auxiliary Air Force
664 AOP Squadron Royal Auxiliary Air Force
666 AOP Squadron Royal Auxiliary Air Force

Additionally, an auxiliary transport squadron, 622 (County of Hampshire) Squadron, was formed at Blackbushe, equipped with the Avro York or the Lockheed Viking, but this squadron floundered due to a lack of recruits and it was disbanded in 1953.

By 1951, the auxiliaries had disposed of their last piston-engine fighters, which were to be replaced by the jet-engine Gloster Meteor and de Havilland Vampire. Early in 1949, the North Atlantic Treaty Organization (NATO) had been formed and SACEUR, the Supreme Allied Commander Europe, needed to know what forces would be available to him. All twenty auxiliary squadrons were declared as fully combat capable. The onset of the Cold War between the western countries and NATO and the Communist countries of the East caused trouble in Berlin, which had been divided between the four allies at the end of the war. This triggered the Berlin Air Lift which involved supplying the people of West Berlin with food, water and medicine until the Russians lifted the blockade of the land and canal routes into Berlin.

The outbreak of the Korean War in June 1950 meant that the RAuxAF fighter squadrons and the five newly formed Air Observation Post (AOP) squadrons were called up for three months active service, representing one

---

82 *The Times*, 13 March 1950, p2.

third of Fighter Command's strength. Their main role was to operate home defence, replacing regular squadrons who were deployed to Korea. The RAuxAF squadrons were then retained for intensive refresher training at their home bases.

However, by 1953, the training requirements had advanced to the point where the auxiliaries could only be classified at Cat B, which meant that they could no longer be regarded as front-line units. Towards the end of 1953 a new pilot training scheme was announced to maintain the strength of the RAuxAF. Commanding Officers of auxiliary squadrons were able to select and recommend youths for aircrew training before their national service, if they were willing to transfer to the RAuxAF after completing their two-year full-time service; their pilot training would occupy nearly all of the period, but the time and expense would be justified by their continued part-time service with an auxiliary service.[83] By 1954, proposals were made which suggested that the auxiliary squadrons should be reduced from twenty to fifteen squadrons and that they should be re-equipped with the Hawker Hunter and the Supermarine Swift, with the de Havilland Venom being a temporary measure pending the availability of the swept-wing types. In the event, the Venom was a non-starter as it only had an airframe life of seven hundred and fifty hours and most of the airframes would be second-hand.

The end of the Royal Auxiliary Air Force

In 1953 the 'Baker-Carr Report', written by Air Commodore John Baker-Carr, stated that because of the limited amount of flying time that was available to an auxiliary pilot, future aeroplanes would be too complex for them to fly proficiently, and the squadrons would therefore have to be manned by ex-regulars. Furthermore, Baker-Carr believed that the auxiliary squadrons should all be disbanded.[84] Arguments flowed back and forth regarding the feasibility of equipping the auxiliaries with sub-sonic swept wing fighters, including the use of war reserve aircraft. The argument was put forward that since the nation was hard pressed to maintain its regular forces, the cost of new aircraft was so great that it would be cheaper to

---

83 *The Times*,4 September 1953, p3.
84 Jefford, *Post-War Reserves to 1960*, p93.

re-equip the fighter defence if there were less pilots, thus equipping with sub-sonic swept wing fighters was seen as the way forward. Harold Macmillan as Defence Minister gained the nickname 'Mac the Knife' in tribute to the sweeping defence cuts he proposed as a solution to Britain's economic malaise. He announced that it would not be possible, or indeed right, for auxiliaries to switch to the expensive new machines, a necessity if they were to remain in the front line of defence. He added that the government had decided to alter the organization of this force to enable those Auxiliary pilots who could give their time to it to train on the swept-wing aircraft themselves as individuals; not to equip the squadrons with these machines, but to train the men. By this means they would provide reserves behind the regular squadrons in war.

Thus, the role of the RAuxAF was questioned in so far as the RAuxAF fighter squadrons were called up for three months training in 1951 to prepare them for the Korean War which upset many employers and the RAuxAF were never called out again. It was calculated that, by mid-1958, twenty-two Hawker Hunters and ten Supermarine Swifts would have been written off and they could not be replaced because they were the replacements. In the end it was decided not to proceed with the swept-wing options which, in any case would be delaying the inevitable as there was no way the auxiliary squadrons would ever get the English Electric Lightning.

Therefore, it was decided that the auxiliaries would be reduced to a training flight, equipped with the Meteors and Vampires and co-located with a regular Hunter squadron and that up to six auxiliaries would train as Hunter pilots. However, by early 1955, it was decided that it was unpalatable that the auxiliaries should not be allowed to fight as formed units, so it was necessary to find a role for them, which would be to deal with an assault on the United Kingdom by Russian Tupolev Tu-4 strategic bombers. The argument was a bit thin but the anti-invasion commitment in support of the Territorial Army sufficed to permit the auxiliaries to retain their Meteors and Vampires.

Problems with the early Hunters meant that only two pilots per squadron were being trained on the type. Moreover, the anti-invasion role had proved extremely unlikely as the Territorial Army (who the auxiliaries were supposed to support) had been reassigned to support the civilian population in the event of a nuclear war. In addition, the cost of running the auxiliary flying squadrons was running in excess of seventy million pounds a year at today's rates.

By 1954 the Air Council and the Auxiliary and Reserve Forces Committee were trying to find ways to sustain the flying squadrons; updating their aircraft was considered a possibility, as was reducing the number of squadrons from twenty to fifteen, however, aircraft technology was so advanced that it was not considered viable to give new aircraft to the RAuxAF squadrons. By mid-1955 the Air Ministry was under increasing pressure to save money and the possibility was again discussed of disbanding the AAF squadrons.[85] By 1956, the Suez affair had strengthened the case for disbandment because of the drain on Britain's gold and dollar reserves. Some newspapers, and particularly those associated with Max Aitken, the former post-war commanding officer of 601 Squadron, who ran the *Sunday Express,* began to leak details of total disbandment. No official comment came from the authorities, resulting in protracted discussion in the press. However, in 1957 there was a major review of defence policy that culminated with a White Paper in 1957 from the Minister of Defence, Duncan Sandys. This was announced in the aftermath of the Suez crisis and showed a major shift in defence policy by enforcing massive cuts in the number of troops and by increasing the dependence of the United Kingdom on nuclear technology. Furthermore, the disbandment of the AAF squadrons would save money immediately. It must also be remembered that the regular RAF squadrons in Fighter Command were also suffering from cuts and the Royal Naval Volunteer Reserve was to lose all of its ten flying squadrons. The decision was made that 'the most effective deterrents for the United Kingdom were V Bombers and surface-to-air missiles.'[86]

The RAuxAF leaders tried to fight the decision and formed a committee of the four metropolitan areas of London, composed of Squadron Leader John Cormack of 600 Squadron, who was an Esso executive, Tommy Turnbull of 604 Squadron, who was a Lloyd's underwriter, Bob Eeles of 615 Squadron, who was an ICI executive and Peter Edelston of 601Squadron, an advertising executive.[87] The aim of the committee was to try to educate people in the role of the RAuxAF in the hope that public opinion could stop the disbandment. They made a television appearance at the Pathfinders' Club in Knightsbridge and answered questions from the BBC air correspondent. They wrote to all Members of Parliament and all

---

85 Jefford, *Post-War Reserves to 1960*, p96.

86 David Brown, *Thornaby Aerodrome and Wartime Memories*, (Stockton on Tees, 1992) p59.

87 Hans Onderwater, *Gentlemen in Blue. 600 Squadron*, (Barnsley, 1997), p365.

national and provincial newspapers. Their letter was therefore published all over the country, highlighting their concern that:

> The country is throwing away an organization whose worth is far greater than its face value, employing people whose time is spent productively five days a week and two days a week in the service of the crown. There is no doubt that the Royal Air Force is short of pilots, and disbanding the Auxiliary fighter squadrons means that the country will lose over 300 fully trained fighter pilots, and in addition more than 2,000 ground crew.[88]

501 Squadron's CO, Squadron Leader Collings wrote to a local newspaper to present his case against the Air Ministry:

> This is an absolute tragedy. They are throwing away a terrific enthusiasm that has always been the keynote of the Auxiliaries. Farmers, airline pilots, bricklayers, bank clerks, printers and railway workers, who give up their weekends to fly or service the aircraft, working and learning with a rare devotion. Now the thirty officers and seventy-five airmen of 501 Squadron must hang up their flying boots.[89]

As no official comment could be wrung from the authorities, a flood of letters took up the case for the part-timers. Some positive, but others breathing a sigh of relief that the petrol wasting joy riders would leave them in weekend peace. 'They have made mincemeat of my nerves with their power dives over my chimney pots, and I've grown so tired of ducking every few minutes while trying to dig in my garden.'[90] In response someone pointed out that 'my heart bleeds for Mr H, he might feel better if he were to go up to the Abbey, look through the Book of Remembrance, and take note of the number of Auxiliary Air Force men who gave their lives for us. They had all been joy-riding young men at weekends.'[91]

---

88 Tom Moulson, *The Flying Sword, the Story of 601 Squadron,* (London, 1964), p178.
89 David Watkins, *Fear Nothing. The History of No 501 (County of Gloucester) Fighter Squadron, Royal Auxiliary Air Force,* (Cowden, 1990), p93.
90 Tom Moulson, *The Millionaires Squadron. The Remarkable Story of 601 Squadron and the Flying Sword,* (Barnsley, 2014) p206.
91 Ibid, p206

They lobbied MPs and were always received with goodwill and sympathy, but effectively they were beaten. In January 1957, the announcement was made by the Minister of Defence stating that the RAuxAF was to be disbanded on 10 March of that year. The Air Ministry Notice stated that:

> In view of the magnificent war record of the auxiliary fighter squadrons, which fully justified the hopes of those responsible for the formation of the Auxiliary Air Force, this decision has been taken with the deepest possible regret…with the growing cost of equipment it has become clear that the auxiliary fighter squadrons could not be retained, even with their present aircraft, at the expense of the regular units which must be regarded as of higher priority.[92]

Thus, the main reason given was partly on operational and partly on economic grounds. Operationally it was argued that it was unrealistic to expect weekend fliers to be able to operate complex modern aircraft. Economically, the cost of training, maintaining the aircraft and keeping up the aerodromes was too much. It was however, made clear that the RAFVR and the UASs would not be affected by this decision. The intention was to abolish the RAuxAF as such and attach its members to the regular force until the supply of National Service pilots dried up, and the last resistance collapsed with the dissolution of squadron entity. Certainly, the squadrons could not survive such a transplanting, for their roots were in their histories, not in the hangers and crew rooms of any aerodrome. To abolish pride of unit was to abolish voluntary service.[93] The decision was made and on 10 March 1957, the twenty Royal Auxiliary Air Force Squadrons were disbanded for the last time.[94]

The editor of *The Aeroplane* noted:

> It is hard to imagine the poverty of imagination that lies behind the decision to disband the Auxiliaries. In these days when financial reward and material gain are alleged to be the only springs of conduct and employment is there nobody in high places who realises that the spirit behind the Auxiliary Air Force

---

92 TNA, Air Ministry Notice No.23, 15 January 1957.
93 Moulson, *The Millionaires Squadron,* p205.
94 Leslie Hunt, *Twenty-One Squadrons – The History of the Royal Auxiliary Air Force 1929-1957,* (London,1972), p429.

is priceless? Nothing could be madder than to discourage those who wish to allocate their spare time to serving their country.[95]

With the hindsight of half a century it is possible to see that in the long run the government was right, and that Britain's long devotion to amateur service had run its course and would have to yield to the reality of technology. Flying ability was no less important, but flair and courageous individualism would yield to technical mastery and relentless learning and practice.[96]

Had it not been for the formation of three Maritime Headquarters Units and a Maritime Support Unit in 1959, it is possible that the Royal Auxiliary Air Force would have vanished for good.

Personal stories

John (Jamie) Morrison 600 (City of London) Squadron

Jamie joined the Royal Air Force Volunteer Reserve after the war was over. As part of this he trained with several regular squadrons. Whenever he served with these regular squadrons, he would complete some forms which would be sent to his unit. This went on for over two years until after a pay parade the pay officer saw Jamie and said that he had never seen him at a pay parade before. Jamie answered that he had never attended a pay parade before as there was no money ever paid to him. The officer got rather upset and told him that he had seen him work very hard over the last two years so why had he never been paid. Jamie responded that he didn't know why. The officer shook his head and walked away. Later in the day Jamie was called to the Adjutant's Office where he was told that a rather strange mistake had been made. Unfortunately, there was no way that Jamie could get back the money that he should have received, but if Jamie agreed he could join the Auxiliary Air Force, which he agreed to and filled out the forms. There was a vacancy at 600 Squadron, so it was all sorted out for him.[97]

---

95 Ian Piper, *We never slept. The story of 605 Squadron*, (Trowbridge, 1996), p229.
96 Moulson, *The Millionaires Squadron*, pp209-10.
97 *Gentlemen in Blue, 600 Squadron*, Hans Onderwater, London, 1997, p366/7

He joined the RAuxAF on 19 May 1951 as a pilot officer. He was also the first and only black volunteer to join the squadron.

His first annual summer camp was to Takali in Malta. Here, whenever there was a break, Jamie sat in the shade, whilst his comrades sat in the sun trying to top up their tan. They could not understand why Jamie always sat in the shade so he explained that his tan had reached a point of saturation, so he would leave them as much tan as possible. A competition was then declared to see which person could get as near as possible to Jamie's tan. Many ended up with sun stroke and so all the men were warned by the Medical Officer that anyone who came to see him to be treated for sun burn or sun stroke would be put on a charge for self-inflicted wounds.[98]

William Francis Blackadder 607 (County of Durham) Squadron

Born on 23 January 1913, and after being educated in Edinburgh before attending Cambridge University, he joined 607 AAF Squadron in early 1937. After a successful career during the Second World War in which he was awarded both the DSO and an OBE, he rejoined the squadron on 5 December 1946.

William had a successful rugby union career as a prop prior to the war. As an amateur he played for Scottish Wayfarers in 1933. He also played for the West of Scotland. In April 1938 he played for the Co-Optimists before moving to play for Newcastle Northern. He started playing for the Scotland Possibles in the second half of 1938 and in January 1939 he went back to playing for Newcastle Northern and represented the county of Northumberland during this time. He was also capped by Scotland in 1938 when he played in the England versus Scotland Test match at Twickenham on 19 March 1938.

Norman Beresford Tebbit

In February 1952, Norman Beresford Tebbit (Service Number 2435575) was interviewed and took on the role of pilot officer in 604 (County of Middlesex) Squadron. He was promoted to flying officer in January 1953.[99]

---

98 Ibid p 368
99 Ian White, *If You Want Peace, Prepare for War, A History of 604 (County of Middlesex) Squadron, RAuxAF, in Peace and War*, 604 Squadron Association, 2005.

On 18 July 1954 he was returning to North Weald to prepare for Exercise Dividend flying a Gloster Meteor F Mk 8, WL132. On attempting to take off he decided to abandon because he felt that the aircraft had not reached flying speed.

'Electing to abandon take-off, Flying Officer Tebbit aged 23, selected wheels-up, whereupon the aircraft left the runway and skidded some 200 yards on its belly, crossing two ditches and catching fire. Flying Officer Tebbit jettisoned the canopy and rapidly exited the burning wreck without serious injury.'[100]

Later, Norman Tebbit became a famous member of the Thatcher Conservative Government of 1979-1990 as a Member of Parliament for Chingford, Essex and Secretary of State for Trade and Industry.[101]

In 1992 he decided not to stand for re-election, and once the election was over he was given a life peerage as Baron Tebbit of Chingford in the London Borough of Waltham Forest, enabling him to sit in the House of Lords.

---

100   aviation-safety.net/wikibase/21329
101   aviation-safety.net/wikibase/21329

Chapter 6

Radar and the Role of the Royal Auxiliary Air Force in the Control and Reporting System 1947–1959

This chapter looks at the development of radar in the Control and Reporting (C&R) system in United Kingdom Air Defence and the part played in its conception by the Royal Auxiliary Air Force from 1947 to 1959. The chapter is presented in three parts. First, it covers the development of C&R in the years of the Second World War before moving on to discuss the air defence threat in the immediate post-war years (the introduction of the 'ROTOR' programme) before concluding with a description of the role of the auxiliaries and their operational tasks and environment. This is not a technical chapter, as it deals with *what* happened, rather than 'how'.

The development of radar and the CR System from 1939

On 26 February 1935, Hitler officially created the German Luftwaffe, appointing Hermann Goering as Commander-in-Chief. A week later, he revealed this potent threat to the world. On that very same day, in an English meadow near Daventry, a group of scientists were parked in a Morris van, peering intently at a cathode ray tube (CRT) when, at eight miles range, they detected the echo of a Heyford bomber, the signal being reflected from the BBC Daventry radio transmitter. These two events were to come together just four years later, in what has been described as 'a wartime miracle.'

It had long been known that aircraft reflected radio waves, but no means then existed to plot that information and to integrate it into a system whereby fighter aircraft could be directed to intercept hostile raids. What is not generally known is that the radar developed from 1935 onwards was primitive by later standards, indeed, the Americans were disparaging in their criticism of early British methods, but what was important was that the Royal Air Force decided to go with what was available at the time and develop a C&R system that incorporated the new radar as one of its component parts, rather than wait for improved technology to be produced and introduced into service. The ability of Fighter Command to respond to the raids during the Battle of Britain is testimony to that foresight and to the enduring debt owed to its Commander-in-Chief Air Chief Marshal Sir Hugh Dowding who was responsible for the introduction of a tried and tested C&R system in time to meet the threat.

The new C&R system was based on a chain of RDF (Radio Detection Finding) stations that ran from the Isle of Wight in the south to Scotland in the north-east. (It was not until later in the war that the name was changed from RDF to 'RADAR' which stood for 'Radio Detection and Range.') A map of the original stations was to indicate that, coverage was later extended later in the war to the west coast and as far north as the Shetlands. Because the coverage consisted of a chain that it was home-based as opposed to overseas, it was known as 'Chain Home' or 'CH'. Unlike rotating radar aerials, which consist of a radio pulse transmitted in the form of a beam, on the 'searchlight' principle, the CH system flooded the approaches to the United Kingdom with a continuous curtain of radio waves, so that any aircraft approaching the coast would blunder into the coverage.

Aerospace being a three-dimensional medium, it was necessary to not only detect an aircraft but to determine its range from the station (how far away it was), it's bearing (where it was) and its height, in order that defending fighters could be directed to its position and, ideally, be directed above the target for an effective interception to be made. Determining the range was the easy bit. Radio waves travel at the speed of light, which is some 186,240 miles per second, therefore it was a simple matter to measure the time it took for a radio pulse to travel to a target and be returned to the receiver. Range scales would then be marked on the screen and the range read off from the echo displayed. Bearing was calculated by the fact that every station in the chain was positioned on a known bearing, what was known as a 'line of shoot'. For example, if a station was facing due east (90 degrees), then an echo was roughly due east of the station and whilst not an exact science, the use of an instrument called a 'Goniometer' or 'Gonio' for short, enabled a skilled operator to 'tweak' the echo until optimum signal strength revealed how far to the left or right, in degrees, the echo deviated from the line of shoot. Considering that some adjacent stations were probably tracking the same raid, it was possible to triangulate the true bearing from shared information.

Finding the height was a different problem, as it depended on several factors; the slope of the ground on which the station was situated, the maximum possible height of the transmitter masts, the wavelengths available at the time and interference from surrounding terrain. Indeed, Ventnor on the Isle of Wight was not able to provide height information at all during the Battle of Britain. Problems were soon overcome but it was not until the introduction of the Magnetron valve in 1940 which led to centimetric radar, and rotating aerials that were supplemented by ones that 'nodded' up and down, later in the war, that height finding was perfected. In the interim, it was possible to improve rudimentary height finding techniques by periodically calibrating results with actual aircraft at known ranges and heights. All that then remained was to determine the strength of the incoming raid and this was done by a skilled operator interpreting the strength of the signal. Those who have seen such films as *Angels One-Five* will recall the plaques on the plotting table that simply said '150 plus' or whatever.

A typical CH station consisted of three or four 360ft high steel masts, some 180 feet apart, with the aerial dipoles strung between them. Three surviving aerials can still be seen at Dover, one stands on a hill at Dunkirk, and one on the outskirts of Canterbury, visible from the M2 motorway. Receiver aerials were about 240 foot high and were made of wood to avoid contaminating the transmitted signal and were placed in the form of a square. Contemporary pictures show a typical east coast RDF station. Mention has been made of the need to site a CH station in a way that maximised performance and it is interesting to quote an extract from a 'Siting Specification for CH – 'RDF' Stations (circa 1935)':

'A site, well back from the coast, with a smooth slope between it and the sea gave good height-finding and good range-finding – there was a rule by which one knew how far inland it was worth going to get height above sea level. But irregularities in the ground were inevitable and these distorted the height-finding properties of the equipment and gave 'permanent' echoes similar to those produced by large aircraft. The chosen sites had also to be accessible to heavy engineering works, to have soil suitable for carrying 360ft steel masts – they had to be convenient for electrical supplies, secure against sea bombardment, inconspicuous from the air and it was furthermore essential that they should not *gravely interfere with grouse shooting.'*

It would appear that the class system that recruited so many senior officers and scientists in the 1930s was getting its priorities right!

RDF was just part of what was to become the most effective C&R system to be devised at the time. Each CH station plotted incoming raids on a plotting table that showed the range, bearing, strength and height of an incoming incursion into UK air space. The plots were reported to the Fighter Command Filter rooms, one of which was at RAF Bentley Priory, using an alpha-numeric grid reference known as 'GeoRef'. The Filter Room then 'filtered' the information, sorting out duplicated plots, known friendly aircraft and combining all the information so that the most concise picture of the threat was obtained. This information was co-ordinated with information received from the Observer Corps inland and the Anti-Aircraft gun organizations and then relayed to the Sector Operations Rooms situated at the Sector airfields situated within the four operational Groups within Fighter Command, the most important of which was 11 Group at Uxbridge which controlled the Sector Operations Rooms at North Weald, Hornchurch, Biggin Hill and Kenley.

Each Sector Operations Room contained a plotting table similar to the ones at the CH stations and the Filter Room and the information that listed all the available squadrons and their state, whether at readiness, in action, or being refuelled and rearmed, was recorded on a 'totaliser' board or 'tote'. Each Sector Operations Room had links with its own Observer Corps and AA cells which were responsible for issuing air raid warnings in their respective sectors. Therefore, it was possible for a sector controller to see at a glance, the nature of a threat in his sector, and the forces at his disposal to meet that threat with the minimum of delay and the maximum application of scarce resources which could be deployed at the right place and time, avoiding the need of expensive and wasteful standing patrols. The whole organization was held in place by a secure network of GPO landlines, whose own personnel contributed so much in maintaining and repairing lines damaged by bombing. This, indeed, was Dowding's legacy. It is interesting to speculate what the situation might have been at Pearl Harbor in 1941 had a similar system been in place there.

This, then, was the system of radar in defence of the United Kingdom that existed, with little change, for the rest of the war, although it is worth mentioning some other developments that took place during that time. First, and most importantly, was the introduction of Ground Controlled Interception (GCI) which, combined with Airborne Interception (AI) radar in aircraft, made compact by the introduction of centimetric radar, finally defeated the Luftwaffe over Britain at night. The system relied on an aerial that rotated through 360 degrees and showed both the echo from the night fighter and the target, on a screen like those today and known as a Plan Position Indicator (PPI). It was thus possible for the ground controller to 'vector' the fighter onto the target to a point where the fighter could pick up the enemy on its own airborne radar. The early rotating aerials on the ground were not powered and had to be rotated by an airman turning a hand-cranked device connected to a motor-cycle chain, or two airmen pedalling a tandem bicycle contraption, which was a real 'bind', hence the name they were known by – 'binders.' However, one advantage was that the aerial could be halted whilst pointing at the target, or even reversed, enabling accurate assessments to be made.

Another innovation was 'Identification Friend or Foe' (IFF) which enabled a friendly aircraft to identify itself by a flick of a switch in the aircraft that added another echo to its signal. Finally, early radar technology limited radar coverage to certain heights, and aircraft flying close to the station and at low heights could remain undetected or lost in the ground returns (clutter) that surrounded every station as the radio pulses were reflected off the ground or sea. It was possible to employ an 'anti-clutter' switch, but that meant losing everything within that area, including any signals. In time, work on anti-shipping and anti-aircraft gun-laying radars, together with wider use of the narrower beams provided by centimetric radar and other wavelengths, led to the development of Chain Home Low (CHL) and Chain Home Extra Low (CHEL) radars that closed the gap in coverage, but never eliminated it entirely. To this day, the maximum possible elevation of an aerial together with the curvature of the earth means that by flying very low near the target, it is still possible for an aircraft to be undetected until it is too late.

The CH network was largely responsible for the demise of Hitler's V-Weapons. The V1 flying bomb could be easily detected and intercepted and the V2 rocket which, although impossible to track and intercept, proved vulnerable when it was discovered that CH radar could pinpoint its launch site (their radar operators could only work for fifteen minutes a time, intent on the screen before them) and subsequent raids by Bomber Command could target these sites. By the end of the war, the CH system had proved its worth, but well before VE day, many of its stations had been closed or run down. It has often been asked why the newer radars in service had not rendered the CH system obsolete by 1945, but the fact is that CH was such an effective early-warning system that, combined with the excellent C&R system of which it was but just a part, the newer radars supplemented, rather than replaced it. However, the system was very manpower intensive, a subject we will return to, and this was the situation as the war ended and thoughts turned to the new threat posed by the Cold War.

The Cold War

In 1945, four US Army Air Force B29 Super Fortresses crash-landed in Siberia, following a raid on Japan. The Russians accepted this unexpected largesse with relish and passed the aircraft on to Tupolev who copied the examples and came up with the Soviet Air Force's Tu-4. On 29 August 1949, the Russians exploded their first atomic bomb and, suddenly, the United Kingdom was vulnerable to attacks from Tu-4s armed with a 20kt nuclear weapon. The decayed state of the UK's air defence network could never have reacted to this threat in time and, in 1949, the Cherry Report recommended a complete overhaul of the UK air defences under the project name 'ROTOR'. The existing network of some 170 radar sites was to be rationalised to some sixty-six sites, the best of which were to be completed to more exacting peacetime standards. The existing wartime C&R system, with filter rooms and sector stations was to be retained. The contract was awarded to the Marconi Wireless and Telegraph Company and was (and still is) the largest government contract awarded to a UK firm.

The project was massive and resulted in improved equipment and reliability, with the range of some radars more than doubling. Meanwhile, research was undertaken to develop a more powerful radar under the code name 'GREEN GARLIC' which later became known as the Type 80, more of which anon. Meanwhile, long-range warning was provided by twenty-eight rebuilt CH sites, with thirty-eight other sites used for other roles, such as CHL or CHEL. These sites were supplemented by the old Type 7 and 11 GCI radars and Type 13 and 14 centimetric height-finding radars. The ROTOR project was divided into East Coast and West Coast areas and, because the threat was seen to be greatest on the East Coast, massive reinforced underground bunkers were built, those on the West Coast being mainly surface bunkers. The underground bunkers were characterised by a distinctive looking bungalow which served as an access and guardroom to the bunker, which concealed an access corridor, leading to a one, two or three-level bunker.

In constructing the bunkers, a massive hole was first dug and usually, extensive de-watering had to take place. The bunker was then constructed and buried under earth. The bunker had 10-foot Ferro concrete walls with a 14-foot-thick roof and came complete with its own borehole, generators and filtered air conditioning system. They were supposed to give protection against a 20kt nuclear weapon. Those on the West Coast were built to a similar specification but were situated on the surface. Four huge Sector Operations Centres (SOCs) were also built, to divide the UK into six sectors. In addition, the Army got twenty-eight protected Anti-Aircraft Operations Rooms (AAORs) in target areas and the whole project consumed 350,000 tons of concrete, 20,000 tons of steel and thousands of miles of telephone and telex cables. Because the whole system was as manpower intensive as had been the wartime one, the RAF calculated that it would need some 10,000 reservists to man the network and planned to recall them annually for training. Then, as now, there was no guarantee that ex-regular reservists, let alone radar qualified ones, would be available in sufficient numbers, so it was decided to form twenty-eight Fighter Control Units (FCUs) and two Radar Reporting units (RRUs) of the Royal Auxiliary Air Force, the first of which was formed in 1947, all within Fighter Command. In the event of war, it was the Fighter Control Units of the Royal Auxiliary Air Force that were formed to provide much of the manpower for the Control and Reporting system for the United Kingdom.

However, two events in the early 1950s were to render the whole new ROTOR system obsolete at a stroke. First, came the introduction into service in 1955, of the magnificent Type 80 search radar. This radar had a range of up to 280 miles at heights of up to 70,000 feet and, because it could be used to control fighters onto their targets, it rendered the old Type 7 and 11 GCI radars obsolete, although the former remained in service as a back-up radar for some years. The second event was the testing of the first Soviet hydrogen bomb, also in 1955 and this, together with the advent of supersonic jet bombers to deliver it, gave insufficient warning for the existing ROTOR system. As a result, many stations closed, along with the SOCs and AAORs, and the remaining stations were converted to Type 80-equipped Master Radar Stations (MRS) supported by one or more Type 13 height radars. The latter were supplemented by American FPS-6 height-finding radars.

No. 3604 (County of Middlesex) Fighter Control Unit RAuxAF was formed in 1948. The unit had its Town Headquarters in Queen's Square Holborn in London (opposite the Great Ormond Street Hospital for Sick Children) and its two operational flights trained at the MRSs at RAF Bawdsey in Suffolk and RAF Wartling in Sussex respectively. Summer camps of fifteen days duration were spent at RAF Sandwich (later RAF Ash), RAF Wartling and elsewhere.

The Town HQs were provided by the Territorial and Volunteer Reserves Association (TAVRA) and the FCUs were based on county affiliations, as were the auxiliary flying squadrons, with the FCUs based in major towns and cities within mobilisation distance from their allocated war appointed radar stations.

Establishment

Structure, personnel, stores, medics, radar ops controllers, mechanics, clerks etc and a synthetic ops room were based on the original earlier ROTOR principle. However, the strength of the early FCUs in 1951/2 was running at about twenty-five per cent of establishment but it should be noted that the RAuxAF as a whole was competing for recruits against the attractions of both the Naval and Army reserves, as well as those of industry and commerce. On the outbreak of war in 1939 the flying squadrons of the AAF were running at about sixty-six per cent.

Training

Training for the FCUs was carried out during the weekends and evenings at their respective Town HQ and frequently at a weekend visit to a Master Radar Station (MRS). Live Practice Interceptions (PIs) were possible, either using CAACU (civilian organization contracted to the MoD), or operational Hunters for day, or Javelin aircraft for night and/or all-weather training. When no flying was possible, an innovative solution was found by using 'Mullards', so named after the maker's name of radio valves, of what can only be best described as agricultural flight simulators. These consisted of two very large grey cabinets with various knobs and switches and located in an adjacent room to the fighter controller's cabin. Two airmen/women would be detailed, one to act as the 'fighter' interceptor and one the target.

Once switched on, signals representing both interceptor and target would be relayed to the controller's radar screen who would then instruct the operators to manoeuvre their 'aircraft' using the controls on the Mullards. It actually worked!

Notwithstanding the source of recruiting for the WAAF during the war, whether it be from ex-ATS personnel in 1939 or from wartime sources, many of the volunteers for the post-war FCUs were former WAAF plotters who had been disbanded in 1945 and whose natural temperament and experience gave them a clear advantage over their male counterparts. By the time the FCUs were finally disbanded in 1958-1961, the FCUs had made a valuable contribution to the air defence of the UK, without whom it could have been seriously under-manned or even overwhelmed.

List of Fighter Control Units

3500 (County of Kent)
3501 (County of Nottingham)
3502 (County of Antrim – later Ulster)
3505 (East Riding of Yorkshire)
3506 (County of Northampton)
3507 (County of Somerset)
3508 (County of Northumberland)
3509 (County of Stafford)
3510 (County of Inverness)
3511 (City of Dundee)
3512 (County of Devon)
3513 (City of Plymouth)
3602 (City of Glasgow)
3603 (City of Edinburgh)
3604 (County of Middlesex)
3605 (County of Warwick)
3608 (North Riding of Yorkshire)
3609 (West Riding of Yorkshire)
3611 (West Lancashire)
3612 (County of Aberdeen)
3613 (City of Manchester)
3614 (County of Glamorgan)
3617 (County of Hampshire)

3618 (County of Sussex)
3619 (County of Suffolk)
3620 (County of Norfolk)
3621 (North Lancashire)
3631 (County of Essex)
3700 (County of London)
3701 (County of Sussex)

The last two units to be formed, Nos. 3700 and 3701, were called Radar Reporting Units. However, their role was essentially the same as that of the Fighter Control Units, without the fighter control element.

Chapter 7

The Royal Auxiliary Air Force Regiment

The Royal Air Force Regiment (RAF Regt) is a specialist airfield defence Corps which was founded by Royal Warrant in 1942. After a twenty-nine week course, its members are responsible for defending airfields and training Royal Air Force personnel in military skills. Members of the Regiment are known within the RAF as 'Rock Apes' or 'Rocks.'

The genesis of the RAF Regiment was with the creation of No. 1 Armoured Car Company RAF in 1921 for operations in Iraq, followed shortly afterwards by Nos. 2 and 3 companies. These were equipped with Rolls-Royce Armoured Cars and were highly successful in ground combat operations throughout the Middle East in the 1920s and 1930s. The RAF Regiment came into existence, in name, on 5 February 1942. From the start it had both field squadrons and light anti-aircraft squadrons, the latter originally armed with Hispano 20mm cannon and then the Bofors 40mm anti-aircraft gun. Its role was to seize, secure and defend airfields to enable air operations to take place. Several parachute squadrons were formed to assist in the seizing of airfields and No. II Squadron retains this capability today. 284 Field Squadron was the first RAF unit to arrive in West Berlin in 1945 to secure RAF Gatow.

It was not until 1946 that the Royal Auxiliary Air Force Regiment was formed. Its members, like their regular colleagues also wore the 'mudguard' shaped RAF Regiment badge on each shoulder as well as, until recently, the Auxiliaries letter 'A.'

The RAF Regiment was formed as a corps within the Royal Air Force to provide ground and short-range air defence for airfields. The concept survived the peace and, when the Royal Auxiliary Air Force was re-established in 1946, it was decided to form twenty Regiment squadrons under the ROTOR plan, although only twelve were actually formed. Each was to be associated with a flying squadron and all were to be Light Anti-Aircraft (LAA) squadrons, equipped with the Bofors L40/60 gun. The first four units formed on 1 May 1947, a fifth on 1 October and the remainder on 1 December. They were:

2501 (County of Gloucester) Squadron
2502 (Ulster) Squadron
2504 (Nottingham) Squadron
2600 (City of London) Squadron
2602 (City of Glasgow) Squadron
2603 (City of Edinburgh) Squadron
2604 (County of Warwick) Squadron
2608 (North Riding of Yorkshire) Squadron
2609 (West Riding of Yorkshire) Squadron
2611 (West Lancashire) Squadron
2612 (County of Aberdeen) Squadron
2629 (City of Lincoln) Squadron

However, by the early 1950s the L40/60 Bofors gun was nearing the end of its useful life and the replacement weapon was deemed too complex for part-time reservists to operate, so in 1953 it was decided to re-role the RAuxAF Regiment units as field squadrons, in effect changing them from air defence to ground defence units, but this was to prove short-lived as, on 10 March 1957, in common with all the flying squadrons, they too were disbanded.

Some twenty years after the RAuxAF had virtually ceased to exist, in March 1979, it was decided to trial three new RAuxAF Regiment Squadrons, 2503 (County of Lincoln) Squadron at Scampton, 2623 (East Anglian) Squadron at Honington and 2622 (Highland) Squadron at Lossiemouth, to provide defence of the main base to which they were assigned. The numbering of the Regiment squadrons followed the pattern of the FCUs, using the same number as their erstwhile flying squadrons but prefixed with the number '2.' The Honington based 2623 Squadron was the first to introduce women into the Regiment as signallers.

In 1981, it was accepted that the first three 'pilot' squadrons had been a success and two more squadrons were formed in 1982, 2624 (County of Oxford) Squadron at Brize Norton, 2625 (County of Cornwall Squadron at St Mawgan, and in 1983, 2620 (County of Norfolk) Squadron at Marham. In 1984, on the phasing out of the V-Force, 2503 Squadron relocated to Waddington.

THE ROYAL AUXILIARY AIR FORCE REGIMENT

By now, there was pressure for all main bases to be provided with an auxiliary Regiment squadron but, under an arrangement with the United States, the RAF Regiment (to some extent by forming additional RAuxAF squadrons) was also to provide defence, including Short Range Air Defence (SHORAD) of USAF bases in the United Kingdom, and at Lossiemouth. Trials were held with auxiliary personnel forming a flight to contribute to the resident RAF Regiment Rapier Squadron. In 1985, a new squadron was formed, 2729 (City of Lincoln) to take advantage of Argentinian Oerlikon guns and Skyguard radar, captured during the Falklands War in 1982.

Despite the reduction of the RAF Regiment, some forty years on, some auxiliary field squadrons remain whilst others, and some new squadrons, have taken on the role of Offensive Support Squadrons which now include 2748 Squadron at Waddington, nominally a RAF Regiment unit but largely manned by auxiliaries. The training wing was created and became 2623 Squadron when the RAF Regiment Depot moved from Catterick to Honington, subsequently becoming a sustainment squadron to the Rapier Force and an element of force protection. The gun squadron and wing which followed 2729 Squadron and the trials at Lossiemouth led to the establishment of more additional squadrons.

In May 2001, 2624 (County of Oxford) Squadron was re-numbered 501 (County of Gloucester) Squadron, following a decision that year to allocate former RAuxAF flying squadron numbers to certain ground units, and operating in the force protection role. The RAuxAF Regiment no longer recruited women, due to combat restrictions and, since the year 2000, members of the Regiment had continued to provide support to their regular 'gunners' in Afghanistan and Iraq.

In 1986, it had been decided that the Warsaw Pact threat to some main RAF bases in the United Kingdom required the formation of four Airfield Defence Force Flights. These were to be at key RAF bases and were to last for eight years until the threat receded with the fall of the Berlin Wall and after. These flights were active from 1986 to 1993 and were located at:

RAF Brampton
RAF High Wycombe
RAF St Albans

Also, members of the Defence Force served the Royal Air Force at RAF Lyneham for eight years between 1986 and 1994.

Finally, RAuxAF Regiment Squadrons which were extant on 1 April 2022 were:

2503 (County of Lincoln) Squadron
2620 (County of Norfolk) Squadron
2622 (Highland) Squadron
2623 (East Anglian) Squadron
2624 (County of Oxford) Squadron

Personal stories

In January 2021 LAC Georgia Sandover became the first female Gunner in the regular RAF Regiment to graduate.

She was nineteen years old and 5 foot 4 inches tall and in January 2020 she passed an incredibly demanding selection course to become the first and only female member of the RAF's frontline infantry regiment, whose job is to defend overseas British bases from attack. Her unit, No. 1 Squadron is now on standby to assist in the guarding of key areas such as Downing Street, the Parliament buildings and the country's nuclear power plants.

She had to complete an exhausting 20-week RAF Regiment selection course with her cohort of forty-two male recruits. To pass the course she had to prove her fitness with tests such as a four-kilometre march carrying over six stone in weight, then speeding up and completing a further two kilometres in the time allowed, which was sixteen minutes. She also had to show that she could get a wounded soldier out of trouble by dragging a seventeen stone sandbag at speed. There were also live fire drills using an L85 automatic rifle. Only eighteen from her cohort passed the course.

She was inspired to join the RAF Regiment by watching programmes like Our Girl on BBC1 and Channel 4's SAS Who Dares Wins.

'We are soldiers because we can end up on the front line,' she says. 'You would go on patrols around the base and surrounding areas to stop people attacking.' She adds that she would be armed with her L85 rifle, which can fire 650 rounds a minute, at all times.[102]

---

102 https://www.dailymail.co.uk/femail/article-8177257/How-Georgia-fought-way-RAF-boys-club.html

Chapter 8

The Maritime Headquarters Units of the Royal Auxiliary Air Force

For nearly forty years there were three Maritime Headquarters Units (MHUs) of the Royal Auxiliary Air Force. From 1959, these three units provided support to Coastal Command and its successors in a variety of roles, and constituted the entire RAuxAF until Regiment squadrons began to be formed some twenty years later. During this period, the RAuxAF, with a total establishment of some 300 personnel, continued to be featured in the annual Festival of Remembrance at the Royal Albert Hall and the annual Lord Mayor's Parade, both in London, as they still do today.

The Maritime Headquarters Units

Following the disbandment of the auxiliary flying squadrons, the fighter control units, the regiment squadrons and other ground support units, the establishment of the RAuxAF had been reduced to fewer than some 300 personnel. This remained the case until 1979, during which period a generation of regular RAF personnel became progressively unaware of the volunteer reserves in their midst. The Force was kept in being, however, through the foresight of Air Marshal Sir Edward Chilton, then Air Officer Commanding-in-Chief of Coastal Command and his Senior Staff Officer, Air Vice-Marshal Will Oulton, who recognized the value of retaining the auxiliaries as trained augmentees to supplement the regular staffs at operational HQs. Thus, three MHUs were established to support HQ Coastal Command (subsequently HQs 18 Group, 11/18 Group and, latterly 3 Group at Northwood and the former Southern and Northern Maritime Air Regions based at Pitreavie Castle, Fife and at Mount Wise, near Plymouth, respectively).

These three units provided reinforcement and support in the operations rooms, intelligence sections and communications centres of their related HQ, all of which had North Atlantic Treaty Organization (NATO) as well as national responsibilities. A fourth unit, the former Ulster Maritime Support Unit undertook similar duties at Aldergrove between 1960 and 1965, when it was disbanded.

As a friend of the author, a former Commodore Royal Navy never tires of reminding me, the UK is an island maritime nation although, as I never fail to remind him, that in the Second World War, more German U-boats were sunk by aircraft than by surface vessels. It is fitting therefore, that the Maritime Headquarters Units of the RAuxAF played such a major part in keeping open the seaways of these islands for forty years.

No. 1 (County of Hertford) Maritime Headquarters Unit (MHU)

No. 1 MHU was formed in January1960 under the command of Wing Commander A.R. Poole. It was initially manned by officers and airmen of the former No. 604 (County of Middlesex) Squadron, No. 3604 (County of Middlesex) Fighter Control Unit and No. 3700 (County of London) Radar Reporting Unit. The unit was also recruited from No. 600 (City of London) and No. 601 (County of London) squadrons and the RAFVR No. 7301 Flight at Northwood. a rich heritage indeed. No. 1 MHU's original task was to provide personnel to man the NATO Maritime Headquarters at Northwood (Commander in Chief, Eastern Atlantic Area), but it subsequently took on the additional responsibility of supporting the Maritime Headquarters and airfield at Gibraltar as well. For many years, the unit was located at Valency House, an Edwardian country house within sight of Northwood, but in 1991 it moved to new purpose-built accommodation at Northwood.

No. 1 MHU fostered close links with both the City of London and the Worshipful Company of Butchers. Its badge, with the motto *Swift to Respond* was approved by HM Queen Elizabeth II in July 1965. The badge was dedicated at St Clement Danes Church in 1970. On 12 June 1989, No. 1 MHU was proud to field Flying Officer John Easton as Colour Bearer when the Sovereign's Colour for the Royal Auxiliary Air Force was presented at a parade held at RAF Benson. The RAuxAF was, incidentally, the first reserve formation to be so honoured.

No. 2 (City of Edinburgh) Maritime Headquarters Unit

No. 2 MHU was formed under the command of Flight Lieutenant R.B. Worthington on 1 November 1959, its original staff being furnished by officers and airmen drawn from the former 3603 (City of Edinburgh) Fighter Control Unit, which had disbanded the previous day. The unit's town headquarters, formerly that of No. 603 Squadron and 3603 Fighter Control Unit, had been used by the auxiliaries since 1925, and still is.

The role of the unit, on its formation, was to provide operations, intelligence and communications personnel to support the joint Royal Navy/ Royal Air Force MHQ at Pitreavie Castle, Fife, particularly during NATO exercises. In 1986, the unit's role expanded to include mission support for aircrew operating from Kinloss, Lossiemouth, Machrihanish, (close to the Mull of Kintyre) and Turnhouse. It would eventually take on even more responsibility, including the provision of operational, intelligence, medical, Regiment, air traffic control and motor transport to support the operations of the Nimrod force at Kinloss, the maritime attack Tornados at Lossiemouth and the air defence operations of the air defence Tornado F3 squadrons at Leuchars. In addition, the unit provided intelligence support for the NATO/ National Joint Intelligence Centre at the Faslane Naval Base.

To train for these various roles, the unit supported the Joint Maritime Operations Training Staff (JMOTS) during Joint Maritime Courses and also provided support for overseas deployment. No. 2 MHU's badge with the motto *Watch Well*, was approved by HM The Queen in July 1963.

No. 3 (County of Devon) Maritime Headquarters Unit

No. 3 MHU was formed at Mount Batten, Plymouth, in January 1960, its initial members being drawn from No. 3513 (County of Devon) Fighter Control Unit, under the command of Wing Commander R.E.G. Van der Kiste. The MHU provided personnel to support HQ 19 Group at the Joint Maritime Headquarters at Mount Wise. Its commitments were later expanded to embrace Chivenor, near Barnstable, Gibraltar and St Mawgan, Cornwall. On the closure of Mount Batten in 1992, the unit moved to St Mawgan where it continued to support Gibraltar and, to a lesser extent Mount Wise, Devonport. Featuring Drake's drum with the motto *Muster*, No. 3 MHU's badge was approved in February 1963.

Roles

RAuxAF personnel from the MHUs were established to augment the regular operations, intelligence and communications staff at HQ Coastal Command during Transition to War (TTW) and during major NATO exercises. Working with their colleagues in the Royal Naval Reserve, the MHU personnel were initially expected to provide the third watch 'down the hole' in the various MHQ bunkers.

MHU personnel also provided expertise in the same fields at Northwood, Gibraltar, Kinloss, Lossiemouth, Machrihanish and St Mawgan. Specific duties included the tasking of maritime patrol, reconnaissance and strike/attack aircraft and the briefing and debriefing of aircrews. The MHUs worked closely together, and personnel were often interchanged for their annual training or exercises, particularly in support of the Joint Maritime Operations Training at Turnhouse (and later at Northwood), during the three annual Joint Maritime Courses (JMCs) to which the MHUs were committed from 1986 onwards, this activity involving personnel working in a variety of capacities at Pitreavie Castle, Machrihanish and Kinloss.

At much the same time as No. 3 MHU moved to St Mawgan in 1992, the locally-based Nimrods moved to Kinloss, so the MHU's primary task thereafter became the support of St Mawgan in its new role as a Forward Operating Base. In addition, it continued to support exercises with unit personnel augmenting the station's own operations and intelligence staff. The unit also supported the Maritime Cell in the joint Operations Centre at Gibraltar, with taskers, controllers, intelligence officers and clerks, and provided the entire operational support staff at the airfield. In short, Gibraltar was totally dependent upon the officers of No. 3 MHU for operational and intelligence support during exercises and they could also be called upon to assist in emergencies, as they did, for instance, in the case of the *Herald of Free Enterprise* disaster, during which the ferry capsized moments after leaving the Belgian port of Zeebrugge on the night of 6 March 1987, killing 193 passengers and crew.

In addition to their primary specializations, the MHUs were expected to furnish some ancillary assistance during TTW, the provision of motor transport drivers and medical support for instance. Although all MHU personnel had specific war roles, the aim was to train them so that they would be capable of filling both headquarters and station posts, thus giving them the flexibility required for both peacetime exercises and war.

As an example of the latter, MHU personnel provided support at Northwood, Kinloss, St Mawgan, Lossiemouth and Pitreavie Castle during Operation Granby, and the Gulf War of 1990-91. More recently still they have supported the RAF effort during operations conducted in Bosnia, and Kosovo (Operations Allied Force, Engadine and Agricola).

Personnel and Training

The three MHUs reflected the traditions of the old RAuxAF fighter squadrons, in that each was an independent unit with its own administrative and training structure. The establishment ranged from seventy to 100 auxiliary personnel commanded by a wing commander. The rank structure within each MHU was determined by the war appointments of its personnel, for example, the CO was expected to fill a Duty Wing Commander Operations slot. Day to day running of the unit and training support was handled by a nucleus of regulars headed by an adjutant. As is customary in the reserve forces, auxiliaries came from many walks of life; teachers, accountants, scientists, engineers, students, public servants, secretaries, train drivers and even members of the Defence Intelligence staff were but a few of the occupations represented. The author served on a fighter control unit which enjoyed the services of a lighthouse keeper and a railway level crossing keeper. Some officers and airmen were ex-regulars, among them former aircrew, engineers, nurses, educators, fighter controllers, Regiment gunners and communicators.

The three MHUs followed a similar annual training programme, although training was varied to suit local requirements. A typical training cycle consisted of one training weekend per month followed by two Sundays and one evening per week, which amounted to a minimum attendance of ninety-six non-continuous hours, the equivalent to twelve full days. In order to achieve and maintain the standards set by their regular counterparts, MHU personnel were each allocated fifty-six-man training days with any individual authorized up to ninety-nine days. All auxiliaries carried out fifteen day's Annual Continuous Training at their war appointments or on courses or attachments. Additional voluntary training could be undertaken if suitable opportunities presented themselves. Finally, all three MHUs participated in an annual 18 Group sponsored exercise, exercise Penny Black, which was designed to test operational procedures and to demonstrate the inter-operability of the MHUs at their TTW locations.

The MHUs adhered to regular RAF training methods and standards. They coordinated their methods to review and restructure their training syllabi, particularly in relation to operations and intelligence, as well as general service training, common skills such as first aid, skill at arms, nuclear, biological and chemical procedures and post-attack recovery training. Auxiliary personnel were eligible for rates of pay and expenses similar to those drawn by their regular counterparts, and a tax-free bounty was paid every year on successful completion of training.

Operations and Intelligence Tasks

Most auxiliary MHU officers were commissioned into the General Duties (Ground) Branch, later the Ops Support Branch, in either flight operations or intelligence specialties. At MHQs, Operations Officers were primarily concerned with the tasking and control of maritime patrol aircraft. At station level, they briefed and debriefed aircrews.

Similarly, there were two types of intelligence posts. One was at MHQs during major exercises for instance, or in support of JMCs. At this level, RAuxAF personnel represented a substantial proportion of the intelligence community, working alongside regulars and reservists from other services, including those of NATO countries. Information on enemy forces reported by ships and aircraft was processed to create the Recognized Maritime Picture (RMP) and used to produce Air and Flag Staff briefings, periodic maritime intelligence summaries and ad hoc intelligence reports.

The station intelligence task involved working closely with maritime aircrew. Operations/Intelligence Officers briefed the crew on the potential threat before their mission and debriefed them on their return. The post-mission report was signalled to the MHQ where it was assessed and integrated into the RMP which was, in turn, relayed to the stations, thus completing a continuous cycle.

Operations/Intelligence Training

MHU operations and intelligence personnel frequently attended RN/RAF courses related to maritime operations alongside their regular counterparts in order to be fully conversant with current levels of risk, operational risks and tactics. They included courses at the Maritime Tactics School at HMS

Dryad, Mission Support System courses at RAF Kinloss and intelligence-related courses at the Defence Intelligence and Security School at Ashford and later at RAF Chicksands.

Interlude 1996–2000

Although they had been formed to support Coastal Command during the Cold War, the three MHUs continued to provide Strike Command's HQ 18 Group with a similar service in the dangerous and uncertain situation that took place in the relative stability of the east-west confrontation which had ended with the collapse of the USSR in 1991. The optimism sparked by the demise of the Warsaw Pact meant that it was almost inevitable that there would be cutbacks in defence spending and 'Options for Change' and the subsequent Strategic Defence Review led to some early reductions in RAuxAF manpower, followed in 1996 by the announcement that Pitreavie Castle, Turnhouse, Mount Wise and Mount Batten were to close.

While No. 1 MHU continued to support the NATO HQ at Northwood, the closure of the MHQs at Pitreavie Castle and Mount Wise had deprived No. 2 and No. 3 MHUs of their main functions. Largely operating on their own initiative, the personnel of the two notionally redundant units exploited other avenues and found continuing employment in support of the JMC's sundry maritime exercises and the air defence operations of the two fighter squadrons at Leuchars.

The upshot of all this was that the MHUs gradually evolved into what amounted to Maritime Support Squadrons, each having much the same establishment as before. It could be said that they always had been 'Role Support Squadrons' decades before the term was officially coined for the multi-role RAuxAF squadrons of the twenty-first century. While continuing to provide operational support staff for maritime HQs and squadrons, their commitments broadened to embrace mission support for the Sentry and for Air-to-Air Refueling (AAR).

Among other innovations, the new Reserve Forces Act of 1996 had made provision for reservists to work full time and to be employed on peacekeeping and humanitarian operations as well as in aid to the civil authorities in time of emergency. It was this new flexibility that enabled personnel to be deployed to Italy and Germany in support of Operation Allied Force to Kosovo, for Operation Agricola and to Saudi Arabia for Operation Jural.

Re-Roling and Re-formation

During 1999, the Air Force Board decided that new squadrons of the expanding RAuxAF should be granted the identities of some of the auxiliary squadrons that had been previously disbanded in 1957, thus reinstating their number plates and badges. On 1 October 1999, the Queen approved the re-formation of No. 603 (City of Edinburgh) Squadron from the personnel of No. 2 MHU and of No. 600 (City of London) Squadron from the personnel of No. 1 and No. 3 MHUs.

No. 600 Squadron's role was to provide trained augmentation personnel for any HQ handling RAF or joint operations anywhere, including the National Permanent Joint Headquarters and within Commander-in-Chief, Eastern Atlantic Area's NATO HQ, both of which are at Northwood, and on the staff of the Joint Force Air Component commander at High Wycombe. The squadron could offer specialists in the fields of intelligence, flight operations, logistics support, motor transport and administration.

The new 603 Squadron has a specialist Survive to Operate role. Alongside logistics and air operations, the squadron's primary role is now a vital element in the operational capability of the RAF. Survive to Operate and Force Protection are now integral elements of current NATO Air and RAF doctrine which embrace the defence and protection of assets involved in expeditionary operations. In addition, the squadron continues to provide mission support for maritime and other RAF and NATO (Air) formations or units wherever and whenever they may be required in peace or war.

Contribution

For twenty years, between 1959 and 1979, the personnel of the MHUs were the sole representatives of the RAuxAF and, as such, they provided foundations upon which the present force was built, starting in 1979 with the formation of some Regiment squadrons in the wake of the Soviet invasion of Afghanistan. Indeed, it is arguable that without the example of the MHUs on which to build, there might not be a Royal Auxiliary Air Force today. [103]

---

103 Sqn Ldr Bruce Blanche RAuxAF, RAF Historical Society on the Royal Air Force Reserve and Auxiliary Forces at the Royal Air Force Museum London in 2002.

Personal stories

Squadron Leader J.B. (Bruce) Blanche QVRM AE

Born in Gainsborough in 1946, Bruce moved to Brunei at the age of two when his father accepted a job as a driller in the oil business. As a young man he attended St John Cass College, University of London, where he graduated with a BSc in Geology and Geography. He then attended Imperial College London and gained an MSc in Petroleum Geology. He began working as a geologist with the British Coal Board, Oil and Gas Division, and then, when the division moved from London to Glasgow, he moved there with his wife and three children. Bruce was made redundant in 1981 and decided to set up a hydrocarbon exploration consultancy with his wife, who was also a geologist. Their company was particularly interested in opportunities abroad in places such as North Africa, South Africa, the Middle East and Asia.

As a well-respected oil man, he was appointed as an Honorary Professor in the Institute of Petroleum Engineering at Heriot Watt University, Edinburgh, where he lectured post graduate students and offered tutorials and mentoring. He was also the Chair of the Mediterranean, Middle East and Africa Scout Group in London. Furthermore, he was a Fellow of the Royal Geographical Society and the Geological Society of London.

He was a member of the Royal Auxiliary Air Force and served during the First Gulf War. He was also a military historian. He joined No. 1 Maritime Headquarters Unit in London in the late 60s. In 1977 he transferred from No. 1 to No. 2 Maritime Headquarters Unit in Edinburgh. He had a major accident when he entered a lift in the Brit Oil building in Glasgow to find there was no floor. He fell down the lift shaft, believing that he would die there until rescued by a fireman. His legs were badly injured, and his wife talked to surgeons insisting that there was to be no amputation. He had to undergo several operations and was in hospital for seven months. He was discharged from hospital and was sent to RAF Headley Court, which was the RAF's rehabilitation unit. Clearly, his determination, focus, drive and loving family helped him to recover.

Bruce was a senior intelligence officer in 603 (City of Edinburgh) Squadron. His grasp of the job was excellent. He held a very high security clearance, and he was pivotal in 'back-room operations' deep underground in the Joint Naval and Air Force Headquarters at Pitreavie where submarine, surface and air reconnaissance tasking was conducted. He also worked in the intelligence section at the Clyde Naval Base at Faslane, home to the Polaris and later Trident nuclear submarines. One of Bruce's greatest military attributes was that he could always see 'the big picture' and this, coupled with his detailed knowledge of Soviet forces and his international experience as a consultant in the oil and gas business made him a most valued asset during exercises and during other operations. Indeed, during the Gulf War, Bruce personally briefed the Commander-in-Chief and other senior staff on the importance of the oil and gas fields in the Middle East and the implications of air attacks in that region.

Bruce worked closely with Bill Simpson and David Ross as a co-author of the history of 603 Squadron entitled *The Greatest Squadron of Them All*, an acclaimed and most detailed aviation publication running to two large volumes and no less than eight hundred pages. Bruce was utterly dedicated to, and promoter of, the Royal Auxiliary Air Force, its ethos and traditions, and it is common knowledge that he knew more of its history than anyone else. We were all delighted when he was invested personally by Her Majesty the Queen, with the Queen's Volunteer Reserves Medal. A rare honour that was fully deserved. Later, he became a founding Trustee of the Force Foundation and subsequently a guiding light in the planning for and installation of the Royal Auxiliary Air Force Memorial at the National Memorial Arboretum at Alrewas and our Roll of Honour at St Clement Danes Church in the Strand. After a short illness, Bruce died in hospital on 7 November 2018, aged 72, leaving behind his wife Jean, daughters Rachel and Sarah, and son Jamie.

Chapter 9

Specialist Squadrons and Units 1979–2021

(All currently active as at 31 December 2021 unless otherwise stated and all have their own web site.)

No. 7006 (VR) Intelligence Squadron RAuxAF

Formed in 1986 at High Wycombe as a Royal Air Force Volunteer Reserve intelligence unit with the specific role of providing linguists necessary during the Cold War. The squadron was accountable to RAF Volunteer Reserves along with No. 7010, No. 7630, and No. 7644 Flights. It also had a responsibility to gather and analyse intelligence as part of the Intelligence Reserve Wing at RAF Waddington. Throughout the Gulf War the flight was deployed along with 7644 (Public Relations) Flight, 4626 (Aeromedical Evacuation) and 4624 (Movements) Squadrons.

During 1997 a major reform took place entitled Front Line First, which resulted in the Royal Air Force Volunteer Reserve being merged into the Royal Auxiliary Air Force. The flight was also expanded to form No. 7006 Squadron RAuxAF. By 2021 the squadron was moved under the command of the new Intelligence Reserve Wing, as part of No. 2 Group RAF. It is based at RAF Waddington and its personnel are spread across RAF Wyton, RAF Brize Norton, RAF High Wycombe and RAF Digby. It remains as one of only three units which provide intelligence support to the regular RAF. Its analysts and officers obtain, analyse and present different forms of intelligence supporting aircraft and other military assets. Its motto is 'Florebo Quocumque Ferar' which means 'I will flower everywhere I am planted.'

No. 7010 (VR) Photographic Interpretation Squadron RAuxAF

Formed in April 1953 as No. 7010 Flight Royal Air Force Volunteer Reserve with the purpose of providing strategic imagery analysis to support the Royal Air Force. The flight's role was expanded in 1965 to include tactical imagery analysis. When the Warsaw Pact collapsed in July 1991, it resulted in a major reduction of NATO forces in central Europe. This then led to a large reduction in, and reorganization of, the United Kingdom's regular and reserve forces. As part of this overall plan, No. 7010 Flight became No. 7010 (VR) Photographic Interpretation Squadron RAuxAF.

The role of the squadron is to recruit and train a reserve cadre of operational imagery analysts capable of the processing and exploitation of all source imagery. It is also administered from Headquarters Intelligence Reserves at RAF Waddington, and its personnel support two units, the Defence Geospatial Intelligence Fusion Centre (DGIFC) at RAF Wyton and No. 1 Intelligence Surveillance and Reconnaissance (ISR) Wing, also at RAF Waddington. It also provides Strategic Intelligence support to the Joint Air Reconnaissance Intelligence Centre (JARIC) based at RAF Brampton, whilst also supporting the tactical operations of Tornado GR1 and Jaguar GRI aircraft. Finally, the squadron supports HQ Allied Rapid Reaction Corps (ARRC) and HQ Allied Air Command (AIRCENT) at Ramstein in Germany. The squadron motto is '*Vocati Veniemus*' which means 'when summoned we shall be there.'

No. 7630 (VR) Intelligence Squadron RAuxAF

Founded in 1958 as No. 7630 Flight, Royal Air Force Volunteer Reserve, its purpose was to provide a pool of Russian linguists to support the RAF. The squadron widened its intelligence roles to provide analysis and briefing capabilities in 1972. In 1997 it formally became 7630 (VR) Squadron RAuxAF and has a dedicated Human Intelligence role with personnel being deployed in support of Operation Telic in Iraq. Telic was the codename under which all of the UK's military operations in Iraq were conducted during 19 March 2003 at the start of the invasion of Iraq and the withdrawal of the last remaining British forces on 22 May 2011. Personnel were also deployed in support of Operation Herrick, which was the codename under which all British operations in the war in Afghanistan were conducted from

2002 to 2014. In 2017 the squadron became an intelligence Subject Matter Expert (SME) squadron within the Intelligence Reserves Wing based at RAF Waddington. Its motto is 'Persevere.'

7644 (VR) Public Relations Squadron RAuxAF

According to A.H. Narracott in his book *War News Had Wings*, the earliest evidence of putting journalists into RAF uniform dates back to September 1938 when a senior civil servant by the name of Charles Pennycook Robertson, the Press and Publicity Officer at the Air Ministry, saw the need – in the light of imminent conflict with Germany – to have uniformed correspondents at the front line. Robertson thought the best way to collect news of what the Air Force was doing was to have trained journalists at the front. He decided that short service commissions as RAF Volunteer Reserve Officers were to be offered to some of Fleet Street's finest, including H.E. Bates, R.F. Delderfield and Hector Bollitho. These would then be sent out to various commands at home and overseas, particularly France, as Service Press Officers attached to the Advanced Air Striking Force.

Robertson wanted to get the scheme underway in peacetime to help breakdown the natural opposition of commanding officers to having 'journalists-come-officers' in their midst and to give the Service Press Officers an idea of how the RAF worked. With some wrangling the idea was finally accepted. On 14 September 1939, four newly commissioned officers set out from RAF Heston for northern France to land at Le Bourget. The scheme worked well. Without it the public would have been left in ignorance of the valiant deeds performed by the RAF in those early days of the war. However, there were muddles over censorship and accommodation, and not least the difficulties caused by the rapidly advancing German army.

A similar idea came from Lord Beaverbrook who realised that in 1940 there was a need to keep the general public informed about the war, not only giving the hard facts, but also introducing servicemen and women who could tell their own stories. He wanted to find information experts who had a service background or an interest in the services and ask them to become officers in each of the Armed Forces.

When the war ended, the RAF realised the benefits of maintaining a small number of journalists in uniform. These public relations specialists became No. 7644 (VR) Public Relations Squadron RAuxAF. Therefore, the key role of the squadron is Media Operations and the squadron is based at

RAF Halton. As the RAF has full-time officers serving in communications, 7644 Squadron personnel support these professionals when they are required. Using its journalistic skills the squadron prepares news releases, stories about individuals and video and audio news releases for the media.

7644 Squadron provides a range of media training to enable RAF officers of all ranks to be confident when accepting interview requests from the media. They are taught to answer questions directly in a friendly manner. This is important as the Royal Air Force is keen to promote its image and to create a reputation for being open and honest. The squadron also produces various individual pieces of work ranging from magazines and other publications to video productions. The Squadron motto is '*vérité a jamais*' which translated means 'the truth always.'

In 1982, following lessons learned from the Falklands War, 4624 (County of Oxford) Movements Squadron was formed at Brize Norton, followed by 4626 (County of Wiltshire) Aeromedical Evacuation Squadron, which formed at Wroughton before moving on to Lyneham via Hullavington. Another initiative at this time was the formation of four Airfield Defence Flights, at Lyneham, St Athan, Brampton and High Wycombe, to provide a low-cost guard force for their parent stations. However, there was a restricted training commitment for these four units and recruiting and retention became a problem as auxiliaries wanted more of a challenge, so the experiment was discontinued.

In 1990, coalition forces, including those of the United Kingdom, were dispatched to the Gulf States to prepare for an operation to eject Iraqi forces from Kuwait, which had earlier invaded that country. A United Nations resolution requiring Iraq to withdraw its forces by January 1991 was ignored so what became known as Operation Granby in the UK and Operation Desert Storm by the USA, was launched to free Kuwait.

The operation required the movement by air of tons of material to support the UK air campaign and other forces. In addition, Saddam Hussein had promised that the campaign would become 'The Mother of all Battles', and the use of chemical and biological weapons was anticipated. Therefore, it was decided that the UK needed to reinforce its air movements capability and because heavy allied casualties were forecast, its Aeromedical Evacuation facilities. Therefore, it was necessary to mobilise the RAuxAF 4624 Movements Squadron and 4626 Aeromedical Evacuation Squadron.

A problem arose when it was realized that the Reserve Forces Act at the time stated that the RAuxAF could only be mobilized by an Order in Council if the UK was threatened by 'actual or apprehended attack' which it clearly

Ornamental tail and gates designed and crafted for the chapel at RAF Thornaby by Flt Sgt Richard Heppell in 1930s. (Louise Wilkinson, private collection)

King George VI visiting RAF Thornaby. (Louise Wilkinson, private collection)

King George VI inspecting 608 squadron. (Louise Wilkinson, private collection)

Two Spitfires of 616 (South Yorkshire) Squadron come into land at Fowlmere during the Battle of Britain in September 1940. The foreground aircraft is X4330, QJ-G. (Ken Delve and Graham Pitchfork, *South Yorkshire's Own, The Story of 616 Squadron*, Exeter, 1990, p9)

Above: RAF personnel pictured at a barrage balloon site during the Blitz. (Louise Wilkinson, private collection)

Right: 3608 (North Riding) Fighter Control Unit. (Louise Wilkinson, private collection)

No. 3608 (North Riding) FIGHTING CONTROL UNIT ROYAL AUXILIARY AIR FORCE

"So vital are these Units to our defences it would be no exaggeration to say that the successful repulsion of an air attack in the event of war would depend entirely on their adequate manning with skilled personnel."

(Air Ministry).

We need women (and some men) to train as Radar Operators and Fighter Plotters in our "spare-time" Unit. You do not need to have had any previous experience in the Services, but you must be willing to learn, and keen to do a vital job.

The demonstrator at the Radar Model (in the Ground Equipment Display) can give you more information, or write to:—
The Officer Commanding. No. 3608 Fighter Control Unit, Royal Air Force, Thornaby,

Twentythree

Group of 609 Squadron pilots in 1941. (Frank H Ziegler, *The Story of 609 Squadron Under the White Rose*, London, 1971)

WAAF air-ambulance orderlies in flying gear in May 1943. (Beryl E Escott, *The WAAF*, Botley, 2012, p17)

No. 2608 LIGHT ANTI-AIRCRAFT SQUADRON
ROYAL AUXILIARY AIR FORCE REGIMENT

Personnel of No. 2608 (N.R.) L.A.A. Sqn., R.Aux.A.F. emplaning for Annual Camp in Germany,
8th August, 1953.

This unit is fully mobile and is equipped with Bofors 40 m.m. A.A. Guns as its main armament.

Other armament includes Rifles, Brens and Stens.

Vacancies exist for keen men, whether ex-service or not, in the following trades :—
    GUNNERS L.A.A.   GUNNER DRIVERS.
              GUNNER SIGNALLERS.
If you have experience on these lines come and put it to good use, if not we will train you.

If you are interested in an active form of service, with good promotion prospects, come and visit the unit and we will show you round, and give you an idea of our activities. Apart from training you for your operational role, the Squadron can offer you many social and recreational amenities, and an opportunity for making new friends. During your fifteen days Annual Camp Training period you will have the chance of visiting new places, and perhaps to travel overseas.

APPLY NOW
to the Recruiting Stand or to Headquarters No. 2608 L.A.A. Squadron, Royal Air Force, Thornaby.

24

2608 Light Anti-Aircraft Squadron Royal Auxiliary Air Force Regiment. (Louise Wilkinson, private collection)

Fully armed and ready – Max Sutherland and pilots of 602 Squadron. (No. 602 (City of Glasgow) Squadron Reformation of Squadron booklet 19 September 2006, p23)

Volleyball at Ternhill with 611 Squadron Spitfire FY:Y in background. (Aldon P. Ferguson, *The history of 611 (West Lancashire) Squadron Royal Auxiliary Air Force*, Reading, 2004, p38)

Right: A WAAF balloon operator. (Louise Wilkinson, private collection)

Below: A WAAF Meteorologist. (Louise Wilkinson, private collection)

Raymond Baxter of 602 Squadron briefs pilots before a V2 strike in early 1945. (No. 602 (City of Glasgow) Squadron Reformation of Squadron booklet 19 September 2006, p22)

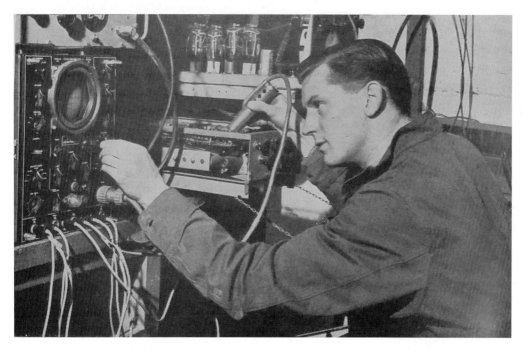

An auxiliary radar fitter at work in the maintenance workshops of a Fighter Control Unit. (Louise Wilkinson, private collection)

Auxiliary airmen refuel Auster aircraft of a RAuxAF AOP squadron. (Louise Wilkinson, private collection)

Marcus Robinson briefs pilots of 602 Squadron on the wing of a Spitfire F21 in 1947. (No. 602 (City of Glasgow) Squadron Reformation of Squadron booklet 19 September 2006, p23)

Flying Officer James W Woolcock with his crew. (Louise Wilkinson, private collection)

Gunners of 2602 Squadron on weekend exercises with a Bofors 40mm gun. (Louise Wilkinson, private collection)

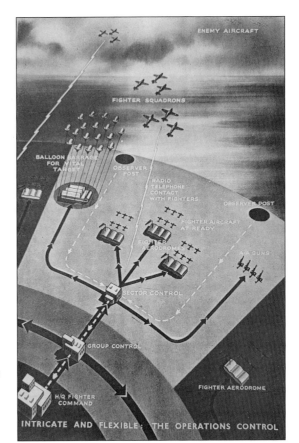

Right: Operations Control.
(Louise Wilkinson, private
collection)

Below: Peter Vaux with the
press on a complementary
flight with 608 Squadron.
(Louise Wilkinson, private
collection)

General repairs and upkeep. (Louise Wilkinson, private collection)

Roger Bushell 601 Squadron. Tom Moulson, *The Millionaires' Squadron, The Remarkable Story of 601 Squadron and the Flying Sword*, Barnsley, 2014, plates

Above: Sqn Ldr Geoffrey Shaw with 608 Squadron personnel. (Louise Wilkinson, private collection)

Right: Formation flying by Vampire jet fighters of 601 and 604 Squadron. (Ian White, *If You Want Peace, Prepare for War, A History of No.604 (County of Middlesex) Squadron, RAuxAF, in Peace and War*, 604 Squadron Association, 2005.)

Above: 607 Squadron at Abbotsinch 1939. L – R Bobby Pumphrey, Francis Blackadder, Joe Kayll, Alan Glover, John Sample and Jim Bazin. (Robert Dixon, *607 Squadron A Shade of Blue*, Stroud, 2008, p65)

Left: The construction of a Tiger Moth being explained to WAAFs. (Louise Wilkinson, private collection)

Above: The CO's Hawker Hind
(K6848) which Pilot Officer
John Dundas crashed at the first
pre-formation take off. (Isobel
Foggitt, *Down Your Way*, Skipton,
2008, p11)

Right: Training in the Auxiliary
Air Force. (Louise Wilkinson,
private collection)

WAAF plotter with Goneo in her left hand. (Louise Wilkinson, private collection)

De Havilland Vampire 1's of 501 Squadron in 1950. (David Watkins, *Fear Nothing The History of No. 501 (County of Gloucester) Fighter Squadron, Royal Auxiliary Air Force*, Cowden, 1990)

Pilot Officer Ken Temple with a Gloster Meteor T7 in 1955. (Louise Wilkinson, private collection)

was not. The only solution was to *ask* the personnel involved to *volunteer* to be mobilized. This had all kinds of implications for employers, job security, families and mortgages. This was less of a problem for the aeromedical people, many of who worked for the NHS, but for the movers, who came from a much broader employment spectrum it was a greater concern; after all, they had joined the RAuxAF, only prepared to be mobilised for a war of national survival if it came. After many telephone calls, the squadron members, both male and female, responded positively, which speaks volumes for their patriotism and unit cohesion, their decision not to let their squadron down, at what must have been a worrying time for many of them.

A new Reserve Forces Act came into being in 1996 which provided for reservists to be deployed for warlike operations, actual or in preparation, aid to the civil powers and other emergencies such as COVID in 2020/2021. In addition, it provided for other opportunities for Full Time Reserve Service (FTRS) and Part Time Reserve Service (PTRS). Since then, hundreds of RAuxAF personnel have served in Iraq, Afghanistan, and other locations in support of operations and two have been killed in action.

In 1997, the four 'war appointable' flights of the Royal Air Force Volunteer Reserve (RAFVR) were amalgamated with the RAuxAF at a ceremony at the RAF College Cranwell in the presence of HRH The Duke of York. They are 7010(VR) Photographic Interpretation Squadron, 7644(VR) Public Relations Squadron and 7006(VR) and 7630(VR) Intelligence Squadrons. Also, in 1997, the auxiliaries took to the air again with the formation of No. 1359 Flight, the Hercules Reservist Aircrew Flight at Lyneham. The flight's role is to provide Hercules crews to augment the RAF Hercules Force in crisis and war and to provide peacetime utility during normal operations. All aircrew are former regular Hercules crews. This squadron was re-numbered No. 622 in 2014.

Four new Role Support Squadrons were formed in 1997/8, an Offensive Support Squadron at Cottesmore, in support of the Harrier Force, a Helicopter Support Squadron at Benson, an Air Defence Squadron at Leeming, and an Air Transportable Surgical Squadron was formed at Leuchars. All these squadrons were originally formed to augment and support operations at their parent bases but, as time went on, with the exception of the Surgical squadron, more and more focus was placed on the Force Protection and Survive to Operate roles.

On 1 October 1999, it was decided to resurrect some of the original RAuxAF flying squadron number plates as it was unlikely that they would ever be used again as originally intended. 1 MHU became 600 (City of

London) Squadron and 2 MHU became 603 (City of Edinburgh) Squadron (3 MHU was disbanded). The Offensive Support Squadron was renumbered 504 (County of Nottingham) Squadron, 2624 Squadron became 501 (County of Gloucester) Squadron and the Helicopter Support Squadron became 606 (Chiltern) Squadron. Finally, the Air Defence Support Squadron became 609 (West Riding) Squadron, and the Air Transportable Surgical Squadron became 612 (County of Aberdeen) Squadron.

During the 1990s, it was mooted that what the regular service needed was guards, to free up regular service personnel for deployment. This suggestion was quietly dropped on the grounds that recruiting and retention would suffer should part-time volunteers not be given more challenging roles to fulfil, although a glance at the recently formed squadrons in the Force Protection and other similar supporting roles may indicate a move in that direction.

An interesting squadron to be formed was No. 3 Provost Squadron of the Tactical Provost Wing at Henlow, in 2002, to provide provost and security support to RAF Police operations worldwide, although 603 Squadron has since formed a detached flight in Glasgow which has been numbered 602 (City of Glasgow) Squadron and plans were well advanced to form another detached flight in Dumfries which came to nothing.

During 2003 the RAuxAF was involved in the first large scale mobilisation for over fifty years. More than nine hundred personnel, which equated to over seventy per cent of its trained strength, were called into full time service and were deployed to support Royal Air Force operations in Cyprus, Kuwait, Iraq, Afghanistan and the Falklands, as well as in the UK. On 19 July 2007, Senior Aircraftman Christopher Dunsmore, serving with 504 (County of Nottingham) Squadron, was one of three men who were killed by a rocket attack on the RAF base at Basrah Airport in Iraq. He was twenty-nine years old and was the first serving RAuxAF member to be killed by enemy action since the Second World War. On 13 April 2008, Senior Aircraftman Gary Thompson of 504 (County of Nottingham) Squadron was killed by a roadside bomb while on patrol in Kandahar. He was fifty-one. He was the oldest British serviceman killed in Afghanistan. Both men are commemorated on the Armed Forces Memorial in Staffordshire and in the RAuxAF Roll of Honour.

In 2013, No. 611 (West Lancashire) Squadron was re-formed at RAF Woodvale as a General Support Squadron and the following year No. 605 (County of Warwick) Squadron was formed at RAF Cosford as a Logistics Support Squadron together with No. 614 (County of Glamorgan) Squadron which was formed at Cardiff as a General Support Squadron. In 2015, No. 607 (County of Durham) squadron was formed at RAF Leeming as a Logistics Support Squadron and finally, a RAuxAF Band was formed in 2017 at RAF College Cranwell in support of RAF Music Services.

There are currently thirty-one RAuxAF units, some of which bear the number plates of their illustrious ancestors and these squadrons and units regularly deploy personnel on operations in Iraq and Afghanistan, as well as other locations in support of RAF operations worldwide. Those squadrons that were formerly flying squadrons pre- and post-war in the squadron number series 500 and 600 and were awarded Squadron Standards, and will qualify for a new Standard on completion of twenty five years cumulative service.

Current Orbat of the RAuxAF at 31 July 2022[104]

Squadron	Formed	Location	Role	Remarks
No. 1 Air Intelligence Unit	1947	London	Air Intelligence	Disbanded.
No. 1 (County of Hertford) Maritime HQ Unit (MHU)	1 November 1959	JHQ Northwood	Maritime Support	To support maritime operations at JHQ. Disbanded 1999 Re-formed as 600 Sqn.
No. 2 (City of Edinburgh) MHU	1960	Edinburgh City	Maritime Support	To support maritime operations in the north of UK. Disbanded 1999 Re-formed as 603 Sqn.
No. 3 (County of Devon) MHU	1960	RAF Mount Batten	Maritime Support	To support maritime operations in the Western Approaches. Amalgamated with 1 MHU 1999.
No. 1 (Ulster) Maritime Support Unit	1960	Belfast	Maritime Support	Disbanded by 1963.

104 With permission from Air-RAuxAF Dep Insp July 2022

Squadron	Formed	Location	Role	Remarks
No. 3 Tactical Police Squadron	October 2002	RAF Henlow	RAF Police	Part of Tactical Police Wing.
No. 501 (County of Gloucester) Squadron	2001	RAF Brize Norton	Logistics Support (LSS)	Formed from 2624 Sqn in 2001 in Ops Support/Force Protection Role. Re-formed as 501 Logistics Support Sqn on 1 April 2013.
No. 502 (Ulster) Squadron	1 September 2013	RAF Aldergrove	General Support Squadron (GSS)	Multi-role Sqn.
No. 504 (County of Nottingham) Squadron	1999	RAF Wittering	Logistics Support Squadron (LSS)	Formed in 1999 as a Role Support Squadron at RAF Cottesmore before becoming a Force Protection Squadron and transferring to RAF Wittering on 1 April 2013.
No. 600 (City of London) Squadron	1999	RAF Northolt	General Support Squadron (GSS)	To support Permanent Joint HQ at Northwood. Formerly No. 1 MHU.
No. 601 (County of London) Squadron	20 April 2017	RAF Northolt	Specialist Support Squadron	Commerce and Industry Liaison.
No. 602 (City of Glasgow) Squadron	1 June 2006	Glasgow City	General Support Squadron (GSS)	Formed from Mission Support Element of 603 Squadron Edinburgh.
No. 603 (City of Edinburgh) Squadron	1 October 1999	Edinburgh City	RAF Police/ RAF Regiment	A RAF Police Squadron with an embedded RAF Regt Flight. Formerly, No. 2 MHU.

SPECIALIST SQUADRONS AND UNITS 1979–2021

Squadron	Formed	Location	Role	Remarks
No. 605 (County of Warwick) Squadron	2014	RAF Cosford	Logistics Support Squadron (LSS)	Part of 85 Expeditionary Wing.
No. 606 (Chiltern) Squadron	1 October 1996	RAF Benson	Helicopter Support Squadron (HSS)	Re-formed as 606 Sqn in 1999 supporting Joint Helicopter Command.
607 (County of Durham) Squadron	5 January 2015	RAF Leeming	Logistics Support Squadron (LSS)	Multi-role Sqn.
No. 609 (West Riding) Squadron	1998	RAF Leeming	Regiment and Force Protection	Initially formed as Air Defence Role Support Sqn. Re-formed in 1999.
No. 611(West Lancs) Squadron	2013	RAF Woodvale	General Support Squadron (GSS)	Multi-role Sqn.
No. 612 (County of Aberdeen) Squadron	1999	RAF Leuchars	Aeromedical Surgical Support Squadron	RAF Medical Reserves.
No. 614 (County of Glamorgan) Squadron	2014	Cardiff City	General Support Squadron (GSS)	Multi-role Sqn.
No. 616 (South Yorkshire) Squadron	1 April 2019	RAF Waddington	Intelligence, Surveillance and General Reconnaissance and Combat Air Support	Multi-role Sqn.
No. 622 Squadron	2012	RAF Brize Norton	Transport and AAR	Originally formed in 1994 as No. 1359 Reserve Hercules Aircrew Flight. Re-formed in 2012 as an OCU for all Transport and AAR roles.

Squadron	Formed	Location	Role	Remarks
No. 1310 Wing RAuxAF Regiment	13 June 1989	RAF Catterick	Wing HQ	Disbanded 1993.
No. 1339 Wing RAuxAF Regiment	13 June 1989	RAF Waddington	Wing HQ	Disbanded 1993.
No. 2503 (County of Lincoln) Squadron RAuxAF Regiment	1 July 1979	RAF Scampton	Regiment Field Squadron	Formed for Ground Defence of the Vulcan Force. Moved to RAF Waddington in 1985 for on-base security and Force Protection duties.
No. 2620 (County of Norfolk) Squadron RAuxAF Regiment	1983	RAF Marham	Regiment Field Squadron	Re-roled as an OSS in 2000. Reverted to Field Squadron in 2004.
No. 2622 (Highland) Squadron RAuxAF Regiment	1 July 1979	RAF Lossiemouth	Regiment Field Squadron	Re-roled as Force Protection in 2004.
No. 2623 (East Anglian) Squadron RAuxAF Regiment	1 July 1979	RAF Honington	Regiment Field Squadron	Disbanded as Field Sqn on 18 April 1994. Re-formed as a Training Sqn on 1 June 1995. Re-formed as a mixed Regular and Reservist Sqn in October 1998 to operate Rapier Field Standard C Missile. Re-roled in 2004 to provide component of the Joint NBC Regiment.

Squadron	Formed	Location	Role	Remarks
No. 2624 (County of Oxford) Squadron RAuxAF Regiment	October 1982	RAF Brize Norton	Regiment Field Squadron	Re-roled in 1998 as a Role Support Sqn (RSS). Became 501 Sqn in 2003. In 2013 reverted to 2624 Sqn as a Logistics Support Sqn (LSS).
No. 2625 (County of Cornwall) Squadron RAuxAF Regiment	1982	RAF St Mawgan	Regiment Field Squadron	Ground Defence of RAF St Mawgan. Disbanded November 2006.
No. 4624 (County of Oxford) Movements Squadron RAuxAF	October 1982	RAF Brize Norton	Air Movements	To accept, prepare and load cargo and passengers for worldwide travel in RAF transport and coalition aircraft. Mobilised for the First Gulf War in 1991.
No. 4626 (County of Wiltshire) Aeromedical Evacuation Squadron RAuxAF	9 September 1983	RAF Wroughton	Aeromedical Evacuation	Casualty Evacuation and Pre-hospital ongoing care. Subsequently relocated to RAF Brize Norton, via Hullavington and Lyneham. Mobilised for the First Gulf War in 1991.
No. 7006(VR) Intelligence Squadron RAuxAF	1 April 1986	RAF High Wycombe	Intelligence Duties	Originally formed as an RAFVR Flight before amalgamating with the RAuxAF on 5 April 1997. Relocated to RAF Waddington in 2000.

Squadron	Formed	Location	Role	Remarks
No. 7010(VR) Photographic Interpretation Squadron	April 1953	RAF Nuneham Park	Imagery Analysis	Originally formed as an RAFVR Flight before amalgamating with the RAuxAF on 5 April 1997. Relocated to RAF Waddington in 2000.
No. 7630(VR) Intelligence Squadron RAuxAF	1986	HQ Strike Command	Briefing and Analysis	Originally formed as an RAFVR Flight before amalgamating with the RAuxAF on 5 April 1997. Relocated to RAF Waddington in 2000.
No. 7644(VR) Public Relations Squadron RAuxAF	1981	RAF High Wycombe	Public Relations	Originally formed as an RAFVR Flight before amalgamating with the RAuxAF on 5 April 1997. Relocated to RAF Halton.
RAuxAF Band	2017	RAFC Cranwell	Musicians	Formed as a band and to supplement regular RAF bands as required.

Chapter 10

Royal Auxiliary Air Force Foundation – History from 2000–2018

The first decades of the twenty-first century saw many developments that enhanced the public and service perception of the RAuxAF, as well as a significant expansion of the Force. In 2002, the Royal Auxiliary Air Force Memorial Trust was established as a registered charity by four former auxiliaries, Group Captain Richard Mighall, Wing Commander Charles Hyde, Squadron Leader Bruce Blanche and Tony Freeman. Its objective was to provide a Memorial dedicated to all those who had served in the Auxiliary Air Force and its successor, The Royal Auxiliary Air Force.

On 23 October 2002 the Royal Air Force Historical Society held a seminar at the RAF Museum, Hendon, on the Royal Air Force Reserve and Auxiliary Forces. This seminar covered all the RAF Reserve and Auxiliary Forces, including the University Air Squadrons and the RAFVR and eight presentations were delivered on the RAuxAF. The record of proceedings from the Seminar were published by the RAF Historical Society in 2003 and are available as a book online.

The RAuxAF National Memorial was established at the National Memorial Arboretum in Staffordshire, and, at the same time, the idea of forming a Trust to oversee this project was agreed. The year 2003 saw the construction of the Memorial, which was dedicated on 25 September 2004 in the presence of HRH The Duke of Gloucester.

Whilst undertaking the Memorial project it became evident to the Trustees that, notwithstanding the Force's distinguished past, there was no formal or centralised public record of its history, achievements, traditions, or organization from its beginnings in 1924 right up to the present day. The Trustees decided to rectify this shortcoming, but as this embraced a wider remit than was originally envisaged for the Trust, it was considered that it would be more appropriate for the Trust to be renamed The Royal Auxiliary Air Force Foundation, a title ratified with the Charity Commission in 2010.

Since its formation, the Foundation has planned and overseen the installation of a Force Roll of Honour at the Church of St Clement Danes in 2012, the introduction of a website in 2013, the renovation of the aforementioned Force Memorial at Alrewas in 2014 and the preparation and installation of a Force pictorial display at Bentley Priory in 2014. The Foundation was honoured when The Duke of Gloucester became its patron in 2012.

The following are extracts from the Foundation web site which illustrate many of the significant events which have taken place since its inception.

In 2001, 501 (County of Gloucester) Squadron RAuxAF was formed at RAF Brize Norton from 2624 Squadron RAuxAF Regiment in the Ops Support/Force Protection role and re-formed as 501 Logistics Support Squadron on 1 April 2013. October 2002 saw the establishment of 3 Tactical Police Squadron RAuxAF at RAF Henlow as part of the Tactical Police Wing, having been formed in 1999.

On 1 June 2006, 602 (City of Glasgow) Squadron was re-formed by splitting the two elements of 603 Squadron, namely Operations and Intelligence, Mission Support and Force Protection. 602 Squadron was given the Mission Support task and 603 Squadron retained the Force Protection task (Regiment and later Police). On 30 September 2006, 2622 (Highland) Squadron was presented with its Squadron Standard. In 2007, No. 600 (City of London) Squadron was granted Privileged Regiment Status by the Corporation of the City of London, a distinction only awarded to eight such formations in its history.

In 2008, the Trustees commenced work on researching the names of all members of the AAF and RAuxAF who had given their lives in the cause of freedom or otherwise on duty. Using records obtained from the Commonwealth War Graves Commission and contemporary records from the post war period, it was possible to complete a Roll of Honour for the AAF/RAuxAF which was dedicated at the RAF Church St Clement Danes in London in 2010 when the Sovereign's Colour for the RAuxAF that had been presented in 1989 was also laid up in the same church. Also, on 18 July 2010, Her Majesty the Queen, Air Commodore in Chief of the RAuxAF presented a new Sovereign's Colour at RAF Marham, together with new Squadron Standards to 2623 (East Anglian) Squadron RAuxAF Regiment and 2620 (County of Norfolk) Squadron RAuxAF Regiment.

In 2010, the name of the RAuxAF National Memorial Trust was changed to the RAuxAF Foundation. In 2012, No. 622 Squadron RAuxAF was re-formed at RAF Brize Norton as an OCU for the Air Transport and Air refuelling fleets. On 8 August 2013, an event took place at the National Memorial Arboretum to dedicate a memorial stone to Squadron Leader Roger Bushell who became a prisoner of war after being shot down over Dunkirk on 23 May 1940. Roger Bushell was a member of 601 Squadron AAF before being posted to form and command 92 Squadron RAF in October 1939. Once captured, he proved to be a thorn in the side of the Germans, being an inveterate escaper who, on two occasions managed to escape before being incarcerated in Stalag Luft III in Poland. He subsequently planned and led the Great Escape in 1944 where he was re-captured and shot by the Gestapo. The dedication of the Memorial Stone was attended by his niece, Mrs Lindy Wilson who travelled from her home in South Africa to attend the occasion.

On 1 September 2013, 502 (Ulster) Squadron was re-formed at RAF Aldergrove as a General Support Squadron. Also in 2013, 611 (West Lancashire) Squadron was re-formed at RAF Woodvale as a General Support Squadron. Furthermore, in the same year, 4624 (County of Oxford) Movements Squadron was granted the Freedom of the County of Oxford. Finally, in 2013, the Foundation launched its own web site at rauxaf.net.

On 16 May 2014, a ceremony of re-dedication was held at the National Memorial Arboretum to mark the renovation of the RAuxAF National Memorial. This renovation was necessary because the inscriptions on the original Memorial were becoming worn and indistinct due to the climatic conditions in the Midlands and, thanks to the efforts of a trustee, Squadron Leader Alfie Hall, and a grant from the National Lottery Heritage Foundation and others, the existing Memorial was clad in black marble with the former inscriptions engraved in gold lettering. In addition, improvements were made to the landscaping at the site, with new paving and additional benches.

The whole design of the new Memorial owes much to Alfie Hall in particular, who worked tirelessly on the concept of the new Memorial and on submitting the various applications for funding. The dedication of the renovated Memorial, together with the dedication of many Memorial Stones to former members of the AAF and RAuxAF, including that of Roger Bushell, which had been laid in August the previous year.

Moreover, in 2014, 605 (County of Warwick) Squadron was re-formed at RAF Cosford as a Logistics Support Squadron. Also in that year, 614 (County of Glamorgan) Squadron was re-formed in Cardiff as a General Support Squadron, now based at JFHQ at Northwood. The 5 January 2015 saw the re-forming of 607 (County of Durham) Squadron at RAF Leeming as a Logistics Support Squadron.

In 2017, a RAuxAF band was formed at the RAFC Cranwell, to support RAF Music Services. Also, on 20 April 2017, 601 (County of London) Squadron was re-formed at RAF Northolt to provide liaison duties between the RAF and commerce and industry.

On 23 June 2018, 607 (County of Durham) Squadron was granted the Freedom of the City of Durham. The next month saw 603 (City of Edinburgh) Squadron granted the Freedom of the City of Edinburgh, and following this ceremony, HM The Queen, Honorary Air Commodore of 603 Squadron, received squadron personnel and their spouses at a Royal Reception at the Palace of Holyrood House. Sadly, Squadron Leader Bruce Blanche, former No. 1 Maritime Headquarters Unit (MHU), No. 3 MHU, 603 Squadron and Foundation Trustee, passed away on 7 November 2018.

Conclusion

As the co-writer of this book, I have the pleasure of owning many, many books on the RAuxAF and the Royal Air Force. Perhaps you as the reader have several books. The one fact that interested me throughout all of my research was that any book on the RAF, in its index would have a couple of references to the Auxiliary Air Force, nothing more. Furthermore, these brief mentions were primarily the same, pointing out the wealth and social status of the men who joined and often their antics. For the first time this book presents all aspects of this voluntary organization to enable readers to see past the 'gentleman's flying club' image that is held by many, showing the full and detailed history of both the men and women who are prepared to be called into action at any time and who give up their evenings and weekends to train and keep up to date with ever changing technology.

We started off with a clear view of how we wanted to tackle the overall subject of the Royal Auxiliary Air Force so that we gave all aspects of the organization an equal and detailed appraisal. By writing chronologically we have made sure that nothing has been omitted due to our errors, and the list of our chapters shows this, I am sure. This book contains ten chapters which discuss all of the branches of the Royal Auxiliary Air Force, from the heady pre-war days of young men who flew, to the clerks, drivers, radar reporters and so many other trades, details of which you will find through these pages. Many people are unaware of the role of the volunteers who flew in the Battle of Britain, who repaired and maintained the aircraft, who warned of the dangers of enemy aircraft overhead, who protected airfields and so many other crucial roles. Most are unaware of the number of these volunteers who lost their lives throughout the existence of the organization, in different theatres of war. Both men and women who enlisted without hesitation. These service personnels' names are listed in the Roll of Honour, which is located towards the back of this book. There is also a timeline which highlights all of the key dates in the development of the Royal Auxiliary Air Force which is also located towards the back of this book.

With flying being relatively new in the 1930s, it is easy to see why young men were so keen to join the Auxiliary Air Force, both those who wanted to fly, and those who wanted to work closely with the aircraft and become the ground crew. As war approached, technology improved and more personnel were needed to meet the station establishment. Women were introduced to the service, along with new more advanced aircraft. The Auxiliary Air Force proved its worth during the war; out of the 3,038 aircrew who flew in the Battle of Britain, 188 of them were auxiliaries. Moreover, fourteen of the sixty fighter squadrons who were part of that battle were auxiliary squadrons. Of the one hundred Balloon Squadrons across the country, half of them were formed of and manned by the AAF.

After the war ended the AAF was disbanded along with the Women's Auxiliary Air Force and the Cold War was just beginning. This state of affairs made those in the Air Ministry realise that the old system of radar was now obsolete and changes needed to be made to enable the country to be fully prepared for what may be to come. So a major construction and re-equipment programme named ROTOR was built by the British Government in the early 1950s to enable the RAF to counter a possible attack from Soviet bombers. This system would modernise and improve the UK Air Defence System; however, the RAF did not have enough personnel to man it. The answer was to establish thirty Royal Auxiliary Air Force Fighter Control and Radar Reporting Units which served from 1947 to 1961. Furthermore, it is a matter of public record that, during the early and uncertain days of the Cold War, the Air Defence of the UK was in the hands of the auxiliaries, many of whom had re-enlisted in their old trades.

By the end of 1945 the decision had been made to re-form the original flying squadrons to bring the order of battle once more up to the strength of the pre-war RAF, plus five Army Co-operation Squadrons which were to be jointly manned by the RAuxAF and the TA. Under the ROTOR programme, twelve RAuxAF Regiment Squadrons were formed to operate anti-aircraft guns. However, by 1957 it had become apparent that it was no longer possible to train auxiliary aircrew, as the fat provided by ex-war aircrew was running out and the modern swept-wing fighters were proving to be too sophisticated to operate for part-timers, so by March 1957 all of the auxiliary fighter squadrons had been disbanded, along with the Fighter Control and Radar Reporting units of the RAuxAF and the Regiment squadrons. So by 1961, the RAuxAF virtually ceased to exist.

Around the same time, the Maritime Headquarters Units of the RAuxAF were being formed which were to cement the continuity of Service of one hundred years that will be commemorated and celebrated in 2024. Unfortunately, until 1979 these few units meant that the RAuxAF was virtually unknown to a generation of RAF personnel and the general public. July 1979 saw the decision to trial three RAuxAF Regiment Field Squadrons, followed by a further three in 1982/3. A Movements Squadron was also formed in 1982 and then an Aeromedical Evacuation Squadron in 1983. Both of which were mobilised for the First Gulf War in 1991, and in addition, four Airfield Defence Flights were formed at key locations in the UK.

In 1997 the War Appointable Royal Air Force Volunteer Reserve Flights were amalgamated into the RAuxAF. At that time there were twenty RAuxAF Squadrons and units which still serve, including their own band, but it was not envisaged that auxiliary squadrons would ever fly their own aircraft again.

So, have we achieved what we set out to do? I think that we are in a position to say yes, we have covered every aspect of the RAuxAF, in some detail, and have presented a detailed examination of an organization which doesn't spring to mind when discussing voluntary organizations, but which has a colourful and comprehensive history and an integral place in the defence of our country. As a whole, the RAuxAF has given one hundred years of valued service to the nation, an achievement which all members, serving, retired and those who are departed should be very proud of.

Timeline
The Auxiliary Air Force/
Royal Auxiliary Air Force
Timeline 1924–2024

1917   Air Force Constitution established
The Air Force Constitution of 1917 was laid down with a provision for an Air Force Reserve and an Auxiliary Air Force.

1918   The Formation of the Royal Air Force
The Royal Air Force was formed on 1 April 1918 by amalgamating the Royal Naval Air Service and the Royal Flying Corps into one independent Force.

A plan for a Reserve Air Force
Sir Hugh Trenchard decreed that a Reserve Air Force should be set up on a Territorial basis. He envisaged the Auxiliaries as a *corps d'elite* composed of the kind of young men who would have been interested in horses but who now wished to serve their country in machines!

1922   A Reserve Air Force Bill
A Reserve Air Forces Bill was drafted to raise six Auxiliary squadrons and seven Special Reserve squadrons with a longer-term plan to raise a total of 20 Auxiliary Squadrons. The Bill was initially opposed, and it did not become law until 1924.

1924   An Order in Council
An Order in Council made in the name of The King was signed 0n 9 October 1924 establishing the Auxiliary Air Force. The First Auxiliary squadrons were formed the following year.

1925   The First Special Reserve Squadron
The first squadron to be formed was No 502 (Ulster) Special Reserve Squadron on 15 May1925, at RAF Aldergrove, later to become an Auxiliary Air Force squadron in 1937.

The First Auxiliary Squadrons
No 602 (City of Glasgow) Squadron became the first Auxiliary squadron to be formed on 12 September at Renfrew. The squadron was equipped with the DH9a bomber aircraft that could carry two 250lb or four100lb bombs. No 600 (City of London) and No 601(County of London), were formed at RAF Northolt, on 14 October, with No 603 (City of Edinburgh which had formed at RAF Turnhouse on the same day. The early bomber squadrons also operated the DH9a aircraft.

1926   A Second Special Reserve Squadron
A second Special Reserve Squadron No 503 (County of Lincoln) was formed at RAF Waddington on 15 October. It was disbanded on 1 November 1938 and moved to Doncaster where it re-formed as No 616 (South Yorkshire) Squadron Auxiliary Air Force.

Further Auxiliary Squadron
On 5 October 1926 No 605 (County of Warwick) Squadron Auxiliary Air Force was formed at Castle Bromwich.

1928   A third Special Reserve Squadron
No 504 (County of Nottingham) Squadron was formed as a Special Reserve light bomber squadron on 26 March at RAF Hucknall equipped

with Hawker Horsleys. 504 Squadron also became an Auxiliary Air Force squadron in 1936.

1929   Expansion of Special Reserve

No 501 (County of Bristol) Squadron was formed at Filton as a Special Reserve Squadron on 14 June equipped with DH9a's that were replaced later with Westland Wapitis. The squadron later became 501 (County of Gloucester} Squadron Auxiliary Air Force.

1930   Additional Auxiliary Air Force Squadrons Formed

On 17 March No 604 (County of Middlesex) at Hendon, No 607 (County of Durham) at RAF Usworth and No 608 (North Riding) Squadrons at RAF Thornaby were initially formed as light bomber squadrons equipped with the DH9a or Avro 504 aircraft but a few years later, they became fighter squadrons, with the Westland Wapiti aircraft.

1931   Final Special Reserve Squadron Formed

On 16 March, No 500 (County of Kent) Special Reserve Squadron was formed at RAF Manston, equipped with the Vickers Virginia light bomber.

1933   First Flight Over Mount Everest

The first flight over Mount Everest, the world's highest mountain at over 29,000 feet, was undertaken by Sir Douglas Hamilton, later The Duke of Hamilton and David McIntyre on 3 April 1933, using specially adapted civilian Westland aircraft. Both officers were members of No 602 (City of Glasgow) Squadron Auxiliary Air Force in what was a private venture financed by Dame Fanny Lucy Huston (Lady Houston).

1936   Further Auxiliary Squadrons Formed

No 609 (West Riding) Squadron formed at Yeadon on 10 February, as were No 610 (County of Chester) Squadron at RAF Hendon and No 611 (West Lancashire) Squadron also at Hendon. These squadrons were formed initially as light bomber squadrons with Hawker Hart biplanes, becoming fighter squadrons two years later.

RAFVR Formed

The Royal Air Force Volunteer Reserve was formed on 1 April 1936 to provide a pool of reserve aircrew for the RAF, unlike the Auxiliary Air Force which consisted of formed squadrons.

Strengthening the Auxiliary Air Force

In 1936 it was decided to transfer 14 Auxiliary squadrons to the newly formed Fighter Command and all other squadrons to their relevant new Commands, eg Bomber, Coastal and Army Co-operation. At the same time, the old No 8 Auxiliary Group was abolished.

1937   RAF Balloon Group Formed

No 30 (Balloon Barrage) Group was formed at RAF Stanmore Park on 17 March. The ten Barrage Balloon squadrons that initially made up the Group were formed at four centres ringed around the Home Counties of London.

Further Auxiliary Air Force Squadrons Formed

On I June, No 612 (County of Aberdeen) Squadron was formed at RAF Dyce, as an Army Co-operation squadron equipped with Hawker Hart and Hector aircraft and No 614 (County of Glamorgan) squadron was formed on the same day at Pengam Moors, as an Army Co-operation unit also equipped with Harts and Hectors. In addition, No 615 (County of Surrey) – 'Churchill's Own' – was formed on the same day at RAF Kenley as a fighter squadron.

1938   Review of AAF Terms and Conditions of Service

In April 1938, a committee issued a report which recommended great improvements to the terms and conditions of the Auxiliary Air Force, not the least of which was to pay and allowances to bring it more in line with that of the newly formed RAFVR.

RAF Balloon Command Formed

On 1 April 1938, RAF Balloon Command was formed and by the outbreak of war in 1939, the Balloon Barrage had increased to 47 squadrons nation-wide recruited and manned as auxiliary squadrons. By the end of the war, a further 52 such squadrons had been formed within the RAF.

1939   No 613 Squadron Formed

On 1 February No 613 (City of Manchester) Squadron Auxiliary Air Force was formed at Ringway, equipped with Avro 504s but transferred only a few days later as a fighter squadron equipped with Gloster Gauntlets as part of No 22 (Army Co-operation) Group, Fighter Command.

War Declared

On Sunday, 3 September, war was declared against Germany and the Auxiliary Air Force ceased recruiting and was 'embodied' (included) with the Royal Air Force. Non-Commissioned Members retained their auxiliary status until their current terms of service expired when they were either transferred to the RAFVR or discharged. They continued to wear the letter 'A' on their uniforms, most personnel continuing to do so for the remainder of the war. Some officers elected to retain the brass letter A on their uniforms.

First Blood to the Auxiliaries

The first German air attack took place over the Forth Estuary on 16 October. Two Junkers 88s were shot down by both 602 and 603 Squadrons. The Chief of the Air Staff sent a message to both squadrons: **'Well done! First Blood to the Auxiliaries'.** The second German aircraft of the war to be shot down and the first to crash on British soil was on 28 October, a victory shared once again by 602 and 603 Squadrons.

1940   Dunkirk

During the period 23 May to 7 June, 11 of the 14 Auxiliary squadrons transferred to Fighter Command since 1936 had fought either over Northern France, southern England, the English Channel or the beaches of Dunkirk.

During this time, five Auxiliary squadrons were either based at, or detached to, airfields in France

The Battle Britain
The Battle of Britain was fought over Southern England from 10 July to 31 October 1940. Of the 62 British squadrons and units that took part, just 14 were Auxiliary Air Force squadrons (23 per cent). Records kept by11 Group which saw the brunt of the action show that of the top scoring 15 squadrons in the Group during the period, eight were Auxiliary with 565 confirmed victories out of 968 (58 per cent).

Public Relations Unit Formed
A RAFVR Public Relations Unit was formed, becoming No 7644 (VR), Flight in 1981 and a RAuxAF squadron in 1997.

1939–1945   The Second World War
The Auxiliary Air Force continued to support air operations throughout the rest of the war. Details of individual operations and locations would be too numerous to be listed here so readers are directed to the chapter on 'The Second World War' elsewhere in this book.

1942   The Air Efficiency Award
The Air Efficiency Award was instituted on 17 August 1942 for all ranks who had completed 10 years efficient service in either the Auxiliary Air Force or the Royal Air Force Volunteer Reserve. The qualifying time was halved for wartime service and the award conferred the post nominals AE for officers.

1945   RAF Balloon Command
RAF Balloon Command was disbanded at the end of the war.

Initial Disbandment
All Auxiliary Air Force flying squadrons and supporting units were disbanded at the end of the war.

1946   Reformation

All the disbanded Auxiliary Air Force flying squadrons were re-formed during the period 1946/1947 plus 48 Air Defence Units, later to become Fighter Control Units, and two Radar Reporting Units.

1947   The Force Becomes 'Royal'

In appreciation of the contribution made by the Auxiliary Air Force during the Second World War, in December HM The King bestowed the title 'Royal' on the Force, it becoming The Royal Auxiliary Air Force (RAuxAF).

1948   RAuxAF Regiment Squadrons

In 1948, twenty RAuxAF Regiment Squadrons were proposed in the light Anti- Aircraft role but only 12 squadrons were formed, armed with the 40mm Bofors anti-aircraft gun, but by 1953, all had been re-roled as Field Squadrons.

1949   Royal Hong Kong Auxiliary Air Force Formed

In 1949, the Hong Kong Auxiliary Air Force was formed, becoming 'Royal' in 1951. Close ties were developed with the RAuxAF in the UK, until the Hong Kong Force was disbanded in 1993.

Air Observation Units Formed

Five Air Observation Squadrons were formed, No 661 at RAF Kenley on 1 May, No 662 at RAF Colerne on 1 February, No 663 at RAF Hooton Park on 1 July, No 664 at RAF Hucknall on 1 July and No 666 at Perth/Scone on 1 May. All were formed within the RAuxAF but were manned jointly by Army pilots and RAuxAF groundcrew.

1950   First Inspector RAuxAF Appointed

Air Commodore Finlay Crerar CBE AE was appointed as the first post-war Inspector of the Royal Auxiliary Air Force.

New Royal Auxiliary Air Force Squadron Formed
On 1 November, No 622 (Transport) Squadron was formed at Blackbushe, equipped with the Vickers Valetta. It was disbanded on 30 September 1953.

1951   First Honorary Air Commodore Appointed
The (then) HRH Princess Elizabeth was appointed Honorary Air Commodore of 603, 2603 Squadrons and 3603 Fighter Control Unit, a position Her Majesty the Queen continued to hold as HAC 603 Squadron until her death in 2022.

The Korean War
All 20 RAuxAF Fighter Squadrons were mobilised for three months extended training during the Korean War, although none were deployed overseas.

1953   HM The Queen Appointed HAC in-Chief
On 1 May, HM The Queen was appointed Honorary Air Commodore-in-Chief of the RAuxAF.

Post-war RAFVR Flights Established
No 7010 (VR) Flight was initially formed as a strategic imagery unit at RAF Nuneham Park in April. No 7630 (VR) Intelligence Flight was also formed with mainly Russian linguists, to support Cold War operations.

Inspector RAuxAF Handover
Group Captain J M Birkin CB DSO OBE DFC AFC was appointed Inspector RAuxAF.

1955   Light anti-aircraft squadrons formed
The 12 Light anti-aircraft squadrons formed in 1948 were re-roled as RAuxAF Regiment field squadrons.

1956   First Honorary Inspector General
Group Captain J M Birkin CB DSO OBE DFC AFC was appointed as the first Honorary Inspector General (HIG) of the Royal Auxiliary Air Force.

1957   Disbandment
The Air Ministry announced that the 20 flying squadrons would cease training and be disbanded on 10 March 1957.

1959 Royal Auxiliary Air Force Units Soldier on
A decision was taken to disband all the RAuxAF Fighter Control and Radar Reporting Units and the 12 regiment squadrons, together with many of the fighter control and radar reporting units. A few FCUs soldiered on and some personnel transferred to four newly formed maritime headquarters units operating from Northwood, Pitreavie Castle (Edinburgh), Mount Batten (Plymouth) in 1959/60 and No 1 Maritime Support Unit in Aldergrove (Belfast) thereby continuing the RAuxAF lineage.

1962   Inspector RAuxAF Appointment
Group Captain The Hon Sir Peter Vanneck GBE CB AFC AE was appointed as Inspector RAuxAF.

1973   Inspector RAuxAF Appointment
Group Captain L E Robins CBE AE* RAuxAF was appointed as Inspector RAuxAF

1974   Honorary Inspector General Appointed
Air Commodore The Hon Sir Peter Vanneck GBE CB AFC AE DL, Lord Mayor of London was appointed as Honorary Inspector General of the Royal Auxiliary Air Force.

1979   Regiment Squadrons Formed

No 2620 (County of Norfolk), No 2622 (Highland) and No 2623 (East Anglian) Squadrons were formed on a trial basis at RAF Marham in 1983, RAF Lossiemouth in 1983 and RAF Honington in1979 as field squadrons to provide airfield defence. No 2503 (County of Lincoln) Regiment Squadron also formed at RAF Waddington to provide airfield defence.

1982   Further Squadrons Formed

No 2624 (County of Oxford) Regiment Squadron was formed at RAF Brize Norton, for airfield defence later becoming a role support squadron for the air transport fleet. No 2625 (County of Cornwall) Regiment Squadron formed at RAF St Mawgan to provide airfield defence and No 4624 (County of Oxford) Movements Squadron also formed at Brize Norton.

1983   Aeromedical Evacuation Squadron Formed

No 4626 (County of Wiltshire) Aeromedical Evacuation Squadron formed on 9 September at RAF Hospital Wroughton, later moving to RAF Lyneham via RAF Hullavington.

Further Field Squadron Formed

A sixth RAuxAF Regiment Field Squadron was formed, two were disbanded and two were re-roled as Role Support Squadrons.

Robins Efficiency Trophy

Group Captain 'Robbie' Robins, Inspector RAuxAF presented the Robins Efficiency Trophy to be presented annually to the unit that had done the most to improve the good name and efficiency of the Force. The first recipient was No 2 (City of Edinburgh) Maritime Headquarters Unit.

Inspector Handover

Group Captain Peter Harris CB AE ADC DL was appointed Inspector RAuxAF.

1984   New HIG Appointed
Air Chief Marshal Sir John Barraclough KCB CBE DFC AFC was appointed Honorary Inspector General RAuxAF.

The Strickland Trophy
Air Commodore Strickland, on his retirement as Director Royal Air Force Regiment, presented the Strickland Trophy to the Force to be competed annually by the RAuxAF Regiment Squadrons by way of a military skills competition. The first recipient was No 2625 (County of Cornwall) Squadron.

1985   No 2729 (City of Lincoln) Squadron Re-Formed
On 1 April, No 2729 (City of Lincoln) Squadron RAuxAF Regiment re-formed at RAF Waddington as a Short-Range Air Defence (SHORAD) squadron equipped with the Swiss made Oerlikon guns and Skyguard radar captured in the Falkland Islands during the war of 1982. The squadron was disbanded in 1993.

1339   RAuxAF Regiment Wing Formed
No1339 RAuxAF Wing was formed at RAF Waddington, comprising 2729 and later 2890 Squadrons.

Airfield Defence Flights
Four Airfield Defence Force units of the RAuxAF Regiment were formed as Defence Force Flights at RAF stations Lyneham, Brampton High Wycombe and St Athan.

1986   Intelligence Unit Formed
With vague links to a 7006 (VR) Intelligence Flight going back to the 1940s, a new Intelligence flight was set up at RAF Hight Wycombe with the same name.

1987   Inspector RAuxAF Handover

Group Captain Michael Tinley CBE ADC was appointed Inspector RAuxAF.

1989   The Sovereign's Colour

At the invitation of ACM Sir John Barraclough, Her Majesty The Queen graciously presented the first Sovereign's Colour for the Royal Auxiliary Air Force (indeed the first such Colour to any reserve force) at a parade held at RAF Benson on 12 June 1989. No 1 Maritime Headquarters Unit provided the Colour Bearer and No 4624 Squadron the escort to the Colour.

No 2890 Royal Auxiliary Air Force Regiment Squadron

No 2890 Squadron was formed on 1 October at RAF Waddington as a Short-Range Air Defence (SHORAD) squadron as part of No 1339 Wing.

1990   New HIG Appointed

The Rt Hon Sir Hector Monro AE was appointed Honorary Inspector General of the RAuxAF on 15 September.

50th Anniversary of The Battle of Britain

A Royal Review and fly-past by over 100 aircraft which was televised, took place at Buckingham Palace on 15 September to commemorate the 50th Anniversary of the Battle of Britain. The Sovereign's Colour for the Royal Auxiliary Air Force was paraded by a Colour Party from 4624 Squadron.

1991   Mobilisation

No 4624 (Movements) Squadron and No 4626 (Aeromedical Evacuation) Squadron were both mobilised in support of Operation Granby (The First Gulf War) in January 1991, the Movements Squadron to support aircraft movements to and from theatre, and the aeromedical evacuation squadron to support a field hospital in Riyadh, Saudi Arabia.

1992   Expansion of No 4626 Squadron

A further Field Support Flight of 4626 Aeromedical Squadron was established in 1992. Initially operating from No 2 MHU's headquarters in Edinburgh, the unit became the re-formed No 612 (County of Aberdeen) Squadron based at RAF Leuchars in 1996.

1993   No 2890 and 2729 Squadrons Disbanded

No 2890 (City of Lincoln) and 2729 (City of Lincoln) Squadrons were disbanded at RAF Waddington along with No 1339 Wing. Personnel from the disbanded squadrons went to Scampton to form and serve on the Rapier Conversion/Cadreisation Unit which eventually became the relocated 27 & 48 Squadrons, a mix of auxiliary and regular personnel.

1994   Disbandment of 2623 Squadron

No 2623 Squadron RAuxAF Regiment was disbanded, re-forming in 1995 as a Regiment Training Unit until subsumed in 1997 into the RAF Regiment Training Wing.

The Inspector's Cup

Group Captain Mike Tinley donated The Inspector's Cup to be awarded annually to the unit that had made a notable achievement in the past year.

New Inspector RAuxAF Appointed

Group Captain Richard Mighall OBE ADC was appointed Inspector RAuxAF.

1996   First RAuxAF Yearbook Published

The Inspectorate published the first RAuxAF Yearbook that was distributed to every member of the Force. The Yearbooks were published annually until 2000.

Helicopter Support Squadron Formed

A Helicopter Support Squadron was formed at RAF Benson on 1 October, later named No 606 (Chiltern) Squadron.

New Reserve Forces Act Introduced
A new Reserve Forces Act 1996 was introduced. It provided new categories of call-out for part-time reserves, short of general war, and introduced new classes of full and part time reserve service

1997   Integration of the RAFVR and The RAuxAF
The Royal Air Force Volunteer Reserve flights, first formed in 1936, were integrated into the RAuxAF as squadrons, retaining their 'VR' suffix. A parade, reviewed by HRH The Duke of York was held to mark the event at RAF Cranwell. The two surviving VCs from WW2, John Cruickshank from Aberdeen and Bill Reid from Crieff attended as Guests of Honour.

Clyde Public Relations Trophy
Group Captain Alex Dickson OBE QVRM AE** presented the Clyde PR Trophy to the Force to be awarded twice annually to the unit that displayed the highest standards in public relations. The first recipient was the Helicopter Support Unit at RAF Benson.

1998   Role Support Squadrons Formed
Four (as yet un-numbered) Role Support Squadrons at RAF Cottesmore, RAF Marham, RAF Brize Norton and RAF Leeming were formed, joining the Helicopter Role Support Squadron (HSS) at RAF Benson. Role Support Squadrons were a new concept, employing multi trades.

Flying Auxiliaries
Following a two-year trial, a reserve flight of Hercules aircrew was formed at RAF Brize Norton, with ex-regular aircrew, later becoming No1359 Flight RAuxAF before becoming No 622 Squadron in 2012.

27 and 48 Squadrons disband
Nos 27 and 48 Squadrons disbanded in August/September. They were the last remaining units using the Field Standard (FS)B1(M) version of the Rapier Ground-to-Air missile, all the regular squadrons having converted to the FSC (Rapier 2000).

Reformation of 2623 Squadron
No 2623 (Anglian) Squadron was re-formed once again, this time being a Ground based Air Defence (GBAD) Rapier Squadron based at RAF Honington armed with the FSC Rapier missile system.

Queen's Volunteer Reserves Medal
The Queen's Volunteer Reserves Medal (QVRM) was instituted by HM The Queen by Royal Warrant on 29 March 1999. The award conferred presentation at an investiture, was announced in the London Gazette and carried the post nominals QVRM.

1999   75th Anniversary at the Royal International Air Tattoo (RIAT)
HRH The Duke of Kent visited the RAuxAF Display at the RIAT at RAF Fairford set up to mark the 75th Anniversary of the Force.

The Air Efficiency Medal
The Air Efficiency Medal was instituted in 1942. The Air Efficiency Medal that conferred the post nominals 'AE' for officers was withdrawn on 1 April and replaced by the tri-service Volunteer Reserves Medal that did not confer post nominals.

2000   New Honorary Inspector General RAuxAF
Air Vice Marshal B H Newton CB OBE was appointed Honorary Inspector General (HIG) RAuxAF.

New Inspector RAuxAF
Group Captain Robert Kemp CBE QVRM AE ADC was appointed Inspector RAuxAF.

2001   No 501 Squadron Re-formed
No 501 (County of Gloucester) was formed as a Logistics Support Squadron at RAF Brize Norton from elements of 2624 Squadron.

Royal Reception in London Guildhall
To mark the re-forming of No 600 (City of London) Squadron, the City hosted a reception in the Guildhall on 15 November. Her Majesty The Queen Mother attended at the age of 101 in her capacity as the Squadron's Honorary Air Commodore. This was her second last public appearance before her death. A recent decision had been made to renumber many existing and new units with those from the pre-war flying squadron days.

RAuxAF Crest Presented to the RAF Club
A carved Royal Auxiliary Air Force badge was presented to the Royal Air Force Club in London by Group Captain Richard Mighall.

2002   Tactical Police Squadron Formed
No 3 Tactical Police Squadron RAuxAF was established at RAF Henlow as part of the Tactical Police Wing to support RAF Lossiemouth and RAF Kinloss.

RAF Historical Society Seminar
A seminar was held at the RAF Museum in London on the Reserves and Auxiliaries of the Royal Air Force, by the RAF Historical Society, since published as a book available on-line.

2006   International Air Reserves Symposium
The Royal Auxiliary Air Force Hosted the International Air Reserves Symposium in Edinburgh. His Grace the Duke of Westminster KG CB CVO OBE TD DL attended in his capacity as Director Reserve Forces.

2007   The Kemp Dirk
Group Captain Robert Kemp, Inspector RAuxAF presented a Scottish Dirk to be awarded annually to the unit that showed the best recruiting figures during the previous year.

New Inspector Appointed

Group Captain Gary Bunkell CBE QVRM AE ADC was appointed Inspector RAuxAF on 24 March.

2008   New HIG Appointed

Lord Beaverbrook Honorary Air Commodore of No 4624 Squadron was appointed Honorary Inspector General (HIG) of the Royal Auxiliary Air Force, in the rank of Air Vice-Marshal.

2010   The Royal Auxiliary Air Force Foundation

The Memorial Trust was re-named the Royal Auxiliary Air Force Foundation, a title ratified by the Charity Commission.

Operation HERRICK

Increasing numbers of Auxiliary personnel were mobilized to support Operation HERRICK, a war in Afghanistan that lasted from 2002 until 2012.

New Sovereign's Colour

A new Sovereign's Colour for the Royal Auxiliary Air Force was presented to the Force by HM The Queen at a parade held at RAF Marham on 1 July. Standards for 2620 and 2623 Squadrons were also presented during the same parade.

2012   The Roll of Honour

A Service of Dedication was held at The RAF Church, St Clement Danes in London on 21 October during which the Royal Auxiliary Roll of Honour was installed and the first Sovereign's Colour presented in 1988 was laid up. The Service was attended by HRH The Duke of Gloucester KG GCVO GCStJ who had become the Patron of the Foundation on February.

No 622 Squadron Renamed

The RAF Standard Committee re-badged No 622 Squadron, formerly No 1359 Flight as No 622 (Reserve Aircrew) Squadron operating from RAF Brize Norton.

2013   General Support Squadrons
No 502 (Ulster) Squadron was re-formed at RAF Aldergrove and No 611 (West Lancs) Squadron was re-formed at RAF Woodvale, both as General Support Squadrons.

Freedom of the County
No 4624 (County of Oxford) Movements Squadron was granted the Freedom of the County of Oxfordshire.

2014   Squadrons Re-formed
No 605 (County of Warwick) was formed at RAF Cosford as a Logistics Support Squadron and No 614 (County of Glamorgan) was re-formed in Cardiff to support JFHQ at Northwood as a General Support Squadron.

Refurbishment of the Memorial
The Royal Auxiliary Air Force National Memorial at the National Memorial Arbortetum was refurbished in black marble to better protect it from the elements.

2015   No 607 Squadron Re-formed
No 607 (County of Durham) Squadron was re-formed at RAF Leeming on 5 January as a Logistics Support Squadron.

HIG Renamed CG
The title of Honorary Inspector General (HIG) was rescinded to be replaced by the title Commandant General (CG). Lord Beaverbrook, HIG RAuxAF was appointed Commandant General of the RAuxAF and confirmed as a member of the Air Force Board in the rank of Air Vice-Marshal.

New Inspector Appointed
Group Captain G P Hellard CBE ADC was appointed Inspector RAuxAF.

Change of ADC

The Appointment of ADC to the Queen which had hitherto been on the list of ADCs as including the Inspector RAuxAF in the rank of Group Captain, was removed and awarded to the Commandant General. .

2016   Removal of Auxiliary 'A's

It was decided that the distinctive letter 'A', worn by officers on No 1 Dress uniform and No 5 Mess Dress uniform for over 90 years was to be removed.

2017   Formation of Royal Auxiliary Air Force Band

A Royal Auxiliary Air Force Band was formed at RAF Cranwell in support of RAF Music Services. No 2622 (Highland) Squadron Pipe Band continues at RAF Lossiemouth whilst No 602 and 603 Squadron Pipe Bands were disbanded in 1957.

No 601 Squadron Re-formed

No 601 (County of London) Squadron was re-formed at RAF Northolt on 20 April to provide liaison duties between the RAF and commerce and industry.

2018   Freedom of the City

No 607 (County of Durham) was granted the Freedom of the City of Durham on 23 June.

Freedom of the City

No 603 (City of Edinburgh) Squadron was granted the Freedom of the City of Edinburgh on 3 July. Immediately following this, Her Majesty the Queen, as the Squadron's Honorary Air Commodore, received members of the Squadron and family members in the Palace of Holyrood House.

2019   No 616 Squadron Re-formed

No 616 (South Yorkshire) Squadron was re-formed at RAF Waddington.

Commandant General
Lord Beaverbrook stood down as Commandant General on 19 July to be replaced by Major General Ranald Munro TD DL in the rank of Air Vice-Marshal.

2020   Appointment of New Inspector RAuxAF
Group Captain Paul White VR was appointed Inspector RAuxAF.

Last Auxiliary who Flew in the Battle of Britain Dies
Flt Lt William Terence 'Terry' Montague Clark DFM AE, born on 11 April 1919 died on 7 Nay 2020 at the age of 101. He is believed to be the last Auxiliary who flew in the Battle of Britain.

Removal of RAuxAF Post Nominals
It was decided that the post nominals 'RAuxAF' worn by officers entitled to use them would be replaced with the term RAF Reserve.

2021   Re-instatement of ADC to The Queen
The Inspector RAF Reserve was reinstated as ADC to HM The Queen and to wear once more the Royal ER insignia and aigrettes.[105]

2022   No. 601 (County of London) Squadron were presented with a new Squadron Standard on 21 July.

No. 602 (City of Glasgow) Squadron were presented with a new Squadron Standard on 19 August.

On 8 September, Her Majesty Queen Elizabeth II, Air Commodore in Chief Royal Auxiliary Air Force since 1954, died at Balmoral, followed by a State Funeral at St George's Chapel, Windsor on 19 October.

---

105 This Timeline was composed by Group Captain R.G. Kemp CBE QVRM AE ADC

Criteria for Inclusion on the
Royal Auxiliary Air Force
Roll of Honour

AAF/RAuxAF Roll of Honour Criteria for Inclusion

The Roll of Honour chronologically lists all those who died in the period 1924 to the present day and includes all those who were commissioned or enlisted exclusively in the pre-war AAF and who were killed in action or died on active service during the Second World War. (The AAF ceased recruiting in 1939 as it was embodied within the Royal Air Force for the duration of the War.) In this respect, it has been possible to identify those casualties by their Service Number which was allocated exclusively to auxiliaries: 90000 series for officers and 800000 series for other ranks. There are a few anomalies, for example, where an airman undertook pilot training and was subsequently commissioned. Moreover, it is possible that some of those who were commissioned or enlisted into the pre-war AAF had previously served in the regular RAF and who may have retained their original Service Number. These few individuals can only be traced if an application is received to do so from their surviving relatives.

The Roll also includes those original members of the early Women's Auxiliary Air Force (WAAF) who were killed in action, on active service, or otherwise on duty. The WAAF was formed in 1939, from the Air Companies of the Auxiliary Territorial Service (ATS), and until 1940, when the RAF undertook all responsibility for administration and training, the WAAF was administered by the AAF. It has been possible to identify those early and original volunteers as they were allocated the 800000 series of AAF service numbers. However, the 800000 series of number allocation persisted until 1941, so it is possible that some wartime members of the WAAF may be included in the Roll of Honour, but as the WAAF were non-combatant, the number of those who lost their lives is likely to be very few indeed.

Whilst it is true that all females who were commissioned or enlisted into the RAF during the war joined the WAAF, this was an administrative convenience as all male members joined the RAFVR and there was no comparable women's service that had been constituted for that purpose. Indeed, during the war, the future role of women in the regular RAF had not been decided and, along with the AAF and the RAFVR, it was decided to disband both forces at the end of hostilities. This proved to be the case and the nascent WAAF was included in the process. It was not until the onset of the Cold War that the Women's Royal Air Force (WRAF) was re-formed (it had existed during the First World War), as was the RAuxAF and those members, including women, of the new RAuxAF squadrons and units who died whilst on duty are also commemorated in the Roll, and on the Armed Forces Memorial. Given that the Roll of Honour was originally conceived as a memorial to those members of the AAF and RAuxAF who had volunteered to serve part-time, on evenings and at weekends, then the exclusion of the wartime WAAF is understood. Moreover, they were wartime conscripts or volunteers and the WAAF was, given the uncertainty surrounding the future of women in the RAF, the only practical place to put them. As a result, the acronym 'WAAF' became a colloquialism for all female members of the RAF that survived the re-formation of the WRAF in 1947 and is still used to this day.

That said, the Roll of Honour is a living document and the subject of including those wartime members of the WAAF who died on duty, is a matter for debate. However, such a debate should be held on the basis of informed opinion, which is the purpose of this document.

Auxiliary Air Force and
Royal Auxiliary Air Force Roll of Honour

25 September 1943	ABERCROMBIE	Flight Sergeant	DAVID	817167		179 Sqn RAF
13 June 1944	ABERNETHY	Aircraftman 2nd Class	JOSEPH SANDERSON	873289		Unknown
31 May 1942	ACTON	Sergeant	NORMAN	810144		405 (RCAF) Sqn
14 August 1940	AINSCOW	Aircraftman 1st Class	RICHARD	857329	MM	
17 November 1942	ALFORD	Leading Aircraftman	RONALD WILLIAM TICKELL	860263		Unknown
20 June 1941	ALLAN	Leading Aircraftman	CHRISTOPHER	870958		942 Balloon Sqn
15 March 1942	ALLAN	Leading Aircraftman	JAMES WATSON FRASER	817078		612 Sqn AAF
13 August 1940	ALLISON	Aircraftman 1st Class	JOHN	871535		943 Balloon Sqn
14 June 1942	AMBLER	Leading Aircraftman	BRIAN CHARLES	805494		Unknown
23 June 1951	ANDERSON	Pilot Officer	ANDREW	2683591		603 Sqn RAuxAF
10 May 1940	ANDERSON	Pilot Officer	MICHAEL HERBERT	90497	MiD	600 Sqn AAF

154

Date	Surname	Rank	Forename(s)	Number	Unit
30 October 1941	ANDREW	Flight Sergeant	JOHN	817097	612 Sqn AAF
25 March 1944	APEDAILE	Leading Aircraftman	EDWARD	867174	942 Balloon Sqn
10 November 1945	APPLETON	Aircraftman 2nd Class	LEONARD	856575	Unknown
03 September 1950	ARMSTRONG	Pilot 2	THOMAS GORDON	2685590	607 Sqn RAuxAF
16 August 1944	ARMSTRONG	Corporal	WILLIAM VIPOND	866588	Unknown
17 May 1943	ARNOTT	Corporal	THOMSON	802570	Unknown
28 April 1942	ARSCOTT	Aircraftman 1st Class	CHARLES HENRY	865254	964 Balloon Sqn
21 July 1943	ARTHUR	Leading Aircraftman	JOHN HALL	817074	Unknown
05 February 1943	ASHMAN	Aircraftman 1st Class	ALBERT HENRY	840851	902 Balloon Sqn
12 January 1941	ASHMORE	Aircraftman 2nd Class	GUILLERMO	840452	901 Balloon Sqn
20 September 1940	ATHERALL	Aircraftman 2nd Class	WILLIAM ERNEST	870911	942 Balloon Sqn
08 November 1942	ATKINSON	Sergeant	JOSEPH	810060	142 Sqn RAF
26 January 1942	ATWELL	Sergeant	WILLIAM JOHN	845508	51 Sqn RAF

Date	Surname	Rank	First Names	Number		Squadron
11 July 1943	AUBREY	Squadron Leader	THOMAS DIXON RODBARD	91170		Unknown
18 September 1940	AUSTEN	Sergeant	DOUGLAS WILLIAM	812247		58 Sqn RAF
03 April 1954	AUSTIN	Flying Officer	PETER MICHAEL	3124626		604 Sqn RAuxAF
17 March 1955	AUSTIN	Flying Officer	WILLIAM GEORGE GRAHAM	3511467		502 Sqn RAuxAF
12 October 1944	AUSTIN	Sergeant	HARRY	810117		31 (SAAF) Sqn
22 October 1941	AUSTIN	Sergeant	ROBERT EDWARD	808407		419 (RCAF) Sqn
30 May 1940	AYRE	Flying Officer	GEORGE DESMONDE	90330		609 Sqn AAF
26 June 1942	BADDELEY	Flight Sergeant	DOUGLAS HIRAM	814205		Unknown
04 July 1941	BAGNALL	Flight Sergeant	RONALD STANLEY	805437		106 Sqn RAF
20 February 1944	BAGSHAW	Flight Sergeant	CHARLES	820005		103 Sqn RAF
03 July 1949	BAILEY	Pilot 2	RAYMOND ARTHUR	2688117		611 Sqn RAuxAF
27 October 1939	BAIRD	Pilot Officer	ARTHUR DENNIS	91062		608 Sqn AAF
22 December 1940	BAKER	Aircraftman 1st Class	CHARLES HENRY	852052		917 Balloon Sqn
11 April 1945	BAKER	Aircraftman 1st Class	JAMES WILLIAM	858861		5011 ACS RAF

Date	Surname	Rank	Name	Number	Unit
25 April 1947	**BAKER**	Aircraftman 2nd Class	WILLIAM	855151	921 Balloon Sqn
31 August 1940	**BALDIE**	Leading Aircraftman	WILLIAM JOHN	803619	603 Sqn AAF
30 January 1943	**BALL**	Leading Aircraftman	JAMES HENRY	854513	920 Balloon Sqn
27 March 1940	**BALSTON**	Flying Officer	JAMES PETER HENRY	90567	500 Sqn AAF
31 October 1939	**BANKS**	Leading Aircraftman	JAMES RODGERS	811104	611 Sqn AAF
28 August 1941	**BANNISTER**	Aircraftman 1st Class	DONALD WILLIAM	819139	616 Sqn AAF
14 April 1957	**BARBER**	A/Flight Lieutenant	WILFRED JAMES	171272	3701 FCU RAuxAF
07 June 1941	**BARBERY**	Leading Aircraftman	FRANK WALTER	851435	Unknown
30 September 1944	**BARKER**	Flight Sergeant	ELEANOR M.	881177	Unknown
09 January 1943	**BARKER**	Sergeant	ISOBEL MARY	889835	Unknown
15 April 1942	**BARKER**	Sergeant	KENNETH WILLIAM	800585	158 Sqn RAF
28 July 1942	**BARKER**	Aircraftman 2nd Class	GEORGE	842252	Unknown
09 December 1934	**BARNABY**	Flying Officer	WALTER COLLINSON	Unknown	Unknown

157

Date	Surname	Rank	Forenames	Number	Squadron
06 March 1945	BARNES	Flight Lieutenant	GEORGE JAMES	91129	Unknown
15 October 1953	BARNES	Aircraftman 2nd Class	ERIC ALBERT	2681648	504 Sqn RAuxAF
28 January 1945	BARRADELL	Sergeant	EDWARD BERTRAM	851307	218 Sqn RAF
11 July 1940	BARRAN	Flight Lieutenant	PHILIP HENRY	90323	609 Sqn AAF
12 August 1940	BARRELL	Corporal	ARTHUR REGINALD OWEN	864073	933 Balloon Sqn
08 February 1946	BARRETT	Aircraftman 1st Class	JOHN WILLIAM	846489	909/910 Balloon Sqn
30 July 1942	BARRETT	Aircraftman 2nd Class	EDWARD	816224	502 Sqn AAF
30 November 1942	BARRON	Sergeant	SAMUEL EDWARD	809003	36 Sqn RAF
17 October 1954	BARWICK	Flying Officer	ERIC STANLEY	91390	501 Sqn RAuxAF
02 March 1941	BAZLEY	Flight Lieutenant	SYDNEY HOWARTH	90359	611 Sqn AAF
01 September 1940	BEADNALL	Aircraftman 2nd Class	GEORGE	808387	608 Sqn AAF
04 September 1941	BEALE	Squadron Leader	WILFRED BENNETT	90240	Unknown
18 July 1940	BEALE	Sergeant	JACK ALLEN	804328	604 Sqn AAF

Date	Surname	First Names	Rank	Number	Award	Unit
01 November 1944	BEAMES	FREDERICK WILLIAM	Corporal	846445		Unknown
26 June 1943	BEASLEY	HERBERT WILLIAM	Sergeant	846474		61 Sqn RAF
05 February 1944	BEATON	STANLEY	Warrant Officer	817076		502 Sqn AAF
01 February 1945	BEATSON	ALEXANDER PURDIE	Sergeant	823242		519 Sqn RAF
29 October 1944	BEEDIE	ROSEMARY	Corporal	884420		Unknown
02 October 1944	BEGGS	JANE GRANT	Sergeant	889112		Unknown
30 August 1940	BELL	JOHN SWIFT	Flying Officer	90051	MiD	616 Sqn AAF
26 April 1941	BELL	GEORGE	Flight Sergeant	802438		Unknown
17 July 1942	BELL	CHARLES ROBERT	Sergeant	808379		Unknown
03 September 1941	BELLINGHAM	HUGH WALTER	Sergeant	819105		Unknown
29 November 1943	BENNETT	ALEC HENRY	Leading Aircraftman	847141		Unknown
24 February 1944	BENNETT	HARRY	Leading Aircraftman	845735		Unknown
14 February 1941	BENSTEAD	PETER CHARLES	Sergeant	800658		223 Sqn RAF
14 December 1941	BERRY	ARTHUR	Sergeant	812133		209 Sqn RAF

159

Date	Surname	Rank	Forename(s)	Number	Award	Squadron
29 July 1944	**BERRY**	Sergeant	JAMES	860340		927 Balloon Sqn
03 August 1942	**BESWICK**	Leading Aircraftman	JAMES HENRY	867274		Unknown
20 February 1944	**BEWICK**	Sergeant	CHRISTOPHER	817070		Unknown
12 November 1940	**BEZZANT**	Aircraftman 1st Class	WILLIAM ERNEST	845153		907 Balloon Sqn
03 October 1943	**BICKEL**	Sergeant	RONALD GEORGE	818010		88 Sqn RAF
06 February 1942	**BIRTWHISTLE**	Sergeant	THOMAS	808338		608 Sqn AAF
08 July 1955	**BISHOP**	Flying Officer	PETER MATILE	205673		600 Sqn RAuxAF
22 March 1992	**BISHOP**	Senior Aircraftman	ANTHONY PAUL	E2640650		2620 Sqn RAuxAF
29 July 1940	**BLACK**	Pilot Officer	BRIAN HENRY	90139		Unknown
25 June 1943	**BLACKIE**	Sergeant	WILLIAM	802586		51 Sqn RAF
18 March 1941	**BLAKE**	Sergeant	FRANK GRENFELL	812264		269 Sqn RAF
11 June 1943	**BLANCH**	Aircraftman 2nd Class	OLIVER JOHN	866300		Unknown
18 August 1940	**BLAND**	Pilot Officer	JOHN WELLBURN	90895		501 Sqn AAF
22 May 1954	**BLOW**	Flight Lieutenant	HAROLD	158577	DFC	616 Sqn RAuxAF
10 January 1943	**BOAK**	Aircraftman 1st Class	RENNIE CHARLES EDWARD	847092		Unknown

Date	Surname	Rank	Name	Number		Unit
23 October 1946	**BODFISH**	Aircraftman 1st Class	BERNARD LUKE	848357		Unknown
27 September 1939	**BOLER**	Aircraftman 2nd Class	ALBERT EDWARD	869258		939 Balloon Sqn
23 May 1941	**BOLLEN**	Sergeant	LEWIS CECIL THEODORE	813019		2 PRU RAF
20 September 1940	**BOND**	Aircraftman 2nd Class	ERNEST JOHN WILLIAM	846519		909 Balloon Sqn
16 November 1943	**BOOTH**	Sergeant	DAVID MORRIS	870803		942/3 Balloon Sqn
30 August 1943	**BOSWELL**	Corporal	FRANK	844142		906 Balloon Sqn
25 November 1940	**BOURNE**	Aircraftman 2nd Class	HENRY FRED	871509		Unknown
13 December 1938	**BOWCOTT**	Leading Aircraftman	CLIFFORD HARTON	813060		501 Sqn AAF
22 November 1944	**BOWDEN**	Leading Aircraftman	PETER	856716		Unknown
08 October 1940	**BOWTELL**	Sergeant	RICHARD THOMAS	805458		Unknown
13 March 1948	**BOYLE**	Flight Lieutenant	RICHARD MALBORNE	120664		504 Sqn RAuxAF
12 January 1941	**BRACHER**	Aircraftman 1st Class	HORACE WALTER	841819		903 Balloon Sqn

Date	Surname	Rank	Names	Number		Unit
02 December 1939	BRADWELL	Aircraftwoman 2nd Class	GLADYS WENDY	884128		941 Balloon Sqn
14 August 1940	BRADY	Flying Officer	BERNARD JOHN RICHARD	90403		615 Sqn AAF
29 April 1946	BRAIN	Leading Aircraftman	CLIFFORD GEORGE	850275		Unknown
11 August 1940	BRANCH	Flying Officer	GUY RAWSTRON	90137	EGM	145 Sqn RAF
17 March 1941	BRAND	Leading Aircraftman	JOHN BASIL	846936		910 Balloon Sqn
13 August 1943	BRANDS	Warrant Officer	FRANCIS WILSON	817042		502 Sqn AAF
01 May 1945	BRAUN	Squadron Leader	ROBERT PERCY	90114		98 Sqn RAF
26 November 1941	BRECKELL	Sergeant	RALPH HOLLESLEY	811144		106 Sqn RAF
28 July 1942	BRECKNELL	Aircraftman 1st Class	LEONARD HAROLD	848393		913 Balloon Sqn
05 August 1944	BRENNEN	Corporal	WILLIAM EDWARD	867113		575 Sqn RAF
06 April 1941	BREWSTER	Flying Officer	JOHN	90995		118 Sqn RAF
31 March 1944	BRICE	Flight Sergeant	ALBERT	811164		158 Sqn RAF
13 February 1954	BRIDGE	Flying Officer	MICHAEL JAMES	2380453		600 Sqn RAuxAF

Date	Surname	Forename(s)	Rank	Number	Unit
14 March 1945	**BRIDGEN**	WILLIAM	Leading Aircraftman	855984	Unknown
03 September 1940	**BROADBENT**	JOSEPH GEORGE	Corporal	861960	930 Balloon Sqn
14 February 1942	**BROADMORE**	JACK ALFRED	Leading Aircraftman	805521	605 Sqn AAF
12 September 1939	**BROCKWAY**	LEONARD THOMAS	Aircraftman 2nd Class	843146	905 Balloon Sqn
05 October 1943	**BROMWICH**	EMERY ESME	Corporal	847310	Unknown
07 June 1944	**BROOKES**	ARCHIBALD	Corporal	869570	974 Balloon Sqn
13 February 1943	**BROUGH**	SIDNEY	Leading Aircraftman	872300	942 Balloon Sqn
17 August 1944	**BROWN**	HERBERT	Sergeant	850186	102 Sqn RAF
30 July 1942	**BROWN**	ROBERT AUGUSTUS	Corporal	816108	502 Sqn AAF
31 May 1943	**BROWN**	FRANCIS FERNEAUX	Leading Aircraftman	849061	Unknown
21 March 1941	**BROWN**	DENYS HUGH	Aircraftman 1st Class	844681	907 Balloon Sqn
22 June 1941	**BROWN**	ELIZABETH	Aircraftwoman 1st Class	884159	Unknown
09 September 1939	**BROWNE**	JOHN MICHAEL GODFREE	Flying Officer	90066	504 Sqn AAF

163

Date	Surname	First Names	Rank	Service No.	Award	Squadron
11 August 1943	BRYAN	ARTHUR	Sergeant	841200		77 Sqn RAF
21 July 1943	BRYAN	GRAHAM HERBERT	Flight Sergeant	805327		Unknown
08 September 1939	BRYDEN	JOHN MARTIN CULLEN	Sergeant	802600		602 Sqn AAF
06 December 1942	BUBB	FRANK LONOY	Corporal	864051		Unknown
04 December 1932	BUCHANAN	JAMES OSMAN	Flying Officer	Unknown		Unknown
02 June 1942	BUCKINGHAM	DONALD WILLIAM ARTHUR	Leading Aircraftman	846296		908/9 Balloon Sqn
24 June 1950	BUGLASS	JAMES ARMOUR	Pilot 3	2685583		607 Sqn RAuxAF
04 August 1955	BUNTING	MATHEW	A/Corporal	1301434		502 Sqn RAuxAF
09 November 1941	BURNHAM	PHYLLIS ANNE	Aircraftwoman 2nd Class	894543		Unknown
12 August 1942	BURRELL	EDWARD FREDERICK	Sergeant	804335		78 Sqn RAF
07 August 1941	BURTON	RONALD LOUVAIN	Flight Sergeant	812221		500 Sqn AAF
22 June 1941	BURTON	HAROLD EDWIN	Corporal	815216		Unknown
29 March 1944	BUSHELL	ROGER JOYCE	Squadron Leader	90120	MiD	92 Sqn RAF
30 December 1947	BUSHELL	FRANK WALTER	Corporal	845004		906/7 Balloon Sqn

21 September 1944	BUTLER	Aircraftman 1st Class	BERTIE	867047	Unknown
15 February 1943	BUTT	Sergeant	THOMAS ALFRED GEORGE	801506	90 Sqn RAF
31 January 1942	BUTTERWORTH	Sergeant	THOMAS ARTHUR	856750	61 Sqn RAF
30 August 1940	BUTTON	Aircraftwoman 1st Class	EDNA LENNA	886553	Unknown
17 December 1943	CAIN	Sergeant	THOMAS EDWARD	856537	100 Sqn RAF
11 April 1940	CALDER	Aircraftwoman 2nd Class	DOROTHY ETHEL	889998	Unknown
06 July 1942	CALLAGHAN	Leading Aircraftwoman	MARGARET	892229	Unknown
24 December 1943	CALVERT	Sergeant	JOSEPH	857444	115 Sqn RAF
22 April 1956	CAMPBELL	Flight Lieutenant	WILLIAM SANDEMAN	1568523	609 Sqn RAuxAF
31 July 1948	CAMPBELL	Pilot 2	JOSIAH	2681060	502 Sqn RAuxAF
18 August 1944	CAMPBELL	Flight Sergeant	IAN	803386	40 Sqn RAF
07 May 1951	CAMPBELL	Sergeant	EDWARD CLINTON	2689068	614 Sqn RAuxAF
17 September 1945	CAMPBELL	Corporal	WILLIAM	873277	Unknown
27 June 1941	CARLILE	Flight Sergeant	SAMUEL SHANNON	816208	102 Sqn RAF

Date	Surname	Rank	Forename	Number	Award	Squadron
27 April 1945	CARLISLE	Corporal	HILDA	892962		Unknown
17 April 1944	CARLOW	Air Commodore Viscount	GEORGE LIONEL SEYMOUR	N/A		600 Sqn AAF
27 March 1945	CARLSON	Corporal	JOHN ARVID	818181		Unknown
25 November 1944	CARLYLE	Sergeant	JAMES CLIFFORD	808181		Unknown
05 February 1943	CARNABY	Flight Lieutenant	WILLIAM FLEMING	90157	DFC	601 Sqn AAF
07 May 1940	CARPENTER	Aircraftwoman 2nd Class	SHEILA URSULA	880889		Unknown
18 June 1941	CARRICK	Leading Aircraftman	DUNCAN	873274		945 Balloon Sqn
26 December 1944	CARRICK	Leading Aircraftman	ROBERT	874113		976 Balloon Sqn
24 August 1950	CARRIE	Squadron Leader	ALLAN LAIRD	84754		2612 Sqn RAuxAF
01 October 1938	CARROLL	Aircraftman 2nd Class	ROBERT	840676		901 Balloon Sqn
20 August 1950	CARTER	Pilot 2	EDWARD ALFRED	2685591		607 Sqn RAuxAF
24 January 1945	CARTWRIGHT	Leading Aircraftman	WILLIAM ERNEST	841596		116 Sqn RAF
29 March 1942	CASSIDY	Leading Aircraftwoman	ETHEL	896633		Unknown

Date	Surname	Rank	Name	Number	Honours	Unit
25 May 1956	CHADWICK	A/Wing Commander	FREDERICK WARWICK	41522	DFC	1 AIU RAuxAF
31 May 1940	CHAMBERS	Flying Officer	GRAHAM LAMBERT	90343		610 Sqn AAF
08 December 1939	CHAMBERS	Aircraftwoman 2nd Class	MADGE WILSON	884655		Unknown
08 November 1941	CHESMAN	Flight Sergeant	GEORGE HALL	808036		7 Sqn RAF
15 January 1945	CHEW	Flight Sergeant	FRANK	810195		235 Sqn RAF
14 June 1958	CHEYNE	Flight Lieutenant	ERIC SHORT	184941		3612 FCU RAuxAF
14 October 1950	CHIPPERFIELD	Pilot 2	EDWARD WILLIAM GEORGE	2680026		500 Sqn RAuxAF
21 April 1940	CHOPE	Pilot Officer	CHRISTOPHER AUGUSTINE	90826		904 Balloon Sqn
12 November 1940	CHOPE	Aircraftman 1st Class	ARTHUR VALENTINE	845095		907 Balloon Sqn
24 November 1943	CHRISTIE	Leading Aircraftman	ROBERT THOMAS	817921		Unknown
27 August 1942	CHURCHILL	Group Captain	WALTER MYERS	90241	DSO DFC	605 Sqn AAF
01 February 1947	CLAPHAM	Sergeant	GLADYS MARY	891633		Unknown
02 July 1942	CLARK	Leading Aircraftman	NORMAN	801812		Unknown

04 January 1943	**CLARKE**	NORMAN LOUIS	813215		173 Sqn RAF
08 November 1941	**CLARKE**	WILLIAM CHARLES	800570		102 Sqn RAF
05 April 1945	**CLARKE**	EDWARD TUCKER	848342		Unknown
18 June 1951	**CLARKSON**	KENNETH PETER HENRY	5004601		600 Sqn RAuxAF
05 May 1941	**CLEGG**	JOHN	855242		921 Balloon Sqn
20 November 1943	**CLEGG**	STANLEY	800655		462 (RAAF) Sqn
21 January 1940	**CLEMSON**	HENRY	819085		615 Sqn AAF
03 January 1941	**COCKS**	DOREEN RITA	894204		Unknown
01 August 1942	**COHEN**	EDWARD CHARLES	840499		Unknown
27 April 1940	**COLEBROOK**	BERTIE ARCHIBALD WALLACE	846872		928 Balloon Sqn
14 August 1940	**COLLARD**	PETER	90402	DFC	615 Sqn AAF
20 March 1943	**COLLIN**	MARJORIE ADA	892026		Unknown
18 May 1942	**COLLINGS**	LESLIE JAMES	847675		Unknown

The rank column (reading with each row): Sergeant; Sergeant; Leading Aircraftman; Sergeant; Corporal; Corporal; Aircraftman 1st Class; Aircraftwoman 1st Class; Sergeant; Leading Aircraftman; Flying Officer; Leading Aircraftwoman; Corporal.

26 September 1943	COLREIN	Corporal	SIDNEY ROBERT	871575	Unknown
14 May 1973	COLVIN	Sergeant	VICTOR HENRY	C2682254	1 MHU RAuxAF
20 November 1941	COMBES	Flight Sergeant	ERIC	808380	38 Sqn RAF
14 September 1942	CONNELLY	Leading Aircraftman	THOMAS	867349	937 Balloon Sqn
19 April 1944	CONNOR	Aircraftman 1st Class	ALBERT EDWARD	855082	Unknown
10 October 1941	COOMBER	Sergeant	RONALD HAROLD	812107	500 Sqn AAF
15 January 1943	COOPER	Corporal	WILLIAM WARREN	842772	949 Balloon Sqn
22 May 1945	COOPER	Leading Aircraftman	BADEN HARRY	850253	914 Balloon Sqn
21 August 1943	CORDEY	Sergeant	LEWIS WOODWARD	813092	Unknown
25 April 1942	CORFE	Warrant Officer	DOUGLAS FREDERICK	810075	229 Sqn RAF
01 September 1940	CORRIGAN	Aircraftman 1st Class	THOMAS EDWARD	808373	608 Sqn AAF
30 July 1945	CORSIE	Warrant Officer	ERIC WILLIAM CLOUSTON	801433	Unknown
05 December 1941	COTTAM	Flying Officer	HUBERT WEATHERBY	77790	607 Sqn AAF

Date	Surname	Rank	First Names	Number		Squadron
25 May 1942	COTTRELL	Aircraftman 1st Class	GORDON	850240		914 Balloon Sqn
10 April 1944	COWELL	Corporal	GEORGE FREDERICK	872406		932 Balloon Sqn
29 October 1940	COWNDEN	Aircraftman 1st Class	ALBERT ERNEST	841926		903 Balloon Sqn
15 April 1942	COX	Sergeant	SAMUEL	869313		214 Sqn RAF
06 January 1941	COYTE	Aircraftman 1st Class	WILLIAM ALFRED	845123		952 Balloon Sqn
28 November 1940	CRAIG	Leading Aircraftman	JOHN EDWIN	867751		938 Balloon Sqn
22 December 1944	CRAIK	Sergeant	ROBERT LAWRIE	803207		Unknown
30 January 1943	CRAVEN	Sergeant	JAMES RICHARD	844256		Unknown
14 February 1948	CRAWFORD	Flying Officer	IVAN KENNETH	115189	DFC	601 Sqn RAuxAF
24 December 1943	CRAWFORD	Sergeant	GEORGE ERNEST	841109		103 Sqn RAF
07 November 1944	CREAN	Corporal	JOHN	803498		BSDU RAF
31 May 1943	CRIDLAND	Wing Commander	JOHN RYAN	90459		Unknown
22 March 1941	CROCKART	Pilot Officer	WILLIAM FINLAY	91231		612 Sqn AAF

Date	Surname	Rank	Forename	Number		Squadron
19 November 1940	CROCKER	Leading Aircraftman	GORDON EDWARD	812067		500 Sqn AAF
12 August 1940	CROKER	Corporal	SYDNEY ALBERT	864272		933 Balloon Sqn
18 August 1940	CROMIE	Flight Lieutenant	ROBERT STEVENSON	90485		615 Sqn AAF
02 June 1940	CROMPTON	Flying Officer	RALPH KENYON	90361		611 Sqn AAF
18 December 1944	CROOK	Flight Lieutenant	DAVID MOORE	90478	DFC	609 Sqn AAF
11 April 1941	CROOKS	Sergeant	JOHN	816150		30 Sqn RAF
30 May 1940	CROOM-JOHNSON	Pilot Officer	OLIVER POWELL	91109		611 Sqn AAF
03 February 1957	CROSSLEY	Flying Officer	JOHN GREENWOOD	2607762		501 Sqn RAuxAF
03 June 1942	CROWTHER	Sergeant	WILLIAM LONGSTER	809173		102 Sqn RAF
12 July 1943	CUMMING	Aircraftman 2nd Class	WILLIAM SEYMOUR	874021		Unknown
28 August 1940	CUNNINGHAM	Flight Lieutenant	JOHN LAURENCE	90194		603 Sqn AAF
20 October 1944	CUNNINGHAM	Sergeant	JOSEPH JOHN	848394		Unknown
16 April 1943	CURTIS	Sergeant	DUNCAN	814139		460 (RAAF) Sqn
11 November 1941	CURTIS	Aircraftman 1st Class	EDWARD JOHN	846369		974 Balloon Sqn

Date	Surname	Rank	Forenames	Number	Award	Squadron
19 October 1942	CURTIS	Aircraftman 1st Class	OLIVER	863404		Unknown
14 May 1940	CUTHBERT	Flying Officer	GERALD IVOR	90133		607 Sqn AAF
30 May 1943	CUTHBERT	Aircraftman 1st Class	WALTER ERNEST	850157		Unknown
21 May 1945	CUTTELL	Corporal	HENRY RICHARD	805094		Unknown
05 July 1942	CUTTER	Sergeant	GEORGE	860457		37 Sqn RAF
03 September 1942	CUTTING	Sergeant	EDWARD JOHN	846953		405 (RCAF) Sqn
01 February 1953	DANIELS	Aircraftman 1st Class	FRANK EDWARD	2680504		2501 Sqn RAuxAF
17 May 1940	DANIELSEN	Flying Officer	PETER JOHN	90248		605 Sqn AAF
30 October 1940	DAVIES	Squadron Leader	ALFRED ERIC	90963		222 Sqn RAF
16 October 1940	DAVIES	Squadron Leader	JOHN ALFRED	90212		604 Sqn AAF
06 June 1945	DAVIES	Squadron Leader	PHILIP EDMUND	90832		Unknown
10 April 1954	DAVIES	Aircraftman 2nd Class	GEOFFREY WILLIAM	2677748		2603 Sqn RAuxAF
06 September 1940	DAVIS	Flight Lieutenant	CARL RAYMOND	90131	DFC	601 Sqn AAF
01 May 1954	DAVIS	Flying Officer	JOCELYN FRANCIS BAVERSTOCK	91372		613 Sqn RAuxAF
29 April 1941	DAVIS	Sergeant	FRANK EDWARD	800559		82 Sqn RAF

Date	Surname	Rank	First Names	Number	Award	Squadron
12 April 1945	DAWE	Corporal	THOMAS HENRY	865060		Unknown
01 June 1940	DAWSON	Flying Officer	JOSEPH	90331		609 Sqn AAF
25 January 1941	DAWSON	Aircraftman 1st Class	GEORGE HENRY	850567	MM	915 Balloon Sqn
31 May 1942	DEAN	Sergeant	JOACHIM CHARLES	812230		150 Sqn RAF
05 March 1947	DEAN	Leading Aircraftman	ALFRED WILLIAM	842903		Unknown
19 March 1944	DEAN	Leading Aircraftman	WILLIAM FREDERICK	843190		904/5 Balloon Sqn
31 July 1946	DELLER	Leading Aircraftwoman	DOROTHY RUBY	889319		964 Balloon Sqn
11 August 1940	DEMETRIADI	Flying Officer	RICHARD STEPHEN	90145		601 Sqn AAF
27 April 1942	DENNY	Flight Lieutenant	BERNARD MORELAND	90993		7 Sqn RAF
17 February 1942	DENTON	Corporal	JAMES WILLIAM	867030		937 Balloon Sqn
06 February 1940	DENTON	Aircraftman 2nd Class	THOMAS	866615		936 Balloon Sqn
18 August 1943	DEUGARD	Sergeant	ROBERT DOUGLAS	864810		619 Sqn RAF
09 May 1943	DEW	Wing Commander	ARCHIBALD HENRY EVERETT	90453		Unknown
31 August 1940	DICKSON	Leading Aircraftman	JOHN ERNEST	803583		603 Sqn AAF

Date	Surname	First Names	Number	Rank	Squadron
06 November 1950	DIVERS	LESLIE PETER	2690050	Aircraftman 2nd Class	3500 FCU RAuxAF
03 June 1940	DIXON	HENRY PETER	90283	Flying Officer	145 Sqn RAF
11 August 1943	DODD	ERIC CHARLES	801585	Corporal	601 Sqn AAF
18 June 1944	DODDS	PERCY	863491	Corporal	901 Balloon Sqn
16 November 1944	DONALD	FREDERICK	864001	Corporal	933 Balloon Sqn
24 April 1947	DONNELLY	JOHN	858934	Aircraftman 1st Class	Unknown
19 August 1943	DONNELLY	CHARLES SWIFT	853679	Aircraftman 2nd Class	Unknown
28 July 1943	DOUGLAS	STANLEY ERNEST ROSS	845654	Sergeant	15 Sqn RAF
31 August 1940	DOULTON	MICHAEL DUKE	90235	Flying Officer	601 Sqn AAF
29 January 1944	DOVE	GEORGE	820031	Flight Sergeant	630 Sqn RAF
23 September 1940	DOWDS	WILLIAM JAMES	816097	Aircraftman 1st Class	614 Sqn AAF
05 September 1943	DOWSON	GEOFFREY GEORGE	847663	Corporal	995 Balloon Sqn
27 December 1944	DRAY	WILLIAM JAMES	841183	Leading Aircraftman	Unknown
21 May 1928	DREW	JAMES PEARSON	Unknown	Pilot Officer	Unknown

Date	Surname	Rank	First Names	Number	Award	Squadron
07 October 1939	**DREW**	Corporal	JOHN FRANCIS	812045		500 Sqn AAF
04 January 1941	**DREW**	Aircraftwoman 1st Class	ETHEL MARY	894681		Unknown
02 September 1942	**DUCKWORTH**	Sergeant	GLADYS	882377		Unknown
16 January 1940	**DUNBAR**	Aircraftman 2nd Class	GEORGE PILLAR WATSON	874780		947 Balloon Sqn
28 November 1940	**DUNDAS**	Flight Lieutenant	JOHN CHARLES	90334	DFC*	609 Sqn AAF
19 July 2007	**DUNSMORE**	Senior Aircraftman	CHRISTOPHER	S2689410		504 Sqn RAuxAF
01 December 1942	**DURK**	Corporal	WILFRID BRAZIER	805454		Unknown
19 January 1958	**DURRANT**	A/Corporal	KENNETH BRIAN	2693594		3619 FCU RAuxAF
15 August 1943	**EARL**	Leading Aircraftman	PHILIP JAMES	843047		2 Sqn RAF
26 June 1943	**EASTHAM**	Corporal	THOMAS CHARLES	862591		Unknown
06 February 1937	**EASY**	Leading Aircraftman	FREDERICK WILLIAM	814016		503 SqN AAF
18 June 1944	**ELDRIDGE**	Corporal	ERNEST ROBERT	840009		901 Balloon Sqn
22 May 1943	**ELGAR**	Squadron Leader	CHARLES ROBINSON	90009		Unknown

Surname	Rank	Forenames	Number	Honours	Squadron	Date
ELGAR	Flying Officer	CHRISTOPHER MAYLAM	91234		500 Sqn AAF	15 August 1941
ELLAMS	Sergeant	THOMAS	858945		Unknown	23 April 1944
ELLIOTT	Pilot Officer	HARRY	2600669		504 Sqn RAuxAF	07 July 1951
EMBLEN	Aircraftman 1st Class	RONALD JAMES	840988		Unknown	05 June 1941
ENGLAND	Wing Commander	RICHARD GEOFFREY	90392	DSO DFC	107 Sqn RAF	22 October 1943
ENGLISH	Pilot Officer	CHARLES EDWARD	77791		605 Sqn AAF	07 October 1940
EVANS	Pilot Officer	HOWARD HUGHES	195753		614 Sqn RAuxAF	17 April 1948
EVANS	Pilot 2	KENNETH JOHN	2687612		610 Sqn RAuxAF	21 May 1950
EVANS	Flight Sergeant	HERBERT WILLIAM	804210		310 (Czech) Sqn RAF	30 July 1941
EVANS	Aircraftman 2nd Class	DAVID	810182		610 Sqn AAF	14 September 1940
EVASON	Leading Aircraftman	CHARLES HERBERT EDWARD	850305		927 Balloon Sqn	25 March 1943
EWIN	Aircraftman 1st Class	HENRY RICHARD	840936		902 Balloon Sqn	06 December 1940
FANCOURT	Leading Aircraftman	ALBERT HENRY	862656		BSDU RAF	06 June 1944
FAULKNER	Sergeant	GEORGE	849211		170 Sqn RAF	29 December 1944

Date	Surname	Forename	Rank	Number	Award	Unit
24 July 1941	FAWKES	JOHN ALBERT	Sergeant	819035		405 Sqn RAF
26 March 1943	FENDER	DAVID RICHARDSON	Leading Aircraftman	867050		937 Balloon Sqn
18 December 1941	FERGUSON	DAVID	Sergeant	803507		15 Sqn RAF
09 February 1943	FINCH	HAROLD JOHN	Corporal	846320	MM	Unknown
09 December 1940	FINNEN	JOHN	Aircraftman 2nd Class	873051		945 Balloon Sqn
06 April 1942	FISHER	WILLIAM ARTHUR	Leading Aircraftman	800615		Unknown
06 April 1941	FITZPATRICK	RONALD	Flight Sergeant	809113		59 Sqn RAF
20 August 1941	FITZPATRICK	JOHN	Aircraftman 1st Class	868044		938 Balloon Sqn
07 March 1945	FITZSIMMONS	FREDERICK	Aircraftman 2nd Class	853628		919 Balloon Sqn
09 March 1941	FLEETWOOD	WILLIAM HENRY	Aircraftman 1st Class	869565		940 Balloon Sqn
14 November 1953	FLETCHER	ARTHUR MICHAEL	Flying Officer	2600580		610 Sqn RAuxAF
25 August 1940	FLETCHER	JOHN GORDON BEWLEY	Sergeant	800635		604 Sqn AAF
03 December 1939	FLETCHER	PERCY	Aircraftman 2nd Class	870969		942 Balloon Sqn

Date	Surname	Rank	First Names	Service No.	Unit
25 August 1942	FOOT	Leading Aircraftman	RODNEY COLLOM	864821	971 Balloon Sqn
11 November 1940	FORD	Warrant Officer	LEONARD ALEXANDER	846347	909 Balloon Sqn
28 August 1941	FORD	Leading Aircraftman	LESLIE ARTHUR	845761	615 Sqn AAF
01 February 1940	FORSTER	Aircraftman 2nd Class	ANTHONY	861128	929 Balloon Sqn
06 February 1937	FORTE	Pilot Officer	MICHAEL PHILIP	Unknown	503 Sqn AAF
06 January 1941	FORTESCUE	Corporal	HENRY ERIC	843166	952 Balloon Sqn
10 December 1944	FOSTER	Corporal	JOHN	871657	945 Balloon Sqn
15 October 1943	FOSTER	Leading Aircraftman	ARTHUR FREDERICK	872388	Unknown
18 October 1940	FOSTER	Aircraftman 1st Class	REGINALD JOHN MARSHALL	819119	615 Sqn AAF
06 September 1943	FOX	Sergeant	TERENCE ROCHFORT	864838	427 (RCAF) Sqn
22 December 1942	FOXLEY	Sergeant	ALBERT CECIL	811126	105 Sqn RAF
17 December 1941	FRADLEY	Sergeant	WILLIAM ARTHUR	90045	Unknown

Date	Surname	Rank	Forename(s)	Number	Award	Unit
17 March 1946	**FRANKLIN**	Leading Aircraftman	CHARLES HAIGH	853790		Unknown
12 May 1940	**FREDMAN**	Flying Officer	LEVIN	90405		615 Sqn AAF
23 November 1940	**FRENCH**	Corporal	RUPERT CHARLES CONNAUGHT	845038		907 Balloon Sqn
12 April 1941	**FRENCH**	Corporal	WILLIAM	859031		917 Balloon Sqn
14 November 1940	**FRIEND**	Sergeant	ARTHUR JAMES WILLIAM	812272		84 Sqn RAF
31 August 1943	**FRIEND**	Corporal	WILLIAM CHARLES HENRY	845843		151 Sqn RAF
05 December 1941	**FRISBY**	Flight Lieutenant	EDWARD MURRAY	90507		504 Sqn AAF
07 December 1944	**FRY**	Flight Sergeant	MARY ELIZABETH	882088		Unknown
31 May 1941	**FURNEY**	Flight Sergeant	GEORGE	816134	DFM	84 Sqn RAF
27 September 1953	**FURNISS**	Pilot Officer	GEORGE	2687094		616 Sqn RAuxAF
12 June 1943	**FURNISS**	Leading Aircraftman	CHARLES ARTHUR	868690		211 Sqn RAF
13 July 1943	**GABB**	Leading Aircraftman	FRANK	849777		84 Sqn RAF
26 September 1942	**GALE**	Corporal	HARRY CHARLES	804302		Unknown
31 July 1944	**GANDY**	Corporal	RICHARD	850285		Unknown

179

Date	Surname	Rank	First Names	Service No	Squadron
23 April 1950	GANT	Pilot 2	RONALD	2681015	502 Sqn RAuxAF
08 August 1941	GARBETT	Flying Officer	LESLIE PERCIVAL	91055	934 Balloon Sqn
14 June 1995	GARDNER	Corporal	MARK CHRISTOPHER	D2631130	2503 Sqn RAuxAF
27 October 1939	GARNETT	Flight Lieutenant	GEOFFREY WHITLEY	90302	608 Sqn AAF
03 September 1942	GASKEN	Sergeant	ROBERT	807051	Unknown
06 May 1945	GATES	Corporal	ALFRED CHARLES	866397	Unknown
15 September 1940	GAUNT	Pilot Officer	GEOFFREY NORMAN	91230	609 Sqn AAF
18 June 1944	GENT	Leading Aircraftman	ERNEST SIDNEY BURRUP	840084	901 Balloon Sqn
18 January 1940	GERRISH	Aircraftman 2nd Class	JOHN WILLIAM	865652	935 Balloon Sqn
07 July 1944	GIBBERSON	Flight Sergeant	FRANK HUBERT	851417	44 Sqn RAF
25 May 1942	GIBBY	Flight Sergeant	JOHN LLEWELLYN	812346	Unknown
22 February 1942	GIBSON	Aircraftman 1st Class	FREDERICK REGINALD FRANCIS	840190	901 Balloon Sqn
16 May 1940	GIFFORD	Squadron Leader	PATRICK	90188	3 Sqn RAF
31 May 1940	GILBERT	Flying Officer	JOHN CHARLES	90327	609 Sqn AAF

Date	Surname	Rank	First Names	Number	Squadron
30 May 1940	GILES	Leading Aircraftman	FRANK HOWARD	812052	500 Sqn AAF
17 April 1942	GILL	Flight Sergeant	HENRY VERDUN	807146	44 Sqn RAF
25 January 1947	GILL	Sergeant	ERNEST ANTHONY	809178	Unknown
15 May 2005	GILL	Senior Aircraftman	BALVINDER SINGH	K8219506	504 Sqn RAuxAF
19 March 1939	GILL	Aircraftman 2nd Class	GEORGE FREDERICK	844759	907 Balloon Sqn
19 March 1941	GILMORE	Sergeant	DANIEL	818024	75 Sqn RAF
03 August 1941	GLADMAN	Aircraftman 1st Class	CHARLES CLIFFORD	842537	Unknown
17 December 1940	GLEESON	Corporal	ARTHUR JOHN	840509	952 Balloon Sqn
29 October 1939	GLOVER	Flying Officer	ALAN OTHO	90286	607 Sqn AAF
23 May 1943	GODDARD	Leading Aircraftman	STANLEY	808390	608 Sqn AAF
18 March 1951	GODSELL	Sergeant	RONALD CLIFFORD CHARLES	2681566	504 Sqn RAuxAF
05 January 1946	GOLIGHTLY	Flight Sergeant	ARNOLD	807147	Unknown
07 November 1944	GOMER	Corporal	WILLIAM HENRY	841392	BSDU RAF

Date	Surname	Forenames	Rank	Number	Award	Unit
27 December 1942	GOOD	JOHN WILLIAM	Aircraftman 1st Class	867139		937 Balloon Sqn
28 May 1944	GOODALL	ALAN FLETCHER	Pilot Officer	91090		420 (RCAF) Sqn
10 December 1946	GOODCHILD	JOAN LUCILLE	Sergeant	895857		Unknown
14 August 1940	GOODWIN	HENRY MACDONALD	Flying Officer	90269		609 Sqn AAF
24 June 1940	GOODWIN	BARRY LAUGHTON	Pilot Officer	90504		605 Sqn AAF
24 January 1956	GOODWIN-TOMKINSON	JOHN JOSEPH	Flying Officer	2695510		3603 FCU RAuxAF
09 January 1942	GOOLD	ROBERT WALLACE GEORGE	Flight Sergeant	818020		90 Sqn RAF
28 September 1940	GORE	WILLIAM ERNEST	Flight Lieutenant	90279	DFC	607 Sqn AAF
15 December 1942	GOSS	HAROLD JOHN	Sergeant	819019		619 Sqn RAF
17 April 1944	GOULDEN	ERNEST OSMUND	Sergeant	842335	MC	Unknown
25 August 1940	GOULDSTONE	RONALD JOSEPH	Sergeant	812360		29 Sqn RAF
28 August 1943	GOURD	ALBERT ERNEST EDWIN	Sergeant	813163		428 (RCAF) Sqn
20 December 1940	GOWERS	ALBERT PENMAN	Corporal	844507		907 Balloon Sqn

Date	Surname	Name	Number	Award	Rank	Squadron
24 March 1940	GRAEME	NIGEL STUART	90254		Flying Officer	607 Sqn AAF
28 May 1944	GRAHAM	ALLAN DELAFIELD	90348		Squadron Leader	Unknown
08 February 1941	GRAHAM	KENNETH ALFRED GEORGE	78737		Flight Lieutenant	600 Sqn AAF
31 March 1943	GRAHAM	GEORGE WILLIAM	808325		Sergeant	95 Sqn RAF
19 February 1946	GRAINGER	ALBERT EDWARD	865548		Aircraftman 1st Class	Unknown
12 August 1940	GRANT	ALBERT EDWARD	861990		Aircraftman 1st Class	930 Balloon Sqn
30 June 1941	GRAY	RAYMOND MARSHALL	808255	DFM	Flight Sergeant	115 Sqn RAF
17 November 1941	GREEN	JOHN JAMES	811075		Sergeant	Unknown
11 February 1941	GREENLEES	RICHARD COOPER	91106		Flying Officer	22 Sqn RAF
18 December 1940	GREIG	ALEXANDER	867836		Aircraftman 1st Class	938 Balloon Sqn
12 November 1940	GREW	LOUIS	844945		Aircraftman 1st Class	907 Balloon Sqn
27 November 1942	GRIEVESON	WILLIAM	866591		Aircraftman 1st Class	Unknown
31 August 1943	GRIFFIN	JAMES RUSSELL	848343		Flight Sergeant	35 Sqn RAF

Date	Surname	Rank	First Names	Number	Squadron
19 November 1943	GRIFFITH	Sergeant	LUCY ELINOR	885519	Unknown
08 May 1948	GRIFFITHS	Flying Officer	ROBERT HUGH PRICE	150160	611 Sqn RAuxAF
28 May 1945	GRIFFITHS	Flight Sergeant	ARTHUR JOHN	859551	Unknown
03 December 1944	GRIGG	Sergeant	HAROLD ERNEST FRANCIS	863337	Unknown
19 February 1942	GRILLS	Corporal	HORACE FRANK	865014	964 Balloon Sqn
23 May 1943	GRIMES	Sergeant	BENJAMIN	808147	608 Sqn AAF
28 March 1942	GRIMMETT	Sergeant	JAMES FREDERICK	805349	7 Sqn RAF
28 August 1929	GROSVENOR	Lord	EDWARD ARTHUR	N/A	601 Sqn AAF
12 February 1943	GUEST	Corporal	ARTHUR ANDREW	851362	916 Balloon Sqn
30 June 1951	GUNTLEY	Leading Aircraftman	HENRY GEORGE	2676313	2603 Sqn RAuxAF
16 March 1945	GWALTER	Flight Sergeant	GORDON EDWARD	847206	61 Sqn RAF
24 August 1942	HAGGER	Flight Sergeant	FRANK	820001	44 Sqn RAF
22 May 1944	HAIGH	Sergeant	ERNEST WALTER	811039	514 Sqn RAF

Date	Surname	Rank	Name	Number		Unit
28 July 1940	HAIGH	Aircraftman 1st Class	JAMES EDWARD	862743		931 Balloon Sqn
27 March 1942	HAILSTONE	Sergeant	KENNETH	820044		138 Sqn RAF
09 February 1945	HALL	Sergeant	JOSEPH WILLIAM	850060		15 Sqn RAF
28 October 1952	HALLETT	Leading Aircraftman	THOMAS	2649517		3511 FCU RAuxAF
01 February 1941	HALLEY	Aircraftwoman 1st Class	EVA MARY CONRY	882967		Unknown
06 January 1941	HALLIDAY	Leading Aircraftman	EDWARD GEOFFREY	840911		952 Balloon Sqn
13 June 1943	HALLOWS	Sergeant	WALTER	858236		102 Sqn RAF
14 May 1941	HAMILTON	Pilot Officer	CLAUDE ERIC	90964	MiD	185 Sqn RAF
14 October 1944	HAMILTON	Leading Aircraftman	WILLIAM CAMPBELL	873206		Unknown
10 July 1941	HAMPTON	Leading Aircraftman	WILLIAM	862716		930 Balloon Sqn
01 October 1939	HANBURY	Pilot Officer	JOHN CHARLES MACKENZIE	90893		615 Sqn AAF
19 March 1951	HANNA	Sergeant	JAMES	2681084		502 Sqn RAuxAF
03 September 1940	HANNA	Sergeant	ROBERT CHARLES	816023		254 Sqn RAF

Date	Surname	Rank	Names	Number		Unit
24 May 1940	HANNAY	Flying Officer	PATRICK CLAUDE	90097		600 Sqn AAF
18 April 1945	HANNETT	Flight Sergeant	JOHN	811087		Unknown
1932/1934	HARDIE	Aircraftman 2nd Class	FREDERICK McDONALD	805302		Unknown
18 January 1941	HARDING	Leading Aircraftman	JACK	853736		919 Balloon Sqn
26 August 1940	HARDY	Corporal	FREDERICK THOMAS	841560		903 Balloon Sqn
11 December 1952	HARLAND	Flight Lieutenant	JOHN WILSON	152618		616 Sqn RAuxAF
13 August 1944	HARLE	Corporal	WILLIAM GEORGE	861869		Unknown
07 November 1944	HARMAN	Warrant Officer	GEORGE STANLEY	848563		RAF
22 October 1941	HARRIS	Sergeant	LEONARD JOSEPH	808394		413 (RCAF) Sqn
08 October 1944	HARRIS	Leading Aircraftman	JOSEPH HERBERT	855895		953 Balloon Sqn
02 July 1941	HARRISON	Flight Sergeant	ANTHONY ROBERT JAMES	812347		149 Sqn RAF
26 March 1942	HARRODINE	Corporal	HENRY WILLIAM	805450		605 Sqn AAF
19 September 1940	HARROLD	Sergeant	ERIC	805497		53 Sqn RAF

08 May 1941	HART	Sergeant	JOHN LEWIS	818222		150 Sqn RAF
08 March 1956	HARVEY	Aircraftman 2nd Class	ARTHUR EDGAR	2603966		3617 FCU RAuxAF
25 November 1951	HARVIE	Leading Aircraftman	WILLIAM	2683129		602 Sqn RAuxAF
09 December 1938	HARWOOD	Aircraftman 2nd Class	DOUGLAS JULIAN	800626		600 Sqn AAF
02 December 1943	HASELDEN	Sergeant	THOMAS	855848		919 Balloon Sqn
04 January 1945	HASSON	Corporal	FREDERICK THOMAS	810002		Unknown
07 December 1941	HATCHWELL	Flight Lieutenant	JOHN BURKE	91002		No 1 PRU RAF
15 August 1942	HATTLEY	Corporal	ARTHUR ERNEST	845039		907 Balloon Sqn
30 August 1943	HATTON	Leading Aircraftman	JAMES	855017		242 Sqn RAF
26 November 1955	HAUSER	Pilot Officer	GRAHAME OTTO	2608819		605 Sqn RAuxAF
17 November 1947	HAVERON	Corporal	DANIEL	816130		Unknown
29 May 1941	HAWKE	Flight Sergeant	STANLEY NELSON	804142		604 Sqn AAF
10 May 1940	HAWKINS	Leading Aircraftman	HERBERT CHARLES WILLIAM	800567		600 Sqn AAF
01 May 1943	HAWLEY	Sergeant	ALBERT	814218		76 Sqn RAF

16 February 1950	HAY	Flight Lieutenant	JAMES GORDON	70286	3510 FCU RAuxAF
09 October 1943	HAY	Warrant Officer	PETER JOHN	817198	431 (RCAF) Sqn
05 February 1940	HAY	Sergeant	STANLEY JOSEPH	812316	Unknown
09 July 1940	HAY-DRUMMOND-HAY	Flying Officer	PETER	90321	609 Sqn AAF
25 September 1939	HAYWOOD	Aircraftman 2nd Class	ERNEST	853845	919 Balloon Sqn
25 May 1940	HEARD	Aircraftwoman 2nd Class	GWENDOLYN MARY	885746	Unknown
06 February 1942	HEAVISIDES	Flight Sergeant	WILLIAM LEONARD	802520	Unknown
22 January 1943	HEESOM	Corporal	JOHN EDWARD STANLEY	856601	922/3 Balloon Sqn
06 January 1943	HEGAN	Leading Aircraftman	ROBERT STANLEY	816245	502 Sqn AAF
14 July 1944	HELLIER	Sergeant	FRANK	863311	150 Sqn RAF
07 May 1941	HESKETH	Corporal	HENRY	855283	Unknown
09 March 1942	HESLOP	Sergeant	JAMES	845752	9 Sqn RAF
04 January 1944	HEWITT	Corporal	ALBERT EDWARD	869290	Unknown

Date	Surname	Forenames	Number	Rank	Unit
08 March 1945	HEWITT	ARTHUR HERBERT	815203	Corporal	Unknown
08 November 1944	HIGGINS	SANDY LEONARD	846785	Corporal	Unknown
22 September 1951	HIGGS	GRAHAM CLIVE	5005404	Leading Aircraftman	2501 Sqn RAuxAF
10 September 1942	HILL	G.A.	819006	Sergeant	61 Sqn RAF
04 January 1941	HILL	ANNIE DOROTHY	886211	Aircraftwoman 1st Class	Unknown
09 December 1940	HILL	JOHN HENRY	841766	Aircraftman 1st Class	903 Balloon Sqn
03 September 1940	HILLCOAT	HARRY BRYAN LILLIE	90256	Flying Officer	15 Sqn RAF
26 February 1943	HINES	ARTHUR VIVIAN DERRICK	804158	Sergeant	90 Sqn RAF
29 June 1953	HINXMAN	DICK	150723	Flying Officer	500 Sqn RAuxAF
05 September 1943	HITCHCOX	EDWARD JAMES	843241	Sergeant	Unknown
19 July 1946	HOBBY	EDITH KATHLEEN	883854	Sergeant	Unknown
24 April 1941	HOCHSTRASSER	ALFRED EMIL	853801	Leading Aircraftman	919 Balloon Sqn
15 July 1942	HODGE	JOHN STEPHEN ARTHUR	812278	Flight Sergeant	159 Sqn RAF

09 December 1939	HODGE	Aircraftman 2nd Class	THOMAS	874806	947 Balloon Sqn
16 August 1943	HODKIN	Corporal	WILLIAM	858933	Unknown
03 January 1944	HOGGARD	Aircraftman 1st Class	JOHN	871725	942/3 Balloon Sqn
28 November 1940	HOHLER	Wing Commander	CRAVEN GORING	90000	Unknown
26 August 1956	HOLDSWORTH	Flying Officer	JOHN OLIVER	2547372	615 Sqn RAuxAF
15 October 1940	HOLLAND	Leading Aircraftman	JOHN JAMES	840423	901 Balloon Sqn
04 February 1942	HOLMAN	Corporal	CYRIL RUSSELL	864902	934 Balloon Sqn
23 January 1941	HOLMES	Flying Officer	ARTHUR PETER BUCKLEY	90038	502 Sqn AAF
26 March 1943	HOLMES	Leading Aircraftman	ARTHUR JOHN	844525	907/8 Balloon Sqn
26 September 1940	HOLMES	Leading Aircraftman	HARRINGTON FRANK	843311	905 Balloon Sqn
26 February 1941	HOLMES	Aircraftman 1st Class	LEONARD HENRY	865135	934 Balloon Sqn
06 January 1951	HOOD	Pilot Officer	THOMAS CHARLES	2689560	615 Sqn RAuxAF

Date	Surname	Rank	First Names	Number	Squadron
26 September 1940	HOOKER	Sergeant	DONALD	812340	114 Sqn RAF
31 January 1941	HOOKINGS	Corporal	ALBERT HENRY JOHN	842777	904 Balloon Sqn
05 July 1941	HOOPER	Leading Aircraftman	STANLEY	808399	200 Sqn RAF
14 October 1940	HOPE	Flying Officer	RALPH	90257	605 Sqn AAF
15 September 1944	HORSFALL	Aircraftwoman 2nd Class	JOAN CHARLOTTE VICTORIA	890847	Unknown
19 September 1944	HORSFIELD	Corporal	ALBERT	872310	953 Balloon Sqn
22 June 1943	HOSKING	Sergeant	ARTHUR LESLIE THOMAS	865141	460 (RAAF) Sqn
02 February 1945	HOWARTH	Sergeant	JOHN	807287	189 Sqn RAF
10 May 1941	HOWELL	Aircraftman 1st Class	ALFRED	846935	Unknown
16 June 1943	HOWIESON	Sergeant	GEORGE	803556	185 Sqn RAF
15 August 1940	HUDSON	Aircraftwoman 2nd Class	MARGUERITE HESTER	882414	500 Sqn AAF
05 October 1941	HUGHES	Sergeant	JOSEPH	874661	Unknown
13 April 1943	HUGHES	Leading Aircraftman	STANLEY ROBERT	801557	Unknown

Date	Surname	Rank	First Names	Number	Award	Squadron
26 June 1941	HULTON	Corporal	ROWENA	888042		Unknown
14 May 1943	HUNT	Leading Aircraftman	THOMAS HAROLD	849827		993 Balloon Sqn
06 February 1941	HUNTER	Flight Lieutenant	ALASTAIR STUART	90222		604 Sqn AAF
01 September 1943	HUTCHINSON	Sergeant	JOHN HENRY	853608		Unknown
31 August 1943	HUXLEY	Sergeant	NORMAN JONES	820050		427 (RCAF) Sqn
28 September 1940	IRVING	Flight Lieutenant	MAURACE MILNE	90277		607 Sqn AAF
12 March 1950	IRVING	Squadron Leader	WILLIAM HERBERT	91236	DFC	614 Sqn RAuxAF
03 September 1939	ISAAC	Pilot Officer	JOHN NOEL LAUGHTON	90721		600 Sqn AAF
10 May 1940	ISAACS	Corporal	LAURENCE DAVID	800520		600 Sqn AAF
30 August 1940	JACKSON	Aircraftman 1st Class	JOHN JOSEPH	810029		610 Sqn AAF
17 November 1941	JAMES	Sergeant	ARTHUR THOMAS	848459		912 Balloon Sqn
04 May 1944	JAMES	Corporal	REGINALD	848460		912 Balloon Sqn
17 December 1941	JAMES	Leading Aircraftman	SAMUEL GEORGE	848537		933 Balloon Sqn

Date	Surname	Rank	First Names	Award	Number	Squadron
24 December 1943	JAMESON	Flight Sergeant	DEREK BELLINGHAM		860478	100 Sqn RAF
08 June 1944	JARVIS	Sergeant	BARRY WENTWORTH		804377	622 Sqn RAF
13 August 1943	JAY	Leading Aircraftman	THOMAS		812137	500 Sqn AAF
12 February 1945	JEANS	Leading Aircraftman	CLEMENT	MM	842271	904 Balloon Sqn
13 February 1949	JEFFREY	Pilot 2	KENNETH ROLAND		2686064	608 Sqn RAuxAF
26 February 1941	JOHNSON	Flight Lieutenant	SIDNEY FREDERICK FARQUHAR		91005	256 Sqn RAF
18 March 1942	JOHNSON	Sergeant	ELEANOR		891600	940 Balloon Sqn
15 August 1943	JOHNSON	Corporal	JAMES SYDNEY		853637	919 Balloon Sqn
28 April 1945	JOHNSON	Corporal	VERA		890975	Unknown
12 July 1943	JOHNSON	Leading Aircraftman	SYDNEY		811151	Unknown
30 July 1944	JOHNSON	Aircraftman 1st Class	WILLIAM		841275	Unknown
22 May 1944	JOHNSTON	Squadron Leader	GEORGE ACHESON BOWEN	MiD	90596	520 Sqn RAF
29 March 1955	JONES	Flight Lieutenant	BOB	DSO	182962	616 Sqn RAuxAF

Date	Surname	First Names	Rank	Number	Unit
13 July 1957	JONES	ROBERT EDWARD	Flight Lieutenant	109635	3611 FCU RAuxAF
12 February 1942	JONES	NORMAN JOHN	Flight Sergeant	818076	408 Sqn RAF
25 February 1944	JONES	PHILLIP LLEWELLYN	Flight Sergeant	865682	61 Sqn RAF
15 May 1943	JONES	WALTER ARNOLD	Flight Sergeant	811070	228 Sqn RAF
14 September 1943	JONES	FREDERICK	Sergeant	842484	115 Sqn RAF
31 May 1942	JONES	HENRY LEOPOLD	Sergeant	874526	9 Sqn RAF
30 October 1945	JORDAN	ALEXANDER	Aircraftman 1st Class	854350	920 Balloon Sqn
31 May 1940	JOYNT	DUDLEY PERSSE	Flight Lieutenant	90322	609 Sqn AAF
08 August 1940	KEAST	FRANCIS JOHN	Sergeant	801399	600 Sqn AAF
28 January 1944	KEEL	ARNOLD THOMAS	Sergeant	850281	115 Sqn RAF
21 July 1942	KEEN	STANLEY ALLAN	Sergeant	844873	35 Sqn RAF
07 November 1953	KEITH	WILLIAM	Sergeant	5004431	500 Sqn RAuxAF
09 May 1944	KEMP	JOSEPH CHARLES	Warrant Officer	805412	35 Sqn RAF
31 December 1944	KENT	SIDNEY	Sergeant	870252	150 Sqn RAF

Date	Surname	Rank	Names	Number	Award	Unit
27 February 1943	KENWRIGHT	Leading Aircraftman	JAMES	856715		Unknown
29 May 1940	KERR	Flying Officer	GERALD MALCOLM THEODORE	90336		610 Sqn AAF
30 November 1940	KERR	Sergeant	JAMES ARCHIBALD	816249		502 Sqn AAF
19 March 1941	KERSHAW	Pilot Officer	ANTHONY	91191		613 Sqn AAF
10 May 1940	KIDD	Corporal	BASIL ARTHUR	800235		600 Sqn AAF
30 June 1945	KIDD	Aircraftman 2nd Class	ERNEST	870215		939 Balloon Sqn
17 February 1959	KILLEN	Senior Aircraftman	THOMAS	2678594		3502 FCU RAuxAF
14 May 1955	KING	Flying Officer	WILLIAM RODNEY STEWART	3120473		3603 FCU RAuxAF
09 May 1941	KING	Corporal	LESLIE	843910		906 Balloon Sqn
06 October 1939	KING	Aircraftman 2nd Class	ALBERT HENRY SHEDDON	842347		904 Balloon Sqn
14 September 1942	KIRK	Flight Sergeant	ELDRED LEONARD	843133		937 Balloon Sqn
22 July 1941	KIRK	Sergeant	THOMAS BRIAN	808416		74 Sqn RAF
01 August 1953	KIRKPATRICK	Flying Officer	PETER ROBERT JOHNSTON	2600605		607 Sqn RAuxAF
11 December 1952	KNEATH	Flight Lieutenant	BARRY	144636	DFC	616 Sqn RAuxAF

Date	Surname	First Names	Rank	Number	Unit
04 November 1957	KNIGHTS	JOHN RICHARD	A/Corporal	2694067	3620 FCU RAuxAF
14 October 1939	KNIGHTS	LESLIE VICTOR	Aircraftman 2nd Class	819059	615 Sqn AAF
26 August 1956	LACEY	WILLIAM MICHAEL	Flying Officer	2455474	615 Sqn RAuxAF
21 May 1943	LAISHLEY	JAMES ERNEST	Corporal	864180	Unknown
08 March 1942	LAMBERT	CHARLES	Sergeant	808244	Unknown
16 April 1941	LANE	JOHN GRAHAM	Flying Officer	91008	252 Sqn RAF
20 March 1943	LAWLEY	HENRY THOMAS HERBERT	Sergeant	813086	100 Sqn RAF
11 May 1941	LAWRENCE	WALTER HAROLD	Corporal	844621	907 Balloon Sqn
18 December 1947	LAWRENCE	WILLIAM NORMAN	Leading Aircraftman	864150	Unknown
09 October 1940	LAWRY	CAROL WINIFRED	Aircraftwoman 1st Class	886111	Unknown
17 August 1942	LAWSON	WILLIAM ALFRED	Sergeant	804306	Unknown
12 March 1944	LAWSON	WILLIAM HENRY	Aircraftman 1st Class	866367	Unknown
04 October 1941	LAXTON	JOSHUA	Corporal	801445	Unknown
12 May 1945	LAYWOOD	ROY LINDSAY	Leading Aircraftman	853001	211 Sqn RAF

Date	Surname	Rank	First Names	Number	Award	Squadron
20 June 1943	LEADBETTER	Leading Aircraftman	CHARLES EDWARD	856046		979 Balloon Sqn
05 October 1943	LEE	Sergeant	REUBEN FREDERICK	804397		434 Sqn RAF
27 May 1940	LEE-STEERE	Flying Officer	CHARLES AUGUSTUS	90129		601 Sqn AAF
27 January 1944	LEIGH-HAY-CLARKE	Flight Lieutenant	DONALD MASSINGBERD	95249		Unknown
27 April 1941	LENNON	Corporal	WILLIAM	855094		921 Balloon Sqn
03 April 1955	LEONARD	Flying Officer	WILLIAM SMITH	2525427		612 Sqn RAuxAF
24 January 1945	LESTER	Leading Aircraftman	GEORGE THOMAS	865023		Unknown
24 October 1939	LEWIS	Flight Lieutenant	REGINALD COPE	90661		918 Balloon Sqn
20 February 1954	LEWIS	Pilot Officer	BRYON JOHN	2531294		604 Sqn RAuxAF
08 July 1941	LEWIS	Flight Sergeant	GEORGE BERTRAM	805396		10 Sqn RAF
21 January 1944	LEWIS	Leading Aircraftman	HAROLD LEONARD	805509		605 Sqn AAF
28 April 1944	LILLEY	Warrant Officer	ROBERT	801556	DFC	141 Sqn RAF
12 June 1943	LITTLE	Wing Commander	JAMES HAWARD	90125	DFC	601 Sqn AAF
02 June 1940	LITTLE	Flying Officer	THOMAS DONALD	90364		611 Sqn AAF
23 January 1944	LIVINGSTON	Flight Sergeant	MATHEW	802523	DFM	161 Sqn RAF

Date	Surname	First Names	Rank	Number	Honours	Squadron
22 June 1940	LLOYD	JOHN RICHARD	Pilot Officer	90569		615 Sqn AAF
19 November 1939	LLOYD	ROBERT WATSON	Aircraftman 2nd Class	841768		Unknown
20 May 1951	LOFTS	KEITH TEMPLE	Squadron Leader	90483	DFC*	604 Sqn RAuxAF
12 July 1947	LOGAN	NORMAN	Sergeant	817018		Unknown
11 June 1950	LOTHIAN	PETER CLARK	Pilot 2	2688089		611 Sqn RAuxAF
25 January 1942	LOW	ROBERT	Flight Sergeant	817273		Unknown
31 August 1941	LUSCOMBE	JACK	Aircraftman 1st Class	864964		934 Balloon Sqn
21 November 1960	LYNAS	THOMAS RODGERS	A/Flight Sergeant	2650786		Ulster MSU RAuxAF
30 December 1940	LYON	CHARLES ERNEST	Leading Aircraftman	814149		616 Sqn AAF
11 February 1941	LYONS	SAUL EDWARD	Corporal	849780		Unknown
19 February 1943	LYSAGHT	PHILIP MICHAEL VAUGHAN	Wing Commander	90385		295 Sqn RAF
07 October 1939	MABEY	DENNIS GUY	Flying Officer	90008		500 Sqn AAF
28 September 1940	MACDONALD	HAROLD KENNEDY	Flight Lieutenant	90193		603 Sqn AAF
25 July 1942	MACDONALD	ALASTAIR HUGH	Sergeant	802508		230 Sqn RAF

Date	Surname	First Names	Rank	Number	Award	Squadron
17 October 1944	MacDONALD	WILLIAM MORRIS	Leading Aircraftman	855066		Unknown
05 March 1941	MACDOUGAL	CHARLES WHITE	Sergeant	811022		261 Sqn RAF
19 December 1943	MACINTYRE	ALEXANDER JOHN	Sergeant	873863		138 Sqn RAF
24 August 1943	MACK	MICHAEL CHARLES XAVIER	Squadron Leader	91224	DFC	35 Sqn RAF
12 June 1940	MACKENZIE	DONALD KENNETH ANDREW	Pilot Officer	90861		603 Sqn AAF
03 January 1941	MACRORY	HARRY IAN	Sergeant	801456		23 Sqn RAF
11 December 1941	MAGUIRE	WILLIAM	Leading Aircraftman	855203		921 Balloon Sqn
05 September 1955	MAINLAND	FRANCIS DOYLE	Flight Lieutenant	91294	MBE	612 Sqn RAuxAF
25 April 1941	MAITLAND	ALEXANDER	Flight Sergeant	817310		612 Sqn AAF
16 January 1947	MALLETT	ARTHUR EDWARD	Aircraftman 1st Class	847248		Unknown
26 June 1944	MANN	RICHARD HENRY	Leading Aircraftman	841284		902/3 Balloon Sqn
28 August 1940	MANTON	EDWARD	Sergeant (Pilot)	810081		610 Sqn AAF
05 May 1944	MARSH	FRANCIS HENRY LEOPOLD	Leading Aircraftman	846618		Unknown

Date	Surname	Rank	Names	Number	Award	Unit
28 July 1943	MARSHALL	Flight Sergeant	JAMES	817011		53 Sqn RAF
05 October 1940	MARSHALL	Sergeant	JAMES DOUGLAS	817236		50 Sqn RAF
29 April 1943	MARSHALL	Sergeant	NORMAN	817293		90 Sqn RAF
04 April 1951	MARSHALL	Leading Aircraftman	ROBERT FRANK	2696023		3603 FCU RAuxAF
23 October 1942	MARSHALL	Aircraftman 1st Class	JOHN	874532		200 Sqn RAF
29 May 1945	MARSHMAN	Aircraftman	HENRY JOHN	865566		Unknown
25 December 1941	MARTIN	Corporal	HELEN PATRICIA	889904		Unknown
17 March 1945	MARTIN	Sergeant	GEORGE EDWARD	840001	DCM MM	Unknown
07 April 1943	MARTIN	Aircraftman 1st Class	WILLIAM HENRY	852819		Unknown
09 October 1945	MARTINDALE	Aircraftman 1st Class	THOMAS ARTHUR	856147		Unknown
07 April 1945	MASON	Corporal	GEORGINA HARCUS	884651	MD	Unknown
19 September 1944	MASON	Leading Aircraftman	SAMUEL	885198		Unknown
31 May 1942	MASSON	Flight Sergeant	EDWARD SAVAGE	817211		12 Sqn RAF
05 April 1941	MATHEWS	Sergeant	JOHN HENRY	810051		50 Sqn RAF

Date	Surname	Rank	First Names	Number	Awards	Squadron
14 December 1958	MATHEWS	Senior Aircraftman	ARTHUR WALTER	2691147		3505 FCU RAuxAF
18 January 1958	MAUDE	Flying Officer	MALCOLM MILTON	2694605		3618 FCU RAuxAF
16 December 1943	MAWSON	Corporal	WILFRED	871786		Unknown
15 May 1943	MAYCOCK	Warrant Officer	EUGENE JAMES	817061		228 Sqn RAF
18 October 1940	MAYO	Aircraftman 2nd Class	AUBREY LESLIE	819009		615 Sqn AAF
13 June 1948	McCAIRNS	Flying Officer	JAMES ATTERBY	91315	DFC**MM	616 Sqn RAuxAF
25 November 1940	McCLINTOCK	Pilot Officer	JOHN ARTHUR PETER	91064		Unknown
19 January 1940	McCLURE	Leading Aircraftman	THOMAS CHRISTOPHER	816021		502 Sqn AAF
22 November 1942	McDERMOTT	Aircraftman 2nd Class	RICHARD	857362		Unknown
01 May 1941	McDONACK	Corporal	JAMES	807154		607 Sqn AAF
15 October 1941	McDONALD	Flight Sergeant	IVOR JOSEPH	818092		40 Sqn RAF
20 June 1945	McINTOSH	Sergeant	ALEXANDER HUGH	819135		Unknown
17 September 1951	McKAY	Pilot Officer	RODERICK	2684054		612 Sqn RAuxAF
01 November 1940	McKELLAR	Squadron Leader	ARCHIBALD ASHMORE	90168	DSO DFC*	605 Sqn AAF

Date	Surname	Forename	Rank	Number	Honours	Unit
01 May 1941	McKENZIE	JAMES BURNETT	Sergeant	817019		612 Sqn AAF
24 April 1945	McKIE	THOMAS	Leading Aircraftman	872318		943 Balloon Sqn
06 April 1943	McLEAN	JOHN	Leading Aircraftman	850161		Unknown
19 December 1941	McLEVY	ALFRED	Sergeant	809126		203 Sqn RAF
13 February 1988	McMILLAN	EUAN BRUCE	A/Flight Lieutenant	2626677L		2 MHU RAuxAF
20 January 1941	McNEIGHT	RUPERT RANDOLPH	Leading Aircraftman	853883		919 Balloon Sqn
03 April 1948	McWILLIAM	HAMISH	Flying Officer	163749		602 Sqn RAuxAF
06 March 1949	MEARS	JOHN MORTON	Flying Officer	141873		603 Sqn RAuxAF
27 May 1940	MEDCALF	ALBERT RUPERT JOHN	Flying Officer	90339		610 Sqn AAF
13 October 1939	MELVIN	HAROLD STEWART	Aircraftman 2nd Class	804282		604 Sqn AAF
10 January 1942	MENNIE	HAMISH	Flight Sergeant	817128		90 Sqn RAF
14 November 1953	MERCER	ANTHONY BASIL	Flight Lieutenant	188288	AFC	610 Sqn RAuxAF
25 October 1942	MERCER	NORMAN ALEXANDER	Flight Sergeant	817193		103 Sqn RAF

Name	Date	Rank	First Name(s)	Number	Award	Squadron
MERRET	10 August 1940	Flying Officer	NORMAN STUART	90381		614 Sqn AAF
MERRITT	16 November 1946	Aircraftman 1st Class	ALFRED WILLIAM	864248		Unknown
MESSENT	13 August 1940	Sergeant	FREDERICK	812073		500 Sqn AAF
METCALFE	03 May 1946	Corporal	KATHLEEN VIVIENNE	895528		Unknown
MEWHA	30 July 1942	Warrant Officer	WILLIAM GEORGE	816190		502 Sqn AAF
MIARA	13 April 1941	Sergeant	SAMUEL	818141		38 Sqn RAF
MIDDLETON	30 December 1941	Squadron Leader	STUART AULDJO	90371	DFC	35 Sqn RAF
MILES	17 April 1941	Corporal	ARTHUR REGINALD	841742		903 Balloon Sqn
MILLBAND	02 October 1942	Sergeant	LEONARD	815171		78 Sqn RAF
MILLER	03 August 1930	Flying Officer	A	Unknown		603 Sqn AAF
MILLER	07 January 1945	Sergeant	THOMAS	873380		170 Sqn RAF
MILNE	25 April 1941	Flight Sergeant	FRANCIS JOHN	817033		612 Sqn AAF
MILNE	17 April 1955	Flying Officer	SAMUEL	2541520		603 Sqn RAuxAF
MINCHER	09 September 1951	Sergeant	HENRY DARRAGH	2686168		608 Sqn RAuxAF
MINSON	25 July 1943	Corporal	JOHN FRANCIS	844532		Unknown

Date	Surname	Rank	Forenames	Number		Unit
11 July 1940	MITCHELL	Pilot Officer	GORDON THOMAS MANNERS	90484		609 Sqn AAF
07 March 1941	MITCHELL	Sergeant	LAWRENCE GEORGE	817187		37 Sqn RAF
13 June 1940	MITCHELL	Sergeant	GEORGE ALFRED	812090		500 Sqn AAF
26 August 1940	MOBERLY	Flying Officer	GEORGE EDWARD	90332		616 Sqn AAF
01 October 1943	MONDAY	Sergeant	NOEL ALBERT	812164		Unknown
15 November 1939	MONROE-HINDS	Pilot Officer	JOHN	90536		92 Sqn RAF
26 June 1944	MOODY	Leading Aircraftman	ERNEST	841049		902 Balloon Sqn
25 October 1943	MOODY	Leading Aircraftman	HORACE PHILIP	862028		Unknown
19 January 1940	MOORBY	Sergeant	HAROLD CHRISTOPHER	816074		502 Sqn AAF
10 May 1940	MOORE	Flying Officer	CHARLES ROGER	90098		600 Sqn AAF
12 October 1942	MOORE	Warrant Officer	WILLIAM NORMAN	816127		502 Sqn AAF
22 July 1944	MOORE	Corporal	JOHN PORTER BARCLAY	807095		607 Sqn AAF
01 May 1944	MOORE	Leading Aircraftman	ERIC	858258		934 Balloon Sqn

Date	Surname	Rank	First Names	Number	Award	Squadron
28 June 1940	MOORE	Aircraftman 1st Class	ROBERT	873758		946 Balloon Sqn
07 December 1947	MORGAN	Pilot Officer	DAVID EDWARD	187267		614 Sqn AAF
03 November 1943	MOSS	Sergeant	ALBERT EDWARD	807289		428 (RCAF) Sqn
26 December 1944	MOYLE	Corporal	WILLIAM WALTER STANLEY	865083		Unknown
13 July 1944	MUIR	Sergeant	MALCOLM	802563		550 Sqn RAF
16 September 1939	MUIR	Aircraftman 2nd Class	JOHN	873061		945 Balloon Sqn
06 November 1940	MUMFORD	Leading Aircraftman	RAYMOND GEORGE	865676		935 Balloon Sqn
24 May 1943	MUNRO	Corporal	JAMES KINLOCH NESS	874674		Unknown
25 April 1953	MUNTZ	Flying Officer	COLIN LEE IRVING	3129265		600 Sqn RAuxAF
25 April 1947	MURPHY	Corporal	JAMES	858139		Unknown
29 May 1943	MURPHY	Leading Aircraftman	JAMES GERARD	855865		919/23 Balloon Sqn
14 May 1940	MURTON-NEALE	Flying Officer	PETER NORMAN	90401		615 Sqn AAF
10 January 1945	MUSPRATT	Aircraftman 1st Class	FREDERICK WILLIAM	858756		Unknown
06 October 1942	MUTTER	Flight Sergeant	LEONARD HARRY	818018	DFM	44 Sqn RAF

31 May 1945	NAPIER	ROBERT	Leading Aircraftman	817109	179 Sqn RAF
13 August 1940	NEALE	WILLIAM	Aircraftman 2nd Class	812304	500 Sqn AAF
09 August 1940	NELSON	WILLIAM	Sergeant	808425	Unknown
08 July 1939	NEWBURY	ERIC WILLIAM	Aircraftman 2nd Class	810944	615 Sqn AAF
16 March 1941	NEWMAN	STANLEY	Sergeant	811173	37 Sqn RAF
24 February 1941	NEWTON	CYRIL HUBERT	Sergeant	812249	500 Sqn AAF
18 January 1945	NICHOLL	JOHN	Corporal	873038	Unknown
18 October 1940	NICHOLLS	SYDNEY THOMAS	Aircraftman 1st Class	819104	615 Sqn AAF
12 November 1940	NICHOLSON	LESLIE	Leading Aircraftman	844631	907 Balloon Sqn
14 April 1944	NIGHTINGALE	LOUIS	Aircraftman 1st Class	855147	Unknown
08 February 1945	NOLAN	WILLIAM JOSEPH	Leading Aircraftman	856576	Unknown
03 April 1941	NORGATE	CHARLES WILLIAM	Leading Aircraftman	871621	943 Balloon Sqn

Date	Surname	Rank	First Names	Number		Unit
28 May 1940	NORRIS	Leading Aircraftman	JOHN LUMLEY	808431		Unknown
13 October 1943	NUNN	Corporal	ARTHUR CLINTON	867088		936 Balloon Sqn
04 December 1949	OATES	Pilot Officer	LESLIE	2685524		607 Sqn RAuxAF
06 August 1942	O'BRIEN	Leading Aircraftman	FRANCIS	855183		921 Balloon Sqn
27 December 1940	OGSTON	Sergeant	DOUGLAS	817057		210 Sqn RAF
27 September 1940	OLDFIELD	Sergeant	TREVOR GUEST	819030		92 Sqn RAF
29 November 1939	OLIVER	Leading Aircraftman	VERNON HENRY	804281		604 Sqn AAF
21 July 1950	OLLIER	Pilot 2	LOUIS	2688577		613 Sqn RAuxAF
20 November 1942	O'RORKE	Sergeant	JAMES LEO	819061		202 Sqn RAF
17 October 1940	ORRISS	Corporal	FRANK	846454		909 Balloon Sqn
02 April 1947	OTTAWAY	Leading Aircraftman	ALFRED WILLIAM	842804		Unknown
18 May 1940	OWEN	Flight Lieutenant	JOHN SAMUEL	90070		504 Sqn AAF
16 January 1947	OWEN	Leading Aircraftman	SAMUEL WALTER	858153		925 Balloon Sqn

28 November 1954	**PALMER**	Pilot Officer	NIGEL GRAEME	2523877		501 Sqn RAuxAF
07 December 1940	**PARISH**	Sergeant	EDWARD FRANCIS	818132		49 Sqn RAF
15 May 1940	**PARNALL**	Squadron Leader	JAMES BOYD	90060		504 Sqn AAF
09 September 1940	**PARNALL**	Pilot Officer	STUART BOYD	90844		607 Sqn AAF
25 September 1940	**PARNALL**	Aircraftman 1st Class	STAFFORD THOMAS	865570		935 Balloon Sqn
05 April 1941	**PARR**	Leading Aircraftman	LESLIE	815257		504 Sqn AAF
11 December 1946	**PARR**	Aircraftman 1st Class	DAVID	870292		Unknown
02 October 1942	**PARSONS**	Squadron Leader	PHILIP TREVOR	90491	MiD	264 Sqn RAF
18 March 1941	**PARSONS**	Sergeant	ALBERT	808419		21 Sqn RAF
21 January 1942	**PASSAGE**	Corporal	HAROLD	811035		Unknown
07 October 1939	**PATERSON**	Pilot Officer	ANDREW MACDONALD	90572		500 Sqn AAF
07 May 1941	**PATTERSON**	Aircraftman 2nd Class	HENRY PITNEY	854403		Unknown
23 September 1951	**PAYNE**	A/Squadron Leader	JOSEPH CHARLES	64378		3513 FCU RAuxAF

Date	Surname	Rank	Name	Number	Honour	Squadron
20 May 1940	PEACOCK	Flight Lieutenant	MICHAEL FITZWILLIAM	90124	DFC	601 Sqn AAF
11 September 1940	PEACOCK	Sergeant	WILLIAM ALBERT	808268		46 Sqn RAF
18 February 1939	PEASE	Pilot Officer	INGRAM EDWARD	Unknown		603 Sqn AAF
18 June 1944	PEDRAZZINI	Sergeant	JOHN CONSTANTINE	847696		901 Balloon Sqn
17 July 1940	PEEL	Flying Officer	CHARLES DAVID	90199		603 Sqn AAF
19 December 1946	PELLATT	Flight Sergeant	ALFRED THORNAMBY	847107		Unknown
11 May 1940	PERCY	Flying Officer	ALISTER CHARLES JOCELYN	90025		501 Sqn AAF
08 May 1947	PERKS	Corporal	JOSEPH HENRY	850572		Unknown
14 February 1942	PERKS	Leading Aircraftman	ALFRED ARTHUR	805493		605 Sqn AAF
27 May 1940	PERRY	Squadron Leader	GEORGE VIVIAN	90263		605 Sqn AAF
13 April 1945	PETTET	Leading Aircraftman	HENRY WILLIAM	850125		Unknown
23 June 1944	PHILLIPS	Sergeant	IVOR LESLIE THOMAS	865127		Unknown
06 November 1943	PHILLIPS	Corporal	IVOR SYDNEY	840330		901 Balloon Sqn
23 February 1942	PHILLIPS	Corporal	WILLIAM JOHN	840963		902 Balloon Sqn

Date	Surname	Rank	First Names	Number	Unit
15 November 1941	PLATTEN	Sergeant	RALPH WILLIAM	846567	115 Sqn RAF
06 January 1941	PLUCKROSE	Aircraftman 1st Class	JOHN ALFRED	845814	Unknown
01 December 1942	POULSON	Sergeant	WILLIAM THOMAS	805342	Unknown
28 April 1941	POWELL	Flight Sergeant	WILLIAM	809129	59 Sqn RAF
27 June 1941	PRATT	Flight Sergeant	ARTHUR	808346	102 Sqn RAF
09 August 1940	PRENTICE	Sergeant	MONTAGUE ADAM	812244	500 Sqn AAF
18 October 1939	PRESCOTT	Flying Officer	EDWARD NEVILLE	90211	604 Sqn AAF
05 August 1940	PRESTON	Aircraftman 1st Class	ALBERT EDWARD	848506	912 Balloon Sqn
22 July 1951	PRICE	Sergeant	THOMAS ARTHUR RIGNOLD	2688178	611 Sqn RAuxAF
03 February 1946	PRIOR	Leading Aircraftman	ALBERT JAMES	841267	902 Balloon Sqn
14 February 1944	PRITCHARD	Leading Aircraftman	PERCY JOHN	849864	927 Balloon Sqn
23 June 1945	PROSSER	Leading Aircraftman	JACK	851402	5016 ACS RAF
08 May 1942	PROTHER	Aircraftman 1st Class	ARTHUR HENRY	856561	923 Balloon Sqn

11 March 1945	PUGH	Aircraftman 1st Class	ERNEST	855856	922 Balloon Sqn
14 December 1940	PULLEN	Aircraftwoman 1st Class	JOAN	889772	Unknown
23 December 1953	PUNSHEON	Corporal	RALPH GOLDEN	2698581	3605 FCU RAuxAF
22 April 1940	PURVIS	Aircraftman 2nd Class	FREDERICK EDMUND COLE	807265	Unknown
04 February 1950	PYNE	Signaller 2	MORRIS ROBERT	2601344	86 RC
22 March 1953	RACE	A/Wing Commander	GEORGE EMERSON	77367	3605 FCU RAuxAF
24 March 1940	RADCLIFFE	Pilot Officer	HARRY PETER JOSEPH	90293	607 Sqn AAF
03 November 1941	RAE	Sergeant	FORBES GRAHAM	817189	612 Sqn AAF
06 November 1944	RAFFAN	Flight Sergeant	ROBERT CHALMERS	817171	Unknown
15 February 1944	RALPH	Flight Sergeant	BASIL WILLIAM	861857	15 Sqn RAF
19 July 1942	RAMSEY	Leading Aircraftman	JOHN	873287	Unknown
09 May 1942	RANCE	Aircraftwoman 1st Class	MARGUERITE ELLEN	892210	Unknown

08 July 1940	RAVEN	Pilot Officer	ARTHUR LIONEL BOULTBEE	91089	610 Sqn AAF
27 September 1940	RAVENHILL	Leading Aircraftman	JOHN WALTER	842476	904 Balloon Sqn
01 August 1942	RAWCLIFFE	Flight Sergeant	PETER WELBURN	814238	156 Sqn RAF
28 May 1945	RAWNSLEY	Sergeant	HERBERT HENRY	809198	Unknown
12 May 1940	RAYNER	Flying Officer	PETER HERBERT	90022	501 Sqn AAF
11 May 1941	REBBECK	Aircraftman 1st Class	JOHN BERTRAM	842019	903 Balloon Sqn
01 November 1947	REDFEARN	Aircraftman 1st Class	HORACE	870149	Unknown
01 November 1943	REED	Leading Aircraftman	ALBERT	859611	957 Balloon Sqn
07 December 1940	REES	Flight Lieutenant	CHARLES WILLIAM	90050	502 Sqn AAF
12 November 1940	REEVES	Aircraftman 1st Class	FRANCIS CHARLES	844716	907 Balloon Sqn
18 December 1942	REGAN	Flight Sergeant	FRANK RICHARD	812251	205 Sqn RAF
31 July 1947	REID	Flying Officer	ROBERT IVOR	91253	602 Sqn AAF
02 November 1945	REID	Corporal	JAMES N	859703	Unknown
21 March 1945	REID	Aircraftman 1st Class	WALTER	874775	Unknown

Date	Surname	Rank	Forename(s)	Number	Award	Unit
12 June 1943	RELPH	Sergeant	HENRY CHARLES	861885		15 Sqn RAF
08 February 1943	REVELL	Corporal	CHARLES WILLIAM	845076		Unknown
17 June 1951	REXWORTHY	Aircraftman 2nd Class	RONALD	2694586		3507 FCU RAuxAF
11 August 1943	REYNOLDS	Flight Sergeant	ALBERT EDWIN	801547		601 Sqn AAF
14 July 1943	REYNOLDS	Leading Aircraftman	HENRY JAMES	805425		Unknown
06 September 1940	RHODES-MOORHOUSE	Flight Lieutenant	WILLIAM HENRY	90140	DFC	601 Sqn AAF
21 January 1940	RICHARDS	Aircraftman 2nd Class	JOSEPH	850654		915 Balloon Sqn
28 January 1944	RINGWOOD	Sergeant	JACK	843261	DFM	625 Sqn RAF
03 July 1942	RITCHIE	Flight Sergeant	ROBERT HENDRY	817140		214 Sqn RAF
25 June 1942	RIXON	Sergeant	WILLIAM PERCY	818034		Unknown
16 December 1940	ROBERTS	Sergeant	DENZIEL SYDNEY	818085		149 Sqn RAF
16 September 1942	ROBERTS	Sergeant	JOHN ROBERT	811009		106 Sqn RAF
18 October 1939	ROBERTS	Leading Aircraftman	ALBERT	804276		604 Sqn AAF
14 November 1940	ROBERTS	Aircraftman 1st Class	THOMAS	852043		917 Balloon Sqn

Date	Surname	Rank	First Names	Number	Squadron
17 September 1951	ROBERTSON	Pilot Officer	DOUGLAS	2684061	612 Sqn RAuxAF
18 September 1954	ROBINSON	Flight Lieutenant	RICHARD JAMES	162945	610 Sqn RAuxAF
12 May 1941	ROBINSON	Flying Officer	JAMES	91041	221 Sqn RAF
18 March 1941	ROBINSON	Sergeant	THOMAS	816103	Unknown
14 June 1943	ROBINSON	Corporal	ERNEST STANLEY	850299	914 Balloon Sqn
05 February 1942	ROBINSON	Leading Aircraftman	ALEXANDER DEY	817180	249 Sqn RAF
12 August 1940	ROBINSON	Aircraftman 1st Class	ARTHUR EDWARD TURNER	840221	928 Balloon Sqn
19 January 1952	ROBSON	Pilot Officer	ALAN	3123317	612 Sqn RAuxAF
26 December 1949	ROCHE	Flying Officer	ANTHONY GEORGE	199330	3512 FCU RAuxAF
29 November 1939	ROCKINGHAM	Aircraftwoman 2nd Class	YVONNE	885756	Unknown
22 May 1953	RODGERS	Sergeant	ARTHUR	2688634	613 Sqn RAuxAF
21 February 1948	ROGERS	Flying Officer	NORMAN BERNARD	91279	501 Sqn RAuxAF
22 November 1943	ROGERS	Flight Sergeant	SAMUEL PHILLIP	818036	10 Sqn RAF
19 March 1941	ROGERS	Aircraftman 2nd Class	STANLEY WALTER	847201	910 Balloon Sqn

Date	Surname	Forename(s)	Rank	Number	Award	Squadron
29 January 1944	**ROLLINSON**	JOHN DUDLEY	Wing Commander	90391	DFC	630 Sqn RAF
02 December 1945	**ROLLISON**	FRANK LEONARD	Corporal	841948		Unknown
07 March 1940	**RONALD**	JAMES	Aircraftman 1st Class	874509		950 Balloon Sqn
13 March 1948	**ROOK**	MICHAEL	Flight Lieutenant	90077	DFC	504 Sqn RAuxAF
06 June 1945	**ROOK**	ARTHUR REGINALD	Leading Aircraftman	863301		5001 ACS RAF
29 June 1953	**ROOKE**	JAMES GARTH	Pilot Officer	2455334		500 Sqn RAuxAF
11 September 1939	**ROSE**	ANTHONY ST CROIX	Pilot Officer	90719		615 Sqn AAF
14 November 1939	**ROSS**	WILLIAM RONALD	Pilot Officer	90913		604 Sqn AAF
15 February 1943	**ROSS**	ELIZABETH	Leading Aircraftwoman	894394		Unknown
04 January 1943	**ROSS**	ALFRED WILLIAM STANNING	Aircraftman 1st Class	800679		Unknown
10 February 1940	**ROUT**	GEORGE ERIC HIRST	Aircraftman 1st Class	868830		939 Balloon Sqn
28 June 1942	**ROWLAND**	SIDNEY BERTRAM	Sergeant	819083		405 Sqn RAF
06 November 1939	**RUSE**	JOHN	Aircraftman 2nd Class	858971		926 Balloon Sqn

Date	Surname	Rank	Forename	Number	Award	Squadron
05 September 1940	RUSHMER	Flight Lieutenant	FREDERICK WILLIAM	90192	MiD	603 Sqn AAF
16 November 1944	RUSSELL	Sergeant	PHILIP CHARLES	842512		207 Sqn RAF
11 August 1943	RUSSELL	Corporal	WILLIAM JAMES	801576		601 Sqn AAF
01 December 1942	RUSSON	Leading Aircraftman	ARTHUR FREDERICK	805512		605 Sqn AAF
27 June 1941	RUTTERFORD	Flight Sergeant	BRIAN ARTHUR	809200		12 Sqn RAF
24 August 1940	SADLER	Pilot Officer	DAVID ALEXANDER	90937		Unknown
28 October 1941	SAMPLE	Squadron Leader	JOHN	90278	DFC	607 Sqn AAF
18 June 1951	SANDEMAN	Flying Officer	PHILIP VICTOR GLAS	131911		600 Sqn RAuxAF
19 November 1940	SANDERSON	Flying Officer	LESLIE ERNEST	90014		500 Sqn AAF
12 November 1940	SANDS	Leading Aircraftman	JAMES ROBERT MERTON	844529		907 Balloon Sqn
14 April 1943	SAYERS	Sergeant	FRANK GORDON	814160		12 Sqn RAF
08 November 1941	SCOTT	Wing Commander	DOUGLAS REGINALD	90246	AFC	616 Sqn AAF
05 November 1940	SCOTT	Squadron Leader	ALAN MILNE	90369	AFC	612 Sqn AAF

Date	Surname	Rank	Names	Service No	AFC	Squadron
08 November 1941	SCOTT	Squadron Leader	DOUGLAS REGINALD	90246	AFC	605 Sqn AAF
19 November 1957	SCOTT	Squadron Leader	JOHN HAY	136060		3603 FCU RAuxAF
19 August 1942	SCOTT	Flying Officer	ALFRED ENOCH	117308		504 Sqn AAF
06 October 1939	SCOTT	Pilot Officer	JOHN	90612		608 Sqn AAF
12 September 1941	SCOTT	Leading Aircraftman	REGINALD WALTER	813106		Unknown
28 September 1941	SCRASE	Squadron Leader	GEORGE EDWARD THOMAS	90675		600 Sqn AAF
17 September 1942	SEALS	Sergeant	FREDERICK KENNETH ARTHUR	814230		15 OTU RAF
10 May 1943	SEELY	Squadron Leader	NIGEL RICHARD WILLIAM	90150		Unknown
01 November 1944	SEILER	Sergeant	FREDERICK MAURICE	863360		44 Sqn RAF
01 February 1947	SELWAY	Corporal	STEPHEN	843887		906 Balloon Sqn
03 March 1947	SEVER	Leading Aircraftman	EDWARD	870910		Unknown
07 June 1943	SHAW	Sergeant	HENRY DOUGLAS GERALD	812088		209 Sqn RAF

Surname	First names	Rank	Date	Service number	Unit
SHEARER	ROBERT	Sergeant	18 December 1941	873227	15 Sqn RAF
SHEPHERD	FREDERICK ERNEST RICHARD	Sergeant	11 September 1940	811129	611 Sqn AAF
SHEPPARD	D'ARCY HERBERT	Corporal	22 July 1945	819050	615 Sqn AAF
SHERIFF	CHARLES WILLIAM	Aircraftman 1st Class	17 April 1947	870849	944 Balloon Sqn
SHEWELL	JOHN MORLAND	Wing Commander	25 August 1942	90191	7 Sqn RAF
SHIELLS	JOHN TEMPLE LYELL	Pilot Officer	07 July 1928	Unknown	603 Sqn AAF
SHINTON	HERBERT JAMES	Aircraftman 2nd Class	16 December 1939	849216	913 Balloon Sqn
SHIRLEY	SIDNEY HARRY JAMES	Flight Sergeant	24 July 1941	804422	35 Sqn RAF
SIEBERT	HORACE FRANCIS	Flight Sergeant	29 June 1944	844040	5011 ACS RAF
SIM	JOHN HART	Corporal	29 November 1943	803509	Unknown
SIMPKIN	ALBERT HENRY	Sergeant	27 September 1943	848625	50 Sqn RAF
SIMPSON	JOSEPH	Flight Sergeant	19 May 1942	844669	Unknown
SKENE	DONALD	Sergeant	10 April 1941	817099	106 Sqn RAF
SKINNER	STANLEY HEWITT	Wing Commander	19 August 1942	90210	HQ Coastal Command

21 September 1945	**SKIPSEY**	Leading Aircraftman	HARRY	808409	608 Sqn AAF
09 April 1941	**SLADE**	Leading Aircraftman	ALFRED GEORGE	851462	916 Balloon Sqn
14 December 1942	**SLATER**	Leading Aircraftman	THOMAS	858845	980 Balloon Sqn
20 November 1944	**SLOCOMBE**	Sergeant	LEONARD	860307	514 Sqn RAF
25 July 1940	**SMITH**	Squadron Leader	ANDREW THOMAS	90337	610 Sqn AAF
15 May 1940	**SMITH**	Squadron Leader	LAUNCELOT EUSTACE	90273	607 Sqn AAF
12 May 1940	**SMITH**	Flying Officer	MICHAEL FAUCONBERGE CLIFFORD	90026	501 Sqn AAF
03 July 1953	**SMITH**	Sergeant	ALAN ALFRED	2687105	616 Sqn RAuxAF
10 December 1942	**SMITH**	Sergeant	ERIC WILLIAM	841279	931 Balloon Sqn
22 June 1944	**SMITH**	Sergeant	FOSTER NELSON	817196	467 (RAAF) Sqn
29 February 1944	**SMITH**	Sergeant	GEORGE WILLIAM	818186	Unknown
11 February 1941	**SMITH**	Sergeant	LESLIE WILLIAM	818148	Unknown
14 August 1940	**SMITH**	Corporal	ROBERT WHITTELL	809010	609 Sqn AAF

Date	Surname	Rank	Forename(s)	Number	Award	Unit
05 October 1940	SMITH	Corporal	WILLIAM JAMES	849877		914 Balloon Sqn
08 April 1947	SMITH	Leading Aircraftman	COLIN GEORGE	870158		940 Balloon Sqn
01 July 1941	SMITH	Aircraftman 1st Class	JAMES	871501		Unknown
18 December 1939	SMITH	Aircraftman 2nd Class	STANLEY CLARENCE	861137		929 Balloon Sqn
11 September 1949	SMITH	Aircraftman 2nd Class	VICTOR ROY JOHN	2676066		2501 Sqn RAuxAF
05 June 1940	SMITH	Aircraftman 2nd Class	WILLIAM JOSEPH	812204		500 Sqn AAF
12 July 1941	SMITHER	Sergeant	ALLAN RALPH	800665		600 Sqn AAF
11 August 1940	SMITHERS	Pilot Officer	JULIAN LANGLEY	90540		601 Sqn AAF
08 September 1947	SMYTH	Leading Aircraftman	MICHAEL	855160		Unknown
07 September 1941	SMYTHE	Sergeant	JOSEPH HUNTER	816010		58 Sqn RAF
13 October 2007	SOUTAR	Senior Aircraftwoman	SUSAN BEVERLEY	K2689011		603 Sqn RAuxAF
12 May 1939	SPANTON	Flying Officer	JOHN FYRLEY	Unknown		500 Sqn AAF
26 July 1941	SPEKE	Flight Lieutenant	HUGH	90223	DFC	604 Sqn AAF
27 May 1943	ST AUBYN	Squadron Leader	EDWARD FITZROY	90055		170 Sqn RAF

Date	Surname	Rank	First Names	Number	Unit
11 May 1941	STAFFORD	Leading Aircraftman	WILLIAM	844793	907 Balloon Sqn
04 July 1943	STANBURY	Aircraftman 1st Class	THOMAS	841799	Unknown
25 April 1942	STANLEY	Wing Commander	MERVYN JOHN CAMERON	90035	RAF Ferry Command
13 March 1941	STANNARD	Pilot Officer	LIONEL EDWARD	90748	50 Sqn RAF
26 March 1938	STARRETT	Aircraftman 2nd Class	R H	Unknown	603 Sqn AAF
26 March 1941	STEELE	Sergeant	LESLIE FERGUSON	817001	612 Sqn AAF
10 March 1944	STEVENS	Corporal	MARY EMILY	893468	Unknown
31 May 1942	STEWART	Flight Sergeant	CHARLES NOEL DOUGLAS	800061	9 Sqn RAF
21 June 1941	STEWART	Sergeant	JOHN CAMPBELL	801590	99 Sqn RAF
01 July 1937	STONE	Corporal	ALBERT ARTHUR FRY	354317	Unknown
10 October 1940	STONE	Corporal	ALEC BERTIE	844066	906 Balloon Sqn
11 February 1946	STONE	Leading Aircraftman	EDWARD	868670	Unknown
18 July 1938	STONE	Aircraftman 2nd Class	THOMAS GEORGE	840017	901 Balloon Sqn

Date	Surname	Rank	First Names	Number	Award	Squadron
27 October 1941	STRICKLAND	Flying Officer	CLAUDE DOBREE	91220		615 Sqn AAF
28 November 1944	SUGDEN	Leading Aircraftman	ERNEST	872425		Unknown
18 October 1940	SUMMERFIELD	Aircraftman 2nd Class	ALEC ALFRED	819151		615 Sqn AAF
23 July 1941	SUTTON	Flying Officer	JAMES RONALD GABERT	90758		611 Sqn AAF
05 October 1940	SUTTON	Pilot Officer	NORMAN	84033		72 Sqn RAF
28 June 1940	SWAINSTON	Pilot Officer	ALAN	90610		500 Sqn AAF
17 May 1941	SWANSTON	Leading Aircraftman	JAMES NICHOLSON	803465		Unknown
20 July 1940	SYLVESTER	Pilot Officer	EDMUND JOHN HILARY	90556	DFC	501 Sqn AAF
03 January 1941	SYNNUCK	Aircraftman 1st Class	GILBERT FRANCIS	859653		927 Balloon Sqn
19 August 1940	TANNER	Leading Aircraftman	WILLIAM JOHN	819076		615 Sqn AAF
14 June 1943	TASKER	Leading Aircraftman	JOHN NORMAN	805411		605 Sqn AAF
15 January 1942	TAYLOR	Sergeant	HERBERT KENNETH	804258		10 Sqn RAF
26 November 1940	TAYLOR	Sergeant	RONALD HENRY WILLIAM	804401		604 Sqn AAF

11 December 1944	TAYLOR	VINCENT NELSON	Sergeant	818137	57 Sqn RAF
21 August 1946	TAYLOR	FREDERICK WILLIAM	Corporal	841555	Unknown
03 November 1942	TAYLOR	PRISCILLA	Leading Aircraftwoman	897210	Unknown
01 June 1943	TAYLOR	JACK	Aircraftman 1st Class	858990	211 Sqn RAF
15 October 1940	TEDEN	DEREK EDMUND	Pilot Officer	90486	206 Sqn RAF
13 August 1941	TEMPLE	HERBERT EDWARD	Sergeant	800532	9 Sqn RAF
19 August 1941	TENNENT	ALEXANDER LINN STORIE	Leading Aircraftman	840591	Unknown
27 August 1940	TERRY	ARTHUR WILLIAM	Sergeant	801454	26 Sqn RAF
20 November 1940	THIRD	HUGH WILLIAM	Sergeant	802490	149 Sqn RAF
08 April 1941	THOMAS	CLAUDE PERCIVAL	Sergeant	818179	61 Sqn RAF
23 January 1945	THOMAS	WILLIAM	Corporal	861962	Unknown
03 October 1938	THOMAS	IVOR JAMES	Aircraftman 2nd Class	813203	501 Sqn AAF
08 June 1943	THOMASON	THOMAS	Leading Aircraftman	855879	Unknown

Date	Surname	Rank	Forename(s)	Number	Squadron
13 May 1940	THOMPSON	Flying Officer	MONTAGU HENRY BRODRICK	90287	607 Sqn AAF
20 September 1942	THOMPSON	Sergeant	THOMAS	807161	61 Sqn RAF
13 April 2008	THOMPSON	Senior Aircraftman	GARY	C9108797	504 Sqn RAuxAF
26 March 1945	THOMPSON	Leading Aircraftman	STEPHEN THOMAS	816056	Unknown
26 March 1938	THOMSON	Flying Officer	C.A.G.	Unknown	603 Sqn AAF
28 July 1951	THOMSON	Flight Sergeant	JAMES McDONALD	2684168	612 Sqn RAuxAF
14 August 1940	THORLEY	Leading Aircraftman	HARRY	809035	609 Sqn AAF
15 July 1943	THORNE	Flight Sergeant	ERIC JOHN	850080	139 Sqn RAF
16 May 1940	THORNLEY	Flight Lieutenant	LESLIE THOMAS WING	90398	615 Sqn AAF
09 August 1941	THOROGOOD	Aircraftwoman 1st Class	PEGGY EILEEN	884820	Unknown
17 November 1941	THRESHIE	Aircraftwoman 2nd Class	KATHLEEN MAY	882841	Unknown
11 December 1941	THURGET	Sergeant	FREDERICK WILLIAM	804398	141 Sqn RAF
07 October 1945	TIMMS	Sergeant	HILDA VICTORIA	883422	Unknown

Date	Surname	Rank	Forenames	Number	Honours	Unit
21 May 1952	TINKER	Sergeant	DAVID HERAPATH	5005203		613 Sqn RAuxAF
24 February 1943	TIPLADY	Leading Aircraftman	WILLIAM	866587		Unknown
08 March 1940	TOBIN	Aircraftman 2nd Class	ALFRED EDWARD RAYMOND	863477		Unknown
21 May 1944	TOMKINSON	Sergeant	ARTHUR	856024		5014 ACS RAF
27 January 1944	TOMKINSON	Sergeant	CLAUDE VERNON	811121		Unknown
29 November 1943	TOOTH	Leading Aircraftman	CYRIL GEOFFREY	805530		605 Sqn AAF
29 March 1953	TOPPING	Flying Officer	JOHN ELGIN	91384		615 Sqn RAuxAF
10 April 1948	TOUCH	Flight Lieutenant	DONALD FRANK	91311	AFC	504 Sqn RAuxAF
17 August 1942	TOUTT	Leading Aircraftman	FRANK WILLIAM	859668		979 Balloon Sqn
31 August 1941	TOWLE	Aircraftman 1st Class	HEDLEY	872451		943 Balloon Sqn
12 November 1940	TOWNSHEND	Flight Sergeant	CHARLES SAMUEL	844509	DCM	907 Balloon Sqn
16 November 1953	TOWNSON	A/Wing Commander	WILLIAM	37072		3613 FCU RAuxAF
15 March 1942	TRACEY	Leading Aircraftman	IVY THERESE	895505		Unknown
20 May 1941	TRACY	Flight Sergeant	HAROLD MERVYN	844976		959 Balloon Sqn

Date	Surname	Rank	Forenames	Service No	Unit
17 June 1940	**TRAHEARN**	Leading Aircraftman	HENRY CORNELIUS	805215	73 Sqn RAF
03 May 1941	**TRIPP**	Pilot Officer	HUGH UPTON HOWARD	91069	44 Sqn RAF
25 November 1940	**TRURAN**	Pilot Officer	ANTHONY JOHN JAMIESON	91019	615 Sqn AAF
30 April 1951	**TUBB**	Flying Officer	WILLIAM ERIC	180390	500 Sqn RAuxAF
12 July 1942	**TURNER**	Leading Aircraftman	SIDNEY JOHN	844830	907 Balloon Sqn
30 December 1944	**TUTILL**	Flight Sergeant	JOHN WILLIAM	808316	156 Sqn RAF
10 April 1943	**TUTT**	Sergeant	NORMAN PERCY	812184	9 Sqn RAF
03 April 1942	**UNDERWOOD**	Leading Aircraftman	RUSSELL EDWIN	843175	Unknown
07 December 1940	**UPHAM**	Aircraftman 1st Class	STANLEY CHARLES	865247	964 Balloon Sqn
04 May 1941	**VANES**	Leading Aircraftman	JOHN	861187	929 Balloon Sqn
11 December 1940	**VAUGHAN**	Aircraftman 1st Class	CUTHBERT CYRIL	840962	902 Balloon Sqn
30 August 1940	**VEAL**	Aircraftman 2nd Class	EDWARD THOMAS	813038	Unknown
15 August 1951	**VEITCH**	Flying Officer	DAWYCK GEORGE McLEOD	178711	504 Sqn RAuxAF

VENNING	Senior Aircraftman	ANDREW PAUL	B8403515S		600 Sqn AAF
VICKERS	Flying Officer	ALBERT ANTHONY	90084		600 Sqn AAF
VILLIERS	Pilot Officer	GEORGE ERNEST	Unknown		Unknown
WALES	Squadron Leader	JACK BERTRAM	44516	OBE DFC TD	613 Sqn RAuxAF
WALKER	Flight Sergeant	CHARLES ALEXANDER	875132		260 Sqn RAF
WALKER	Sergeant	ALFRED LIONEL DAVID	2680093		500 Sqn RAuxAF
WALKER	Corporal	JOSEPH	863295		932 Balloon Sqn
WALLEY	Sergeant	PETER KENNETH	819018		615 Sqn AAF
WARD	Leading Aircraftman	ALBERT EDWARD	840231		901 Balloon Sqn
WARD	Aircraftman 2nd Class	MICHAEL JAMES	873302		945 Balloon Sqn
WARD-PURKIS	Aircraftman 1st Class	ERNEST EDWARD	846373		952 Balloon Sqn
WARNER	Flight Lieutenant	WILLIAM HENRY CROMWELL	90344		610 Sqn AAF
WARREN	Flying Officer	JOHN HENRY	90253		605 Sqn AAF
21 August 2017					
16 November 1939					
07 June 1930					
07 December 1956					
26 November 1944					
24 February 1952					
02 December 1941					
18 August 1940					
17 September 1940					
14 June 1940					
17 December 1940					
16 August 1940					
19 September 1939					

09 March 1943	**WARREN**	Sergeant	RICHARD HALL	842606	207 Sqn RAF
05 March 1941	**WARREN-SMITH**	Aircraftwoman 2nd Class	LILIAN KATE	896583	Unknown
13 October 1939	**WARRY**	Aircraftman 2nd Class	JACK	804336	604 Sqn AAF
13 August 1940	**WATCHOUS**	Aircraftman 1st Class	LESLIE AUSTEN	812240	500 Sqn AAF
14 December 1944	**WATERMAN**	Corporal	JOHN HERBERT	863254	932 Balloon Sqn
17 January 1941	**WATERS**	Aircraftman 1st Class	CYRIL HENRY	865245	927 Balloon Sqn
31 August 1940	**WATERSTON**	Flying Officer	ROBIN McGREGOR	90197	603 Sqn AAF
06 September 1943	**WATLING**	Sergeant	FREDERICK	840146	76 Sqn RAF
03 November 1941	**WATSON**	Sergeant	JOHN HENRY	817073	612 Sqn AAF
14 March 1945	**WATSON**	Corporal	WILLIAM	803608	603 Sqn AAF
02 March 1941	**WATSON**	Leading Aircraftman	ROBERT LAUGHLAN	873026	945 Balloon Sqn
05 May 1943	**WATSON**	Aircraftman 1st Class	FRANK DEAMAN	846871	Unknown

Date	Surname	Forename	Rank	Service Number	Honours	Squadron
13 December 1941	WATSON	CHARLES WALTER	Aircraftman 2nd Class	868030		Unknown
25 April 1941	WATT	CHARLES CHAMBERLIN MacCULLOCH	Flying Officer	90546		612 Sqn AAF
25 February 1941	WATT	DAVID GEORGE	Sergeant	844595		103 Sqn RAF
19 April 1942	WATTEN	EDWIN	Corporal	871673		Unknown
27 August 1944	WATTS	DOUGLAS HAIG	Flight Sergeant	815235		44 Sqn RAF
16 May 1942	WEAVER	THOMAS	Leading Aircraftman	860303		Unknown
02 May 1945	WEBB	GEORGE FRANCIS HERBERT	Wing Commander	90987	DFC & BAR	181 Sqn RAF
17 February 1942	WEBB	GEORGE FRANCIS	Flight Sergeant	812243		500 Sqn AAF
20 March 1941	WEBB	JAMES SAMUEL	Aircraftman 1st Class	841347		902 Balloon Sqn
20 September 1940	WEBB	WALTER ERNEST	Aircraftman 1st Class	846574		909 Balloon Sqn
21 February 1954	WEBSTER	RONALD	Pilot Officer	3135026		608 Sqn RAuxAF
10 May 1941	WEDDLE	GEORGE	Corporal	808250		Unknown
08 April 1943	WEEDON	ALBERT CHARLES HENRY	Corporal	856015		185 Sqn RAF

Date	Surname	Rank	First Names	Number	Unit
05 October 1937	WEEKS	Flight Lieutenant	REGINALD VICTOR	Unknown	Unknown
26 June 1942	WEIGHTMAN	Sergeant	WILLIAM	866405	Unknown
10 May 1940	WELLS	Squadron Leader	JAMES MICHAEL	90081	600 Sqn AAF
05 April 1947	WELLS	Corporal	ALFRED	855279	Unknown
06 May 1945	WELSBY	Leading Aircraftman	WINDSOR JAMES	865681	Unknown
18 May 1944	WENHAM	Leading Aircraftman	LESLIE WILLIAM BADEN	842086	Unknown
16 August 1940	WEST	Aircraftman 2nd Class	WILLIAM FREDERICK GEORGE	813222	Unknown
09 February 1947	WESTRAN	Corporal	LESLIE	869476	906 Balloon Sqn
01 October 1941	WESTWOOD	Sergeant	DOUGLAS ERIC	805525	115 Sqn RAF
29 November 1939	WHEELER	Flying Officer	PHILIP CLIFTON	90213	604 Sqn AAF
07 June 1945	WHEELER	Leading Aircraftman	JOHN ALFRED	842515	901/5 Balloon Sqn
05 July 1943	WHEELER	Aircraftwoman 2nd Class	MARJORIE JOAN	895047	Unknown
30 May 1940	WHEELWRIGHT	Pilot Officer	IRVINE SYME	91003	500 Sqn AAF
19 December 1946	WHITBREAD	Aircraftman 1st Class	PERCY WILLIAM	845342	Unknown

Date	Surname	Forename	Rank	Number	Squadron
11 February 1947	**WHITE**	JOHN HENRY	Leading Aircraftman	862502	Unknown
18 March 1945	**WHITE**	JAMES WILLIAM	Aircraftman 2nd Class	871022	944 Balloon Sqn
19 November 1941	**WHITEHEAD**	ROBERT HENRY	Aircraftman 1st Class	853649	919 Balloon Sqn
22 July 1946	**WHITTAM**	PETER CHRISTOPHER	Corporal	853658	Unknown
30 August 1941	**WICKHAM**	GEORGE ARTHUR	Flight Sergeant	863430	Unknown
02 August 1944	**WILKINS**	JOHN	Sergeant	858830	467 (RAAF) Sqn
15 August 1941	**WILKINSON**	HENRY SIDNEY	Flying Officer	91156	914 Balloon Sqn
29 November 1940	**WILKINSON**	GEORGE MILLER	Corporal	841738	Unknown
05 August 1942	**WILLIAMS**	ALBERT EDWARD	Flight Sergeant	818241	44 (Rhodesia) Sqn RAF
15 December 1940	**WILLIAMS**	CYRIL	Sergeant	818161	77 Sqn RAF
09 November 1943	**WILLIAMS**	RICHARD LONGFORD	Sergeant	813209	Unknown
26 October 1945	**WILLIAMS**	GILBERT GEORGE	Corporal	818237	Unknown
05 June 1944	**WILLIAMS**	MOLLIE ISABEL	Corporal	889601	Unknown

Date	Surname	Rank	Forename	Number	Unit
06 November 1944	WILLIAMS	Leading Aircraftman	GWYLIM MATHEWS	842401	5003 ACS RAF
02 May 1943	WILLIAMS	Leading Aircraftman	THOMAS JOHN	855234	Unknown
20 June 1940	WILLIAMS	Aircraftwoman 1st Class	BARBARA SARAH WATLIN	883075	Unknown
25 June 1942	WILLIAMSON	Flight Sergeant	DOUGLAS GEORGE	817226	102 Sqn RAF
01 May 1943	WILLIAMSON	Sergeant	ERIC FORD	815223	Unknown
12 September 1952	WILLIS	Flight Lieutenant	THOMAS ALLAN	91247	608 Sqn RAuxAF
25 August 1940	WILMOTT	Leading Aircraftman	EDWARD VENNER	846488	949 Balloon Sqn
21 February 1940	WILSON	Flight Lieutenant	ANTHONY NEVILLE	90300	616 Sqn AAF
29 May 1940	WILSON	Flying Officer	JOHN KERR	90338	610 Sqn AAF
11 November 1940	WILSON	Sergeant	GEORGE ROBERT	808414	83 Sqn RAF
10 June 1940	WILSON	Corporal	JOHN	807066	608 Sqn AAF
27 October 1939	WILSON	Corporal	RICHARD ANDREW	808180	608 Sqn AAF
26 November 1942	WILSON	Corporal	SARAH ELIZABETH	894014	Unknown
06 May 1941	WILSON	Corporal	WALTER SABLICK	871702	938 Balloon Sqn
14 August 1940	WILSON	Leading Aircraftman	KENNETH	809140	609 Sqn AAF

Date	Surname	Rank	First Names	Service Number	Squadron
17 November 1941	WILSON	Aircraftman 1st Class	WILLIAM	871652	974 Balloon Sqn
06 February 1940	WILSON	Aircraftman 2nd Class	ARCHIBALD	874565	947 Balloon Sqn
14 September 1947	WILTSHIRE	Corporal	CHARLES ALBERT	841648	Unknown
02 December 1940	WINDER	Leading Aircraftman	ROY	814127	616 Sqn AAF
11 May 1941	WINGFIELD	Sergeant	VICTOR JOHN	801551	500 Sqn AAF
17 December 1940	WINSBORROW	Aircraftman 1st Class	LESLIE THOMAS	845292	952 Balloon Sqn
23 September 1951	WITHERS	Senior Aircraftman	ERIC ROY	2684640	604 Sqn RAuxAF
21 January 1959	WOLSTENHOLME	Flying Officer	JOHN ALAN	3131451	Unknown
17 December 1940	WOOD	Sergeant	ALEXANDER MILNE	817163	49 Sqn RAF
12 April 1944	WOOD	Sergeant	LAWRENCE ALBERT	812291	547 Sqn RAF
04 October 1941	WOOD	Leading Aircraftman	JOHN JAMES	867843	938 Balloon Sqn
23 May 1943	WOOD	Leading Aircraftman	NORMAN	808077	608 Sqn AAF
01 September 1940	WORTHINGTON	Aircraftman 1st Class	JAMES	803601	603 Sqn AAF

Date	Surname	Forename(s)	Rank	Number	Unit
22 May 1940	WRIGHT	GILBERT FRANCIS MONCREIFF	Flying Officer	90265	605 Sqn AAF
15 June 1949	WRIGHT	NORMAN MONTAGUE	Pilot 2	2682638	601 Sqn RAuxAF
10 April 1941	WRIGHT	JOHN THOMPSON	Sergeant	817188	106 Sqn RAF
07 March 1941	WRIGHT	BETTY	Aircraftwoman 1st Class	897565	Unknown
30 August 1940	WRIGHT	WILLIAM	Aircraftman 1st Class	810068	610 Sqn AAF
26 April 1943	WRIGHTAM	THOMAS WILLIAM	Aircraftman 1st Class	871037	942/3 Balloon Sqn
04 August 1942	WYNNE	GEORGE HENRY	Sergeant	847519	Unknown
26 January 1943	YARDLEY	WILLIAM GEORGE	Leading Aircraftman	842390	Unknown
29 June 1951	YARROW	ERIC THOMPSON	Sergeant	2686184	608 Sqn RAuxAF
10 April 1943	YATES	FRANK	Sergeant	820019	Unknown
17 September 1942	YATES	KENNETH	Sergeant	811209	Unknown
02 August 1942	YATES	HORACE JOHN	Corporal	813260	69 Sqn RAF
16 August 1943	YOUNG	JOHN	Aircraftman 1st Class	850544	Unknown
06 August 1940	YOUNG	DONALD JAMES	Pilot Officer	91232	Unknown

Bibliography

The National Archives

Air 1, Air Ministry, Air Historical Branch: Papers, Series 1, discovery. nationalarchives.gov.uk

Air 2/253 Associations of the Auxiliary Air Force, 25 July 1924

Air 2/273 Formation of Territorial Air Force 20 May 1919

Air 2/273 Formation of Auxiliary Air Force 24 January 1925

Air 2/696 Re-organization of Special Reserve Squadrons as Auxiliary Air Force Squadrons

Air 2/13172 Future of the Royal Auxiliary Air Force

Air 19/725 Royal Auxiliary Air Force

Air 19/743 Royal Auxiliary Air Force

Air 20/932 Auxiliary Air Force Reconstitution

Air 27 Air Ministry, Series details: Air Ministry and Successors; Operations Record Books, Squadrons 1911–1972

Air 41/4 RAF Monograph, Flying Training 1934-1942, Air Historical Branch

Air 41/23/30 Conclusions of a meeting of the Cabinet held at 10 Downing Street, SW1 on Tuesday, 11 July 1922

Air 41/24/165 Auxiliary Air Force and Air Force Reserve Bill, 3 March 1924

Air 41/24/164 Letter from Secretary of State for Air to the Secretary, Cabinet, 5 February 1924

Air 41/24/138 Formation of an Auxiliary Air Force, 13 September 1922

Air 41/24/267 Plan for Further Expansion of First Line Strength of the Royal Air Force, January 1937

Air 41/65 Royal Air Force Manning Plans and Policy

Air 41/129/19 Needs of the Armed Forces and the Ministry of Supply for Land for Training and Other Purposes, June 1947

Air 41/129/44 Defence Programmes 1951–54, January 1951
WO 296/21 Territorial and Reserve Forces Act 1907

Newspapers

Daily Telegraph, 1937.
Eastern Weekly News, 1948.
The Gazette, 1937–1941.
The Guardian Digital Archive, 1821–2000.
The London Gazette, 1926–1957.
North Eastern Daily Gazette, 1930–1958.
North Eastern Weekly News, 1947.
Northern Daily Mail, 1947.
Northern Echo, 1946–1947.
The Times Digital Archives, 1925–1985.
Flight Magazine Digital Archive.
RAF Quarterly.

Books

Addison, Paul & Crang, Jeremy A. (eds)	*The Burning Blue. A New History of The Battle of Britain*, (London, 2000)
Armitage, Michael	*The Royal Air Force – An Illustrated History* (London, 1993)
Bailey, David J.	*610 (County of Chester) Auxiliary Air Force Squadron, 1936–1940*, (Stroud, 2019)
Beauman, Katherine Bentley	*Partners in Blue. The Story of Women's Service with the Royal Air Force*, (London, 1971)
Beck, Pip	*A WAAF in Bomber Command*, (Manchester, 1989)
Bialer, Uri	*The Fear of Air Attack and British Politics, 1932–1939*, (London, 1980)
Bishop, Patrick	*Fighter Boys Saving Britain, 1940*, (London, 2004)

BIBLIOGRAPHY

Bond, Brian	*British Military Policy Between the Two World Wars*, (Oxford, 1980)
Boog, Horst (Ed)	*Conduct of the Air War in the Second World War. An International Comparison*, (London, 1992)
Bourne, J.M.	*Britain and the Great War 1914–1918*, (New York, 1989)
Bowman, Timothy & Connelly, Mark L.	*The Edwardian Army: Recruiting, Training and Deploying the British Army, 1902–1914*, (Oxford, 2012)
Bowyer, Chaz	*The History of the RAF*, (London, 1977)
Bowyer, Chaz	*The Royal Air Force 1939–1945*, (Barnsley, 1996)
Bowyer, Michael J.F.	*Aircraft for the Few. The RAF's Fighters and Bombers in 1940*, (Yeovil Somerset, 1991)
Boyle, Andrew	*Trenchard*, (London, 1962)
Brooks, Robin J.	*Kent's Own. The History of 500 (County of Kent) Squadron Royal Auxiliary Air Force*, (Gillingham Kent, 1982)
Brown, E.	*Wings on My Sleeve*, (London, 2006)
Buckley, John	*Air Power in the Age of Total War*, (London, 1999)
Buckley, John	*RAF and Trade Defence 1919–1945 Constant Endeavour*, (Staffs, 1995)
Burns, M.G.	*Bader, the Man and his Men*, (London, 1990)
Carr, S.J.	*You are not Sparrows*, (London, 1975)
Chamier, John Adrian	*The Birth of the Royal Air Force*, (London, 1943)
Chorlton, Martyn	*Airfields of North-East England in the Second World War*, (Newbury, 2005)
Clark, Alan	*Aces High. The War in the Air over the Western Front 1914–1918*, (London, 1973)
Clayton, P.B. (MC, FSA)	*Tales of Talbot House: Everyman's Club in Poperinghe & Ypres 1915–1918*, (London, 1919)

Clayton, T. & Craig, P. — *Finest Hour*, (London, 1999)

Coombs, L.F.E. — *The Lion has Wings. The Race to Prepare the RAF for World War II: 1935–1940*, (Shrewsbury, 1997)

Cross, J.A. — *Lord Swinton*, (Oxford, 1982)

Davidson, M. & Taylor J. — *Spitfire Ace. Flying the Battle of Britain*, (London, 1988)

Dean, Sir Maurice — *The Royal Air Force and Two World Wars*, (London, 1979)

De Groot, Gerard J. — *Blighty. British Society in the Era of the Great War*, (Harlow Essex,1996)

De Groot, Gerard J. — *The First World War*, (Basingstoke, 2001)

Deighton, L. — *Fighter. The True Story of the Battle of Britain*, (London, 1977)

Delve, Ken & Pitchfork, Graham — *South Yorkshire's Own. The Story of 616 Squadron*, (Exeter, 1990)

Devine, David — *The Broken Wing – A Study in the British Exercise of Air Power*, (London, 1966)

Dickson, Wing Commander Alex (ed) — *The Royal Air Force Volunteer Reserve – Memories* (RAF Innsworth, Gloucester, 1997)

Dixon, Robert — *607 Squadron, A Shade of Blue*, (Port Stroud, 2008)

Dundas, H. — *Flying Start. A Fighter Pilot's War Years*, (London, 1988).

Edgerton, David — *England and the Aeroplane: Militarism, Modernity and Machines*, (London, 2013)

Escott, Beryl Y. — *The WAAF*, (Oxford, 2012)

Eyre, Richard — *National Service Diary: Diary of a Decade,* (London, 2003)

Ferguson, Aldon P. — *Beware Beware! The History of 611 (West Lancashire) Squadron Royal Auxiliary Air Force*, (Reading, 2004)

Ferguson, Norman — *For the Love of the Air Force, A Companion*, (London, 2017)

BIBLIOGRAPHY

Francis, Martin	*The Flyer. British Culture and the Royal Air Force*, (Oxford, 2008)
Fredette, Raymond H.	*The First Battle of Britain 1917/1918 and the Birth of the Royal Air Force*, (London, 1966).
Goodson, James	*Tumult in the Clouds. The Classic Story of War in the Air*, (London, 2003).
Grant, R.G.	*Flight. 100 Years of Aviation*, (London, 2004)
Hall, Roger DFC	*Clouds of Fear,* (London, 1977)
Halpenny, Bruce Barrymore	*Action Stations: 4, Military Airfields of Yorkshire*, (Cambridge, 1982)
Hering, Sqn. Ldr. P.G.	*Customs and Traditions of the Royal Air Force*, (Aldershot, 1961)
Hickman, Tom	*The Call-Up. A History of National Service*, (London, 2004)
HMSO	*Coastal Command. The Air Ministry Account of the Part Played by Coastal Command in the Battle of the Seas 1939–1942*, (London, 1942)
Hoare, Samuel (Viscount Templewood)	*Empire of the Air. The Advent of the Air Age 1922–1929*, (London, 1957)
Howarth, Stephen	*The Royal Navy Reserves in War And Peace 1900–2003,* (Barnsley, 2003)
Howes, S.D.	*Goosepool. The History of RAF and RCAF Middleton St. George and Teesside Airport*, (Darlington, 2003)
Hunt, Leslie	*Twenty-one Squadrons. The History of The Royal Auxiliary Air Force 1925–1957,* (London, 1972)
Hyams, Jacky	*The Female Few, Spitfire Heroines*, (Port Stroud, 2012)
Hyde, H. Montgomery	*British Air Policy Between the Wars 1918–1939,* (London, 1976)
James, John	*The Paladins. A Social History of the Outbreak of World War II*, (London, 1990)
Johnstone, Sandy	*Enemy in the Sky*, (London, 1976)

Johnstone, Sandy	*Diary of an Aviator*, (Shrewsbury, 1993)
Jones, Neville	*The Beginnings of Strategic Air Power. A History of the British Bomber Force 1923–1939,* (Abingdon, 1987)
Kennedy, Paul	*The Realities Behind Diplomacy. Background Influences on British External Policy 1865–1980,* (London, 1981)
Knight, Dennis	*Battle of Britain Sketch Book,* (Walton on Thames, 2015)
Lucas, Laddie (ed)	*Voices in the Air 1939–1945. Incredible stories of the World War II Airmen in Their Own Words*, (London, 2003)
Mackay, Robert	*Half the battle. Civilian Morale in Britain during the Second World War*, (Manchester, 2002)
Millin, Sarah Gertrude	*General Smuts*, (London, 1976)
Moggridge, Jackie	*Spitfire Girl, My life in the Sky*, (London, 1957)
Mosley, Leonard	*The Battle of Britain,* (London, 1969)
Moulson, Tom	*The Flying Sword. The Story of 601 Squadron*, (London, 1964)
Moulson, Tom	*The 'Millionaires' Squadron. The Remarkable Story of 601 Squadron And The Flying Sword*, (Barnsley, 2014)
Mowat, Charles Loch	*Britain Between the Wars 1918–1940*, (London, 1955).
Murray, W.	*War in the Air 1914–1945*, (London, 1999)
Nancarrow, F G	*Glasgow's Fighter Squadron*, (London, 1942)
Nesbitt, Roy Conyers	*Coastal Command in Action 1939–1945*, (Gloucestershire, 1997)
Nesbitt, Roy Conyers	*An Illustrated History of the RAF*, (Surrey, 1990)
Newton, Tony	*Pins and Needles and Paperclips: Treasures from the Royal Aero Club Archives*, (London, 2006)

BIBLIOGRAPHY

Omissi, David E.   *Air Power and Colonial Control. The Royal Air Force 1919–1939,* (Manchester, 1960)

Onderwater, Hans   *Gentlemen in Blue. 600 Squadron,* (Barnsley, 1997)

Ottler, Patrick   *Yorkshire Airfields in the Second World War,* (Newbury 1998)

Parker, M.   *The Battle of Britain July–October 1940. An Oral History of Britain's 'Finest Hour',* (London, 2000)

Parker, R.A.C.   *Chamberlain and Appeasement. British Policy and the Coming of the Second World War,* (London, 1993)

Peden, G.C.   *British Rearmament and the Treasury 1932–1939,* (Edinburgh, 1979)

Peden, G.C.   *Arms, Economics and British Strategy. From Dreadnoughts to Hydrogen Bombs,* (Cambridge, 2007)

Piper, Ian   *We Never Slept. The History of 605 (County of Warwick) Squadron Royal Auxiliary Air Force 1926–1957,* (Tamworth, 1996)

Pitchfork, Graham   *The RAF's First Jet Squadron, 616 (South Yorkshire),* (Port Stroud, 2009)

Powers, Barry D.   *Strategy without Slide Rule. British Air Strategy 1914–1939,* (London, 1976)

Pushman, Muriel Gane   *We All Wore Blue, Experiences in the WAAF,* (Port Stroud, 2006)

Rawlings, John D.R.   *The History of the Royal Air Force,* (Feltham, 1984)

Richards, Denis   *Royal Air Force 1939–1945, Volume 1 – The Fight at Odds,* (London, 1974)

Richey, Paul DFC   *Fighter Pilot,* (London, 1990)

Ross, David, Blanche,   *The Greatest Squadron of them all,*
  Bruce, and   *The Definitive History of 603*
  Simpson, William   *(City of Edinburgh) Squadron RAuxAF, Volume 1. Formation to the end of 1940,* (London, 2003)

Ross, David, Blanche, Bruce, and Simpson, William — *The Greatest Squadron of them all, The Definitive History of 603 (City of Edinburgh) Squadron RAuxAF, Volume II, 1941 to Date,* (London, 2003)

Ross, Tony — *75 Eventful Years. A Tribute to the Royal Air Force 1918–1993,* (London, 1993)

Royal Air Force Historical Society — *Royal Air Force Reserve and Auxiliary Forces,* (Oxford, 2003)

Royal Air Force Historical Society — *Defending Northern Skies 1915–1995,* (Oxford, 1996)

Royal Air Force Volunteer Reserve — *Memories,* (Gloucester, 1997)

Royle, Trevor — *National Service. The Best Years of Their Lives,* (London, 2008)

Sarkar, Dilip MBE — *Letters From the Few, Unique Memories From the Battle of Britain,* (Barnsley, 2020)

Saward, Dudley — *'Bomber' Harris,* (London, 1984)

Schindler, Colin — *National Service. From Aldershot to Aden. Tales From the Conscripts 1946-1962,* (London, 2012)

Sharpe, M. — *History of the Royal Air Force,* (London, 1999)

Shores, Christopher and Williams, Clive — *Aces High, A Tribute to the Most Notable Fighter Pilots Of the British and Commonwealth Forces in WWII,* (London, 1994)

Shores, Christopher — *Those Other Eagles, A Companion Volume to Aces High. A Tribute to The British, Commonwealth and Free European Fighter Pilots who claimed between Two and Four Victories in Aerial Combat 1939–1982,* (London, 2004)

Smith, David J. — *Britain's Military Airfields 1939–1945,* (Yeovil Somerset, 1989)

BIBLIOGRAPHY

Smith, H.L. (Ed)	*War and Social change. British Society in the Second World War,* (Manchester, 1986)
Smith, Harold	*Britain in the Second World War. A Social History,* (Manchester, 1996)
Smith, Malcolm	*British Air Strategy Between the Wars,* (Oxford, 1984)
Smithies, Edward	*Aces, Erks and Backroom Boys. Aircrew, Ground Staff and Warplane Builders Remember the Second World War,* (London, 2002)
Smuts, J.C.	*Jan Christian Smuts,* (London, 1952)
Steel, Nigel and Hart, Peter	*Tumult in the Clouds. The British Experience of the War in the Air 1914–1918,* (London, 1997)
Stevens, J.R.	*Searching for the Hudson Bombers. Lads, Love and Death in World War II,* (Victoria, 2004)
Taylor, Les	*BANFF Strike Wing at War,* (London, 2010)
Taylor, Roy	*RAF National Service in Six Movements. A Conscript's Experiences in the RAF in the 1950s,* (London, 2006)
Tedder, The Lord G.C.B.	*Air Power in War – The Lees Knowles Lectures by Marshal of the Royal Air Force,* (London, 1947)
Terraine, John	*The Right of the Line: The Royal Air Force in the European War 1939-1945,* (London, 1985)
Turner, John	*Macmillan,* (London, 1994)
Turner, John Frayn	*The WAAF at War,* (Barnsley, 2011)
Vinen, Richard	*National Service. A Generation in Uniform 1945–1963,* (London, 2015)
Watkins, David	*Fear Nothing. The History of No. 501 (County of Gloucester) Fighter Squadron, Royal Auxiliary Air Force,* (Cowden Kent, 1990)
Wellum, G.	*First Light,* (London, 2003)

White, Ian — *If you want Peace, Prepare for War. A History of No. 604 (County of Middlesex) Squadron, RAuxAF, in Peace and in War*, (London, 2005)

Whittell, Giles — *Spitfire Women of World War II*, (London, 2008)

Wilkinson, Louise — *The Kipper Patrol, The History Of 608 (NR) Squadron Royal Auxiliary Air Force 1930–1957*, (Dartford, 2009)

Wilkinson, Louise — *The Territorial Air Force, The RAF's Voluntary Squadrons 1926–1957*, (Barnsley, 2020)

Wynn, Kenneth, G. — *Men of the Battle of Britain*, (Norwich, 1989)

Wynn, Stephen — *Air Transport Auxiliary at War, 80th Anniversary of its Formation*, (Barnsley, 2021)

Ziegler, F.H. — *The Story of 609 Squadron. Under the White Rose*, (London, 1971)

Journals

Blanche, B. — 'Weekend Fliers', *Aeroplane* 27, 8 (1999)

Bowyer, M.J.F. — 'Royal Auxiliary Air Force'. *Scale Aircraft Modelling* 7, 1 (1984)

Crowson, N.J. — 'Contemporary Record', *The Conservative Party and the Call for National Service, 1937–1939: Compulsion Versus Voluntarism* 9, 1 (1995)

Dewey, P.E. — 'Military Recruiting and the British Labour Force during the First World War', *The History Journal,* 27, 1 (1984)

Douglas, R. — 'Voluntary Enlistment in the First World War and the Work of the Parliamentary Recruiting Committee' *Journal of Modern History* 4, (1970)

Farr, Martin	'A Compelling Case for Voluntarism: Britain's Alternative Strategy 1915–1916', *War in History* 9, 2 (2002)
Hartigan, J.	'Volunteering for the Army in England. August 1914–May 1915' *Midland History* 24 (1999)
Mansell, Dr. A.	'Professionals, Amateurs and Private Armies. Pilot Entry Portals in the RAF Expansion of 1934 to 1939', *Proceedings of the RAF Historical Society* 11 (1993)
Mansell, Tony	'Flying Start: Educational and Social Factors in the Recruitment of Pilots of the Royal Air Force in the Inter-War Years' *History of Education* 26, No. 1, (1997)
Paris, M.	'The Rise of the Airmen: The Origins of Airforce Elitism c. 1890–1918', *Journal of Contemporary History* 28 (1993)
Petler, Martin	'" Temporary Gentlemen" in the aftermath of the Great War: Rank, Status and the Ex-officer Problem', *The Historical Journal* 37, 1 (1994) *Historical Research* 76, 193 (2003)
Samuel, Raphael	'Middle Class Between the Wars (Parts 1 and 2)', *New Socialist* (1983)
Smith, Malcolm	The Royal Air Force, Air Power and British Foreign Policy 1932–1937 *Journal of Contemporary History,* 12, No. 1, (1977)
Whitmarsh, Andrew	British Army Manoeuvres and the Development of Military Aviation, *War in History,* Vol 14, Issue 3 July 2007

Collections

Freeman, Squadron Leader A.F.	'The Post-War Royal Auxiliary Air Force' in Royal Air Force Historical Society *Royal Air Force Reserve and*

	Auxiliary Forces, (Oxford, 2003)
Jefford, Jeff	'Post-War Reserves to 1960' in Royal Air Force Historical Society *Royal Air Force Reserve and Auxiliary Forces*, (Oxford, 2003)
Mansell, Dr. Tony	'Royal Air Force Volunteer Reserve 1936–1939' in Royal Air Force Historical Society *Royal Air Force Reserve and Auxiliary Forces*, (Oxford, 2003)
Shores, Christopher	'The Auxiliary Air Force in WW II' in Royal Air Force Historical Society *Royal Air Force Reserve and Auxiliary Forces*, (Oxford, 2003)
Terraine, John	'Theory and Practice of Air War: The Royal Air Force' in Horst Boog (Ed) *The Conduct of the Air War in the Second World War: An International Comparison.* (Oxford, 1992)

Web Addresses

National Archives	Air Ministry Series Details: Air Ministry and Successors: Operations Record Books, Squadrons, 1911–1972. www.nationalarchives.gov.uk
Charles Gambier Jenyns	www.rogerco.freeserve.co.uk/
Jack Elkan David Benham	www.roll-of-honour.com/ www.uk-cigars.co.uk
William Henry Rhodes-Moorhouse	www.carpages.co.uk/news
Arthur Hammond Dalton	www.cwgc.org/search 6 August 2011
Edward Lawrence Colbeck-Welch	www.kcl.ac.uk 6 August 2011
Peter Kenneth Devitt Anthony Henry Hamilton Tollemache	www.hyderabad.co.uk www.ww2awards.com

BIBLIOGRAPHY

Paul Richey www.tangmerepilots.co.uk

Geoffrey Ambler www.rafweb.org//biographies

Kenneth Maxwell Stoddart www.bowringpark.co.uk

*Various AAF officers www.thepeerage.com

Walter Leslie Runciman and www.norav.50megs.com
 Lancelot Eustace Smith

Cecil Leonard Knox www.remuseum.org

Various AAF officers http://en.wikipedia.org

RAF Air Bases in England www.anti-aircraft.co.uk

Flight Magazine www.flightglobal.com
 Digital Archive

RAF Quarterly Archive www.flightglobal.com

Index

INDEX

INDEX